Kenneth Burke and the 21st Century

SUNY series in Speech Communication
Dudley D. Cahn, editor

Kenneth Burke
and the 21st Century

Edited by Bernard L. Brock

STATE UNIVERSITY OF NEW YORK PRESS

The volume editor thanks Priscilla Meddough for her exacting work in preparing the index for the book.

Published by
State University of New York Press, Albany

© 1999 State University of New York

For information, address State University of New York Press,
State University Plaza, Albany, N.Y., 12246

Production by Cathleen Collins
Marketing by Patrick Durocher

Library of Congress Cataloging in Publication Data

Kenneth Burke and the 21st century / edited by Bernard L. Brock.
      p.   cm. — (SUNY series in speech communication)
   Papers of the Second Triennial Conference held by the Kenneth
Burke Society, May 1993, in Airlie, Va.
   Includes bibliographical references and index.
   ISBN 0-7914-4007-9 (alk. paper). — ISBN 0-7914-4008-7 (pb: alk.
paper)
   1. Burke, Kenneth, 1897–   —Contributions in philosophy of
rhetoric—Congresses.   2. Rhetoric—Philosophy—Congresses.
3. Criticism—Congresses.   I. Brock, Bernard L.   II. Kenneth Burke
Society.   Conference (2nd : 1993 : Airlie, Va.)   III. Series.
P85.B85K46   1998
818'. 5409—dc21   98–10475
                                        CIP

10 9 8 7 6 5 4 3 2 1

Contents

Part IV. The Burkean System

Introduction

Bernard L. Brock

Kenneth Burke's imaginative and creative criticism earned for him the 1981 National Medal for Literature for his "distinguished and continuing contribution to American letters." Challenging the established ideas of his day, Burke's criticisms made him an influential writer and gave him the reputation for being a "truly speculative thinker." Celebrating and extending this tradition, the Kenneth Burke Society held its second triennial conference in Airlie, Virginia, in May 1993. The conference theme, "Extensions of the Burkean System," created the dialogue that brought forth this volume, *Kenneth Burke and the 21st Century*.

Even though Kenneth Burke died on November 19, 1993, his work lives on through his many books and articles as well as in the activities of the Kenneth Burke Society and the many scholars he influenced. One important reason why the Burke project will continue to grow is that ideas inherent to his theory of dramatism are central to the conversation that is launching the twenty-first century.

The Evolution of Burke's Critical Thought

Kenneth Burke's critical thought, as it evolved over a seventy-year period through his many articles and books, made him an influential thinker in the transition between the twentieth and twenty-first centuries. Understanding this evolution will help us see the role he has and will play in this important period. Throughout his entire life Burke attacked the conventional wisdom of his time as he reflected a concern for both micro- and macroscopic issues. As a critic, he microscopically focused on individual texts to gain insight into the author's ideas and/or life, as he did with Coleridge's writing. He also analyzed the symbolic nature of

1

institutions, as he did with capitalism and technology; or he projected symbolic systems into the future, as in "The Rhetoric of Hitler's 'Battle,'" his criticism of *Mein Kampf*. Then, macroscopically, he transcended individual thought, and, from a critical perspective, constructed a theory of the evolution of society. Always assuming the stance of the critic, he shifted his attention in three fairly clear stages from epistemology to ontology until he had not only discussed the important issues of his day, but also had developed a series of rhetorical methods into a complete rhetorical system or theory.[1]

Burke as Critical Realist

In Burke's first stage, which included his early essays and his first four books on rhetoric, he acted as a critical realist. Generally using specific literary texts as a springboard, Burke commented on the work itself, society, and the nature of language or communication. Always proceeding inductively, Burke built insight upon insight as he discovered specific principles and methods for understanding human symbolic action.

In his first book of this period, *Counter-Statement*, Burke starts by examining the life, thought, and techniques of three writers (Flaubert, Pater, and de Gourmont) and concludes by outlining and illustrating "principles underlying the appeal of literature" (123). In his discussion of these principles, Burke makes two important points that undermine the positivist assumptions of his time. First, when experience is converted into a symbolic equivalent, the symbol itself "becomes the guiding principle" (157). Second, magic, religion, and science are all ideological "in that they foster a body of thought concerning the nature of the universe and man's [sic] relation to it" (163). At this point, through his commentary on literary texts, Burke gains insight into the nature of symbolic action.

Burke's next two books, *Permanence and Change* and *Attitudes Toward History*, can be considered companion volumes. These works extend the nature of symbolic action by, again, using literary texts in an examination of the world and its problems. Also, in these books Burke makes his strongest attacks on capitalism and technology, as he articulates a theory of the evolution of Western thought. In these volumes Burke assumes the role of a social as well as a literary critic.

In *Permanence and Change*, Burke starts from the perspective of the individual as he argues that all living organisms are critics. He then, again inductively, presents a general critical method around framing or "perspective" as a procedure for discovering motives within human symbolic action. Employing terms like "trained incapacity" and "scape-goat mechanism," Burke constructs the following critical method:

> (a) There is a sense of relationships, developed by the con-tingencies of experience; (b) this sense of relationships is our orientation; (c) our orientation largely involves matters of expectancy, and affects our choice of means with reference to the future; (d) in the human sphere, the subject of expectancy and the judgment as to what is proper in conduct is largely bound up with the subject of motives for if we know *why* people do as they do we feel that we know *what* to expect of them and of ourselves, and we shape our decisions and judg-ments and policies to take such expectancies into account. (18)

Having constructed a general critical method, Burke transcends the individual perspective to present three societal rationalizations as self-sustaining means of control—magic, "control over the primitive forces of nature"; religion, "attempts to control the specifically *human* forces"; and science, "the attempt to control for our purposes the forces of technology, or machinery" (44). He then explains how "philosophic correctives" arose from outside each rationalization, which in turn combined with and transcended the original one to form a new orientation. In this orderly fashion Burke presents Western thought as religion replacing magic and science supplanting religion as societal rationalizations (59–65).

Burke's analysis of the evolution of Western thought does not stop with science because he predicts that correctives arising out of the weaknesses of technology and overspecialization within capital-ism will result in the new orientation called poetic humanism that will be characterized by subjective, poetic thought, decentralization or pluralism, spirituality, and humanism. Burke describes it as an "art of living" (66).

Attitudes Toward History is a companion volume because Burke applies the societal rationalizations established in *Permanence and Change* to Western culture and describes the "curve of history." Consis-tent with his abiding concern for symbolic action, before charting the curve of history, Burke integrates into his general critical method the concepts of frames of acceptance, rejection, and passivity and poetic categories. In his analysis of acceptance and rejection, Burke develops experience or reality as being essentially symbolic, and his poetic categories reveal comic thought as essential to human cooperation. In his curve of history, Burke emphasizes the weaknesses of capitalism and treats collectivism as salvation.[2]

The final book from this first stage is *The Philosophy of Literary Form*. In this volume Burke advances understanding of the nature of symbolic action itself. The lead article and title of the book departs from his earlier, more inductive approach and starts by presenting a sophisticated analysis of symbolic action, which stands as a strong attack on a scientific, positivist approach to language. Burke argues that "critical and imaginative works are answers to questions posed by the situation in which they arose . . . they are *strategic* answers, *stylized* answers" (3). He extends his position when he indicates that "facts" of historical assertion "are but a strategy of inducement . . . they are themselves a dramatic act" (6). Essentially, Burke argues that "the symbolic act is the *dancing of an attitude*" (9). In the remaining essays, Burke critically responds to the important people and ideas like Mead, Freud, and Dewey as well as pragmatism and liberalism, including one of his most acclaimed essays, "The Rhetoric of Hitler's 'Battle.'" During this first period of critical realism, Burke attacks the reigning beliefs of logical positivism, capitalism, and technology, advances understanding of symbolic action, and develops a theory of the stages for the evolution of society.

Burke as Conceptualist

In Burke's second stage, which also includes four major works on rhetoric, he can best be described as a conceptualist. Burke continues his role as critic and his interest in symbolic action and epistemology, but he reverses his pattern of thought from induction to deduction as he presents three major critical methods.

In this second stage Burke focuses single works on the deductive development of a single critical concept—*A Grammar of Motives* to the pentad, *A Rhetoric of Motives* to identification, and *The Rhetoric of Religion* to terms for order. His fourth work, *Language as Symbolic Action*, is a collection of diverse essays and serves as a transition to his third stage.

A Grammar of Motives develops and applies the pentad, Burke's most widely understood and applied critical method. Burke argues that the pentad is a tool for discovering motive: "What is involved, when we say what people are doing and why they are doing it?" (xv). His definition of the pentad is very brief: "any complete statement about motives will offer *some kind of* answer to these five questions: what was done (act), when or where it was done (scene), who did it (agent), how it he did it (agency), and why (purpose)" (xv). The rest of the book is devoted to brilliantly explicating and illustrating this concept from literature and society in general.

A Rhetoric of Motives develops and applies the concept identification which, Burke argues, should become the key term in rhetoric
and replace the traditional term, *persuasion* (xiv). Again, early in the
work Burke establishes the nature of identification: "A is not identical
with his colleague, B. But insofar as their interests as joined, A is
identified with B. Or he may identify himself with B even when their
interests are not joined, if he assumes that they are, or is persuaded to
believe so" (20). The rest of the book applies identification, first, by
relating it to the traditional principles of rhetoric, and, second, by
locating it within the symbols used to "order" society. In contrast with
the *pentad* which is a tool for microscopic analysis through transcendence upward, identification is a tool for either micro- or macroscopic
analysis. Burke illustrates this use for identification in the conclusion to
the book when he explains "ultimate order" (328).

In *The Rhetoric of Religion*, Burke extends his discussion of transcendence upward and his consideration of "order" by presenting and
applying his logological "terms for order." In an extended comparison of
theology and logology, Burke argues that the terms taken from the
creation myth in the biblical book of Genesis are "intrinsic to the idea of
Order" as well as disorder (4). He presents the terms in the form of a
poem:

> Here are the steps
> In the Iron Law of History
> That welds Order and Sacrifice:
>
> Order leads to Guilt
> (for who can keep commandments!)
> Guilt needs Redemption
>
> (for who would not be cleansed!)
>   Redemption needs Redeemer
> which is to say, a Victim).
>
> Order
> Through Guilt
> To Victimage
> (hence: Cult of the Kill). (4–5)

This symbolic Cult of the Kill can be simplified into the terms *order,
pollution, guilt, purification,* and *redemption.* Humans order their
experience by symbolically establishing hierarchies. Pollution results
when either intentionally or unintentionally the order is rejected. Then,
guilt must be assigned to purify the pollution and gain redemption.

Burke presents these terms for order as a cyclical, psychologically balanced process.[3]

Burke establishes a context for understanding these terms for order by developing six analogies for "the word" (wholly naturalistic, empirical references) and "The Word" (references to the "supernatural") (7). These analogies highlight the tendency of symbol-using to transcend the natural into the supernatural. This comparison between God or "The Word" and language or "the word" enables Burke to distinguish between two strikingly different uses of language—"dramatism" based on human action and form and "scientism" rooted in motion and knowledge (38). Out of this distinction Burke presents his four-clause definition of human beings:

> Man is
> (1) The symbol-using animal
> (2) inventor of the negative
> (3) Separated from his natural condition by instruments of
> his own making
> (4) And goaded by the spirit of hierarchy (40)

This definition is perfectly compatible with the other elements of Burke's critical perspective. Throughout the rest of the book he critically demonstrates that his "terms for order" and definition of humans are consistent with the Bible and Christian theology in general. The final application of Burke's "terms for order" is found in a dialogue between the Lord and Satan that illustrates beautifully his logological analysis.

The final and transitional book in this period is *Language as Symbolic Action*, a collection of previously published essays. This volume extends Burke's thinking in such areas as his definition of humans, where he adds a fifth clause "rotten with perfection" (16), but, more important, this volume provides greater unity to his rhetorical system.

The essay "What Are the Signs of What?" illustrates Burke's movement toward unifying his rhetorical theory and methods. By focusing on the concept of context, Burke is able "to reverse the usual realistic view of the relationship between words and things" (362). He identifies three stages of enlarging contexts: "factual certainty," "equations," and "entitlements." The first stage "is the perfect certainty that ranges from sheer word-counting to a comparison of all the contexts in which a given word appears." The second stage is the "radiations of a term" that "begin to build up equations whereby the terms are treated as overlapping . . . and maybe even identical" (369). The third stage is the series of titles assigned to steps or stages in a work (369–70). What makes this a unifying article is that the three stages parallel Burke's three special methods—pentad, identification, and terms for order. This correlation means that the pentad can be used to establish identification(s) for the terms for order within the process of pollution, guilt, purification, and redemption. In the second conceptual period of his career, Burke presents his special methods as independent of each other, but he also moves toward unifying them as he continues his interest in critiquing language and epistemology.

Burke as a Coherentist

In the third period of his career, starting in the late 1960s, Burke's interest, reflected in a series of articles, continued to shift from epistemology to ontology. Burke distanced himself from traditional, dualist philosophies and moved toward a more coherent philosophy of rhetoric. This move essentially gave Burke two rhetorical systems that required two distinct labels. He called his early epistemology "logology" and his later ontology "dramatism." In describing the two systems, Chesebro argues that they functioned dialectically.

Burke's article, "Dramatism" in the *International Encyclopedia of the Social Sciences* launched his philosophy of symbolic coherence. This article is really the first time he presents his rhetorical theory as a unified system.

This article becomes significant partially because it is his first complete statement, but also because Burke modifies a number of his basic rhetorical concepts—pentad, metaphor, substance, and definition of humans.[4] The pentad, initially in his epistemic system of logology, is a tool for microscopic motive analysis that allows any of the five elements to be featured or dominate. In his ontological system of dramatism, the pentad is still a tool for assessing motives, but "act" becomes the central term from which the other four terms radiate. Additionally, Burke adds a sixth term, *attitude*, to make it a hexad.

In "Dramatism" Burke also modifies his attitude toward metaphor. In the earlier work, *Permanence and Change*, metaphor is equated with "orientation" and "perspective" as a general view of reality (89). However, in "Dramatism" metaphor loses its stance as reality when Burke answers "no" to the question, "Is dramatism merely metaphorical?" At this point, language is no longer metaphorical; it is "literal." Burke argues that the human being "is defined literally as an animal characterized by his special aptitude for 'symbolic action,' which is itself a literal term. And from there on, drama is employed, not as a metaphor but as a fixed form that helps us discover what the implications of the terms 'act' and 'person' *really are*" (448). The shift from "reality" to "literal" allows symbolic action to remain an internal system while also accepting the existence of something external.

Another important modification in Burke's "Dramatism" is that he drops the term *substance* and replaces its function with attitude. In *A Grammar of Motives*, substance is what is beneath or the context in a pentadic analysis. In this approach, substance ties symbol-using to an external reality, making Burke's rhetorical system dualistic: "The transformations which we here study as a Grammar are not 'illusions,' but citable realities. The structural relations involved are observable realities" (57). In "Dramatism" substance is never mentioned; however, attitude is introduced as the *incipient* action that replaces substance as the internal link to an external world of experience.

Burke also modifies his definition of human being. Earlier Burke had made more complex his four-clause definition of humans as symbol-using animals separated from their natural condition by adding that they were "rotten with perfection." In "Dramatism," he reduces the definition to "man is defined literally as an animal characterized by his special aptitude for 'symbolic action,' which is itself a literal term" (448). Later, he simplifies the definition even further to "bodies that learn language" (Brock et al., 32). These revisions in Burke's definition of the human being are another move away from a dualistic rhetorical system toward a more unified one.

In his article "(Nonsymbolic) Motion/(Symbolic) Action," Burke completes the process of unifying his rhetorical system as symbolic coherence. First, he argues that "symbolic action" unifies these concepts: "I have said that the only transcending of the permanent 'split' between the two realms (of symbol and nonsymbol) would be as in some ultimate condition like that which orthodox Western religions imagine, in promising that the virtuous dead will regain their 'purified' bodies in heaven. . . . And the merger with 'symbolic action' is embedded in the very constitution of the poetic medium that celebrates her [Lucy's] oneness with nature as the ground of all physiologic bodies. . . . hence all is as *verbal* as with God's creative word in Genesis" (830–31). Then Burke describes how "symbolicity" transcends all polar divisions. He achieves this unity by merging "Self," a person as an individual, with "Culture": "The Self, like its corresponding Culture, thus has two sources of reference for its symbolic identity: its nature as a physiological organism, and its nature as a symbol-using animal responsive to the potentialities of symbolicity that have a nature of their own not reducible to a sheerly physiological dimension" (815). Finally, Burke explains how "symbolic-action" transcends and unifies the "two realms (of symbol and nonsymbol)" (830) and makes them one "with nature as the ground of all physiologic bodies" (831). In this third period, in which Burke focuses on the ontological nature of symbolic-action, he creates a symbolically coherent rhetorical system. Throughout his career as a critic, Burke focused on symbolic-action even though his interest shifted from epistemology to ontology as he constructed two rhetorical systems—the first he labeled "logology," and the second "dramatism."

Issues Ushering in the Twenty-first Century

Just as Kenneth Burke challenged the conventional wisdom of his time, the postmodern critics are challenging the conventional wisdom of today. The conversation initiated by the postmodernists has raised issues central to ushering in the twenty-first century. Throughout his career, Burke anticipated many of these issues, and his writing may continue to be influential and even point the way for the future of postmodernism.

The debate that has raged for more than two decades now is over whether modern theories and methods are dead and what ideas will succeed them.[5] The new postmodern critics, associated with Nietzsche, Heidegger, Derrida, Rorty, Lyotard, and others, react against the industrialization, commodification, rationalization, and secularization of modern society. They argue that capitalist industry divides the world into "haves" and "have-nots," resulting in the oppression of its victims, ranging from peasants, the proletariat, artisans, and minority cultures to women. They, further, argue that this control takes the form of establishing rules, practices, and institutions that reverse reason into a form of domination (Best and Kellner, 3). Beneath these surface conditions is the postmodern rejection of modern theories of knowledge and notions of causality in favor of concepts of multiplicity, plurality, fragmentation, and indeterminacy.

Defenders of modernity argue from the work of Descartes and the Enlightenment to the social theory of Comte, Marx, and Weber as they point to the progress made in the human condition in the nineteenth and twentieth centuries. Scholars such as Habermas and Grassi acknowledge problems with modern thought based on reason and accumulation of knowledge, but they offer programs to salvage modern thought. Modernists also attack postmodernism for its relativism, irrationality, and nihilism as a theoretical dead-end.

Rhetorical scholars place Kenneth Burke near the center of this postmodern–modern debate. In fact, debates have been held on whether Burke is postmodern even though he himself rejected the label. Cary Nelson acknowledges two Burkes—one humanist (modern) and the other poststructuralist (leaning toward postmodern). Williams discusses Burke as a deconstructionist; Chesebro compares Burke's debunking to Derrida's deconstruction; and Brown argues that a postmodern rhetoric should consider Burke's poetic-metaphoric view of language. Burke places symbol-using and postmodernists place language as central to the study of the human condition, providing a comparable focus of interests.

Not only does their interest in language throw them together, but the postmodern perspectivist and relativist positions do as well. In *Permanence and Change*, Burke introduces "orientation," which he argues is synonymous with "perspective" as the foundation for symbol-using. He also coins the terms *perspective through incongruity*, *trained incapacity*, and *impiety*, which could be viewed as specific forms of deconstruction. In *Attitudes Toward History*, Burke develops "acceptance," "rejection," and "passivity" as alternative frames for language use. This approach is consistent with a postmodern relativist position. Extending the concept of framing, Burke introduces a variety of poetic and comic frames as strategies for deflecting the world in less oppressive ways than the traditional frame of tragedy. These concepts, likewise, could be viewed as deconstructive strategies. Burke's relativism extends into *A Grammar of Motives*, where he presents metaphors of a molten mass of ore and a fluid party conversation as models for continual change in symbol-using.

These similarities between Burke and postmodern thought place his work as central to the conversation launching the twenty-first century, but they do not necessarily make Burke postmodern. It is important to note that most examples of Burke's similarities to postmodern come from his epistemic writing when he was attacking the positivist, conventional wisdom of his day and establishing his critical methods— which is essentially what postmodernists are doing today. As his thinking and writing evolved, Burke shifted from an attack strategy to the construction of a symbolically coherent theory that could be viewed as an alternative to positivism.

Burke's evolution in thought could foreshadow the direction for postmodern thinking. This more constructive position can be seen in Steven Seidman's *The Postmodern Turn: New Perspectives on Social Theory*, particularly in the definition he presents from Lyotard: "I define postmodern as incredulity toward metanarratives" (27). This suggests acceptance of local theories in contrast to modernist grand ones. Seidman also argues that postmodern social analysis would "consider social, moral, and political consequences, the practical purposes of knowledge, and their situational impact" rather than the nature of knowledge and empirical or interpretive conflicts (17). Postmodernism appears to be moving away from its earlier anti-theoretical posture associated with Derrida toward a plurality of approaches and conceptual strategies, which is similar to the evolution of Burke's thought.

Certainly, Burke anticipated many of the issues central to the conversation with either old and new postmoderns, but are there issues in this conversation he did not anticipate? Two important postmodern issues Burke does not address directly are feminism and multiculturalism. Burke's use of language reflects that of a patriarchal society, and he never spoke to the oppression resulting from the gender framing/roles in society. More recently, Burkean scholars have addressed the issue, and this volume will speak to the issue of the adaptability of Burke's theory to feminist concerns.

Multiculturalism is an even more recent issue in the postmodern conversation. Again, Burke does not address the issue directly, probably because he accepted the conventional wisdom of his day that society had a fairly unified, single culture. Today, people are beginning to accept that society is made up of a variety of cultures—thus multiculturalism. Even though Burke does not address cultural pluralism, his perspectivist approach to symbol-using could provide some basis for future Burkean scholars to deal with this issue. One essay in this volume will consider multiculturalism in Burke's rhetorical system directly, while others will treat the issue more indirectly.

Pattern of the Book

This book is divided into four sections that include significant issues for rhetoric as we enter the twenty-first century: Symbolic Action, Burke and Feminism, Postmodern and Multiculturalism, and The Burkean System. The essays within these areas will make it evident that not only did Kenneth Burke anticipate many of the issues leading into the twenty-first century, but also his dramatistic theory and method will remain strong during this period.

Symbolic action is the central concern of Burke's dramatism and was the focus of his writing throughout his entire career. Three essays draw heavily on Burke's earlier critical realist writing as they label and position dramatism for the twenty-first century. Richard Thames, in "Nature's Physician: The Metabiology of Kenneth Burke," presents Burke from an organic perspective as a balance to our current mechanistic orientation. Thames argues that the Burkean system is a metabiology that can restore health to both individuals and the earth. Star Muir's "Toward an Ecology of Language" also sees an organic metaphor as an alternative to a scientific one and as possessing the appropriate balance for the requirements of language in the twenty-first century. Both essays raise issues that are now identified with the New Age. David Blakesley, in "Kenneth Burke's Pragmatism—Old and New," focuses on Burke's ideas of the "unending conversation," analogy, and comic as he describes the Burkean system and places it at the juncture between the old and new pragmatists. Blakesley also clarifies the Burkean system's relationship to the current poststructural and postmodern approaches.

The second section of the book focuses on feminism, an important issue in the twenty-first century that Burke did not anticipate. Because he addressed issues of technology, ideology, and the epistemic nature of language, Burke's failure to comment on the patriarchal nature of language is quite noticeable. In this respect Burke's writing reflects the social values of his time. Two essays consider the usefulness of Burke's dramatism for feminist scholarship. Karen Foss and Cindy White, in "'Being' and the Promise of Trinity: A Feminist Addition to Burke's Theory of Dramatism," see Burke's motion-action duality as too hierarchical and suggest a motion-being-action trinity, which disrupts the polarity of the terms and thus softens the implicit hierarchy to make it more compatible with a feminist perspective. They also see this addition as consistent with the triadic tendencies in Burke's later writing. Then, Phyllis Japp in "'Can This Marriage Be Saved?': Reclaiming Burke for Feminist Scholarship" examines Burke's male orientation to assess if dramatism is salvageable for feminist use or whether it needs to be cast aside. Her tentative conclusion is that Burke's discussion of the four master tropes, from his middle conceptual period, are quite compatible with feminist thinking. In an essay later in this book, James Klumpp speaks indirectly to the issue of feminism as he describes the complexity of hierarchy and argues that sexism is not inherent to the Burkean system.

The third section, three essays on postmodern and multiculturalism, deals with two issues central to the discussion of rhetoric leading into the twenty-first century. Burke anticipated postmodernism, but never mentioned multiculturalism. George Cheney, Kathy Garvin-Doxas, and Kathleen Torrens, in "Kenneth Burke's Implicit Theory of Power," focus on the postmodern concept of "power." They argue, drawing primarily on Burke's middle conceptual period, that he has a fully developed language system for talk about both individual and societal power. Then, Greig Henderson, in "Dramatism and Deconstruction: Burke, de Man, and the Rhetorical Motive," compares the interaction of Burke's grammar and rhetoric to de Man's deconstruction. Henderson, relying most heavily on Burke's *A Rhetoric of Motives* in his conceptual period, argues that Burke goes beyond deconstruction to the demonstration of the suasive power of representation. He also suggests that Burke anticipates deconstruction but is not himself a postmodernist. Finally, James Chesebro, in "Multiculturalism and the Burkean System: Limitations and Extensions," analyzes Burke's concept of form from his early critical realist writing, and argues that his system is monocultural and thus less effective in dealing with multicultural contexts.

In the fourth and final section, three essays present the Burkean system as a more unified theory as they underscore the complexity of dramatism. These essays rely heavily on Burke's later writing. Burke's concern that language is tied to action, not just attitude or motion, places him in the company of the European philosophers who are currently raising critical issues for the future of rhetoric. Dina Stevenson, in "Lacan, Burke, and Human Motive," opens this section by reenforcing the importance of Burke's "terms for order" as a unified language system. Stevenson provides a theoretical and psychological grounding for the terms from Lacanian and Saussurian theory. James Klumpp, in "Burkean Social Hierarchy and the Ironic Investment of Martin Luthur King," focuses on "hierarchy" and creatively applies it in a criticism of King's "I Have a Dream" speech. Klumpp takes a sociological perspective as he also responds to the issues of racism, feminism, and multiculturalism and defends the relevance of Burke's dramatism in the twenty-first century. Finally, Dennis Ciesielski, in "'Secular Pragmatism': Kenneth Burke and the [Re]Socialization of Literature and Theory," explains how Burke's emphasis on "text," his observation that all action is symbolic, and his concept of "terministic screens" anticipate the postmodern concepts of "transcendent signifier" and "philosophical hermeneutics." He also focuses on *A Rhetoric of Motives* in describing Burke's identification as a tool for the [post]modern critic's action as an investigation and a sociopolitically revealing process.

These essays taken together make a strong argument that even though Kenneth Burke did not anticipate all the important issues that are moving us into the twenty-first century, his ideas will continue to be taken seriously. They suggest that Burke's dramatism will remain a force in the "unending conversation" about rhetoric.

Notes

1. For a more detailed discussion of Burke's evolution, see Bernard L. Brock, "Evolution of Kenneth Burke's Criticism and Philosophy of Language," in *Kenneth Burke and Contemporary European Thought: Rhetoric in Transition* (Tuscaloosa: University of Alabama Press, 1995).

2. For an analysis of these stages, see Bernard L. Brock, "Kenneth Burke and the 21st Century," *Kenneth Burke Society Newsletter* 6 (1990): 4–9.

14 Bernard L. Brock

3. For a discussion of these terms, see Bernard L. Brock, "Dramatism," in *Method of Rhetorical Criticism: A Twentieth Century Perspective* (Detroit, Mich.: Wayne State University Press, 1990).
4. For a more detailed discussion of Burke's modification of basic concepts, see Brock, "Evolution."
5. A more detailed development of this debate may be found in Steven Best and Douglas Kellner, *Postmodern Theory: Critical Interrogations* (New York: Gilford, 1991).

References

Best, Steven, and Douglas Kellner. *Postmodern Theory: Critical Interrogations.* New York: Gilford, 1991.
Brock, Bernard L. "Dramatism." In *Method of Rhetorical Criticism: A Twentieth Century Perspective.* Detroit, Mich.: Wayne State University Press, 1990.
———. "Epistemology and Ontology in Kenneth Burke's Dramatism." *Communication Quarterly* 33 (1985): 94–104.
———. "Evolution of Kenneth Burke's Criticism and Philosophy of Language." In *Kenneth Burke and Contemporary European Thought: Rhetoric in Transition.* Tuscaloosa, Ala.: University of Alabama Press, 1995.
———. "Kenneth Burke and the 21st Century." *Kenneth Burke Society Newsletter* 6 (1990): 4–9.
Brock, Bernard L., et al. "Dramatism as Ontology or Epistemology: A Symposium." *Communication Quarterly* 33 (1985): 17–33.
Brown, Richard Harvey. "Rhetoric, Textuality, and the Postmodern Turn in Sociological Theory." In *The Postmodern Turn: New Perspectives on Social Theory.* Edited by Steven Seidman. Cambridge: Cambridge University Press, 1994.
Burke, Kenneth. *Attitudes Toward History.* Boston: Beacon, 1961 [1937].
———. *Counter-Statement.* Chicago: University of Chicago Press, 1957 [1931].
———. "Dramatism." In *The International Encyclopedia of the Social Sciences,* edited by D. L. Sills. New York: Macmillan/Free Press, 1968 ed.
———. *A Grammar of Motives.* Berkeley: University of California Press, 1969 [1945].
———. *Language as Symbolic Action: Essays on Life, Literature, and Method.* Berkeley: University of California Press, 1966.
———. "(Nonsymbolic) Motion/(Symbolic) Action." *Critical Inquiry* 4 (1978): 809–38.
———. *Permanence and Change: An Anatomy of Purpose.* Berkeley: University of California Press, 1984 [1935].
———. *The Philosophy of Literary Form: Studies in Symbolic Action.* Berkeley: University of California Press, 1973 [1941].
———. *A Rhetoric of Motives.* Berkeley: University of California Press, 1969 [1955].

————. *The Rhetoric of Religion: Studies in Logology.* Berkeley: University of California Press, 1970 [1061].

Chesebro, James W. "Epistemology and Ontology as Dialectic Modes in the Writings of Kenneth Burke." *Communication Quarterly* 36(1988): 175–91.

————. "Kenneth Burke and Jacques Derrida." In *Kenneth Burke and Contemporary European Thought: Rhetoric in Transition.* Edited by Bernard L. Brock. Tuscaloosa: University of Alabama Press, 1995.

Desilet, Gregory. "Nietzsche Contra Burke: The Melodrama in Dramatism." *Quarterly Journal of Speech* 75 (1989): 65–83.

Fisher, Walter, and Wayne Brockriede. "Kenneth Burke's Realism." *Central States Speech Journal* 35 (1984): 35–42.

Jay, Paul. "Modernism, Postmodernism, and Critical Style: The Case of Burke and Derrida." *Genre* 21 (1988), 339–58.

Nelson, Cary. "Writing as the Accomplice of Language: Kenneth Burke and Poststructuralism." In *The Legacy of Kenneth Burke.* Edited by Herbert W. Simon and Trevor Melia. Madison: University of Wisconsin Press, 1989.

Seidman, Steven. *The Postmodern Turn: New Perspectives on Social Theory.* Cambridge: Cambridge Universiyt Press, 1994.

Williams, David Cratis. "Under the Sign of (An)Nihilation: Burke in the Age of Nuclear Destruction and Critical Deconstruction." In *The Legacy of Kenneth Burke.* Edited by Herbert W. Simon and Trevor Melia. Madison: University of Wisconsin Press, 1989.

Part I

Symbolic Action

1

Nature's Physician

The Metabiology of Kenneth Burke

Richard H. Thames

Introduction: "Back to the Future"

Kenneth Burke, to the casual reader, appears opposed to science and technology; the more careful reader knows he resists only their enshrinement. Burke, however, is concerned with more than having science know its place. In conjunction with Whitehead, he complains that "scientific method categorically makes the discovery of purpose impossible." Medieval Catholic notions of causality were fundamentally purposive, says Burke; scientific notions emerging from the Renaissance were mechanistic. In the new perspective, even human motives were explained by the *vis a tergo*, or force from behind. Men were no longer drawn as to a beacon but pushed by the compulsion of prior circumstance (Burke, *Permanence*, 170–71). Burke spent his lifetime fighting to restore the old perspective, to reinstate purpose as a primary term of human motivation (*Permanence*, 168).

Restoring the old perspective requires returning to an *organic* rather than a mechanistic orientation, because the former is more congenial than the latter to teleology. Burke complains that the modern world, convinced of machinery's absolute goodness, has assumed that the mechanistic metaphor possesses universal interpretive value and therefore has employed it to explain even biological behavior (Burke, *Permanence*, 207). But *we are animals*, not machines. And as Burke notes in *Permanence and Change*, every "biological organism has 'purposes' intrinsic to its nature" (168).[1] Accordingly, Burke's model science is *biology*, not physics, and his system a metabiology rather than a metaphysics. In this

19

regard he is much like Aristotle—more than 25 percent of whose writings are devoted to biology and in whose system entelechy is central and the organism paradigmatic for understanding being and becoming. Like Aristotle, Burke extends the organic beyond biological being. He shares with Aristotle, Plato, Plotinus, and the Stoics, as well as with Whitehead and Bergson, indeed with the classical and the medieval worlds, a conception of *Nature as an organism*, not a machine.

But fully grasping Burke's metabiology involves recognizing Nature not only as an organism but as an organism human beings are related to in a particular way. Quite simply Burke is a *pantheist* (similar in many respects to Spinoza).[2] His vision of ultimate being is a projection of human being; the concept of an all-inclusive "Nature that itself contains the principle of speech" grows out of the concept of "bodies that (are genetically endowed with the ability to) learn language." What we can know of Nature begins with what we can know of ourselves, because we are a part (perhaps the synecdochic part) of It. What harm is done to Nature is done in effect to us given the intimacy of our relationship and interactions. Thus *Burke's pantheistic metabiology leads to a concern for ecology*.

The intent of this essay is not to examine Burke's concern for ecology per se but the systematic relationship among biology, language, sociology, pantheism, and ecology that exists in Burke's thought—that is, to generate an overview of his metabiology.

The Death of God and Nature

In *A Grammar of Motives* Burke professes to have found Spinoza's pantheism particularly engrossing because it "characterizes to perfection the great watershed moment in Western thought when men were narrowing the scope of their terminologies." This narrowing involved a shifting "from a poetic or moralistic vocabulary of action and passion to a scientific or mechanistic vocabulary of motion." Spinoza's key equation, *Deus sive Natura* (God or Nature), serves to bridge the gap (Burke, *Grammar*, 138).[3]

As the metaphysical scene or ground of Nature's existence, God is traditionally considered the term of wider scope. The relationship can be imagined in terms of two concentric circles, with God (the larger circle) surrounding and containing Nature (the smaller circle). As a pantheist, Spinoza conceives of God and Nature as equals; he imagines the two circumferences as identical in scope. But God and Nature can be equated in either of two ways. The larger circle, God, can be reduced to coincide with the smaller, Nature; or the smaller enlarged to coincide with the greater. Thus the equation raises the question: Has Spinoza naturalized God or deified Nature? The ambiguity is captured in *Webster's* definition as quoted by Burke in the *Grammar*: "the doctrine that there is no God but the combined forces and laws which are manifested in the existing universe [i.e., naturalized God]; the doctrine that the universe, taken or conceived as a whole is God [i.e., deified Nature]" (72).[4] Materialists stressing Nature in the equation (as in the following centuries Western thought itself was progressively to do) can claim Spinoza as one of their own (*Grammar*, 72). Idealists stressing God (as nineteenth-century Romantics were to do) can consider him a mystic. Thus the ambiguity of Spinoza's pantheism provides "a perfect transition from theistic to naturalistic vocabularies of motives" (*Grammar*, 138)—or, as we shall see with Burke's pantheism, from naturalistic to theistic.

When Spinoza equates God and Nature, the stage is set for modern science to omit God in obedience to Occam's contention that "entities should not be multiplied beyond necessity." Burke considers Occam's "law of parsimony" the keystone of scientific terminologies (Burke, *Grammar*, 81). When two circumferences coincide, he claims, the wider set of terms is usually found guilty of multiplying entities beyond necessity.

> If we say, for instance, that the weight fell because God willed laws according to which the weight would fall when we pushed it, and the wood burned because God willed laws according to which wood burns when we light it, we can quickly become parsimonious enough to say that the weight fell because we pushed it and the fire burned because we lit it. And thereby we have significantly reduced the scope of our motivational terminology. (*Grammar*, 98)

For the sake of scientific explanation, God can be ignored as an invariant term and therefore omitted. Although omitting an invariant term may not be unreasonable, such parsimony automatically reduces the circumference of one's terms and can result in terms' getting narrower and narrower (*Grammar*, 99).[5]

When God the Creator and Nature his Creation are made synonymous in pantheism, the former can be dismissed as an unnecessary duplication. In medieval theology the Creator's purpose is embodied in the act of Creation. Consequently, when the Creator is eliminated, purpose is eliminated too. When the Creator is gone, only the Creation remains, not as an act but a concatenation of motions. Stress is shifted from final to efficient cause—the kind of cause, says Burke, "that would reside not in a 'prime mover,' but in a 'last mover' (as the lever with which a man moves a stone could be called the 'last mover' of the stone)." The circumference of terms for motivation is reduced to the orbit of *vis a tergo* cause prominent to theories like behaviorism which treat motivation in compulsive terms of instinct, drive, reflex, and stimulus–response (Burke, *Grammar*, 79).[6] Thus the quality most strongly characterizing our own feelings with regard to our actions is eliminated. "The spontaneous words for human motivation all imply the element of choice," says Burke, "but the scientific words all imply compulsion" (*Permanence*, 218).

So Nature ceases as an organism and becomes instead a machine, a clock occupying space and keeping time. Action becomes motion and purpose agency; final cause gives way to efficient cause. When modern science performs its surgery on medieval thought, excising God with a quick flick of Occam's razor, Nature lies diminished, a cadaver for scientists to dissect. The operation is successful *because* the patient dies.

Metabiology

According to Burke, any "orientation" approaching complete political embodiment will call forth the corrective it requires (*Permanence*, 62, 181–82).[7] Thus, a new orientation correcting the scientific must show some affinity for the religious orientation, because religion stresses the humanistic or poetic aspects of culture eliminated or minimized by science (*Permanence*, 63). At the same time, the corrective must frame its arguments in terms that enjoy prestige in the orientation it would replace. Thus, an orientation correcting the scientific must to some degree resemble it (*Permanence*, 66). The new orientation Burke proposes approaches human motives in terms of action that leads not only into ethical and poetic realms but scientific ones as well "by reason of the fact that 'symbolic' acts are grounded in 'necessitous' ones," that the verbal is grounded in the nonverbal (Burke, *Permanence*, 168).

But this new orientation is more than an orientation per se. To emphasize the shifting particularities of different orientations is to approach human problems *historically*, as in a philosophy of becoming; to emphasize their underlying similarities is to approach human problems *ontologically*, as in a philosophy of being. *Burke's approach is ontological.*

Burke considers "all of man's historic institutions" to be "the externalization of biologic, or non-historic factors" (*Permanence*, 228).[8] Temporal events may cause man "to stray far from his sources," but "he repeatedly struggles to restore, under new particularities, the same basic patterns of the good life." Orientations change, but "the essentials of purpose and gratification" do not, for they are grounded in man's neurological structure and that remains the same (*Permanence*, 159, 162–63).[9]

Burke calls this search for a *philosophy of being* a metabiology because it transcends biology in the strict sense of the term. He argues that "each biological organism has 'purposes' intrinsic to its nature (a specific nature which aims at some kinds of 'good' rather than others)." But man has motives that are more than mere projections of his nature as a biological organism; he is an animal typically given to linguistic motives (*Permanence*, 168) (or motives made possible by language—i.e., human purposes).[10] Thus the term *metabiology*.

The term itself is easily misinterpreted when "meta" is construed strictly in terms of action and "biology" in terms of motion.[11] In their rush to explore the realm of action, Burke's interpreters often exile biology to the realm of motion and assign that realm to science. Burke himself is not as anxious. He has serious things to say about science and Nature. Failing to listen means failing to recognize the full circumference of his system. He complains that the machine metaphor has been assumed to have universal interpretative value and has therefore been used to explain biological behavior totally different from mechanistic (*Permanence*, 207).

A distinction must be made "between a motive in some measure intrinsic to living things and the purely scenic explanation for the motions of a bubble rising to the surface." Because living things make claims on areas covered by the term *agent*, Burke argues that the biologist's "organism" is equivalent to "agent-minus" (*Grammar*, 157, 159).[12] Thus he rescues biology and a considerable part of Nature from the realm of pure motion and mechanistic explanation.

Burke's reading in biology during the late 1920s and early 1930s (perhaps in conjunction with his research on drugs)[13] appears to have been extensive. His notion of metabiology probably develops out of his reading J. H. Woodger, the foremost proponent of organismic biology.[14] According to Morton Beckner, Woodger and the organismic biologists contend that a living organism (1) consists entirely of chemical constituents but constituents organized in such a way that the organism exhibits behavior and properties above the chemical level; (2) possesses directiveness "understood to include the relation between structure and function, goal-directed behavior, and behavior that subserves any of the biological ends of maintenance, reproduction, or development"; and (3) possesses a "historical character," for example, "develops" through "growth, elaboration, and differentiation, accompanied by the appearance of new potentialities at a higher level of organization" (Beckner, *The Biological Way*, 5–7).[15]

Burke appears not only to have adopted the positions of organismic biology but also to have applied them to language. The biological characteristics of organization (the pun on "organism" is intended), directiveness, and development become characteristics of language for Burke. Language exemplifies a higher level of organization than the strictly biological and therefore cannot be explained by reference to lower levels any more than the biological can be explained by the chemical. The telos of human being is language, the end for the sake of which we are born. We are "bodies that are genetically endowed with the ability to learn language" (Burke, personal interview).[16] The potentiality of speech, says Burke in *Counter-Statement*, is inborn in the germ plasm just as the potentiality of barking is inborn in the germ plasm of a dog (48). Born speechless, we develop speech as we mature.

The development of a symbol-system resembles nothing so much as the growth of an embryo into an adult. Form unfolds, whether in a fiction or philosophy or scientific treatise, progressively revealing the potentialities implicit in a work's key terms. Tracking down the implications within a symbol-system or contemplating the systematic interrelationships that develop among terms engrosses and gratifies us because we are symbol-using animals (Burke, "The Poetic Motive," 59–60).

The process of entitlement that ends in a summarizing term (Burke, *Rhetoric of Religion*, 25), containing within itself all terms that it transcends, is entelechial and biological. The process "attains its ultimate identification" in the Aristotelian vision of a "universal order" in which

> all classes of beings are hierarchically arranged in a chain or ladder or pyramid of mounting worth, each kind striving towards the perfection of its kind, and so towards the kind next above it, while all the strivings of the entire series head in God as the beloved cynosure and sinecure, the end of all desire. (Burke, *Rhetoric of Motives*, 333)

The "god-term," implicit in all other terms and toward which all other terms strive, is the ultimate "organizing" term. Whether terms develop from or toward the ultimate "title of titles" makes no difference. The process is organic.

Pantheism

Burke seeks to describe more than the character of human being; he is concerned with ultimate being too. His metabiology possesses the same scope as metaphysics (*Permanence*, 228–29). Unfortunately, because he refuses to refer to his system in traditional terms or develop it along conventional lines, its full circumference is not recognized.

Burke characterizes Spinoza's metaphysics as a bridge across which we passed from the medieval into the modern world. I would characterize Burke's metabiology as a bridge across which he would have us return to the act-substance philosophies of the medieval and classical worlds rather than the scenic philosophies of modern science, to an emphasis on ontology rather than epistemology. If Spinoza's pantheism provided the opportunity for science to reduce the concept of nature, Burke's own pantheism provides the opportunity to expand it again; rather than reduce God to Nature, he seeks to make Nature God.

For Spinoza there is the one infinite divine substance, "God or Nature," possessing an infinite number of attributes of which we know two, *thought* and *extension*. Spinoza arrives at this description by beginning with the human attributes of *mind* and *body*, projecting them onto the universe, then redefining those finite beginnings as modifications of infinite being. Finite minds become modes of the attribute *thought* and finite bodies modes of the attribute *extension*.

Burke begins with the hyphenated "mind-body" (the equivalent of thought-extension) and points toward "a somewhat Spinozistic conception of substance as possessing two integrally interlocking modes" (*Permanence*, 261). Human beings as "bodies genetically endowed with the ability to learn language" are ultimately grounded in "nature . . . containing the principle of speech"—an odd phrase occurring in a critical passage from the *Rhetoric of Motives* (180), where Burke identifies the ultimate ground of speech not as nonverbal nature but more-than-verbal nature, hence "nature as itself containing the principle of speech" (hereafter NATURE).[17] This all-inclusive NATURE, the ultimate ground of mind-body, functions as Burke's "title of titles," his own "god-term," the ontological referent to which is his equivalent to Spinoza's "God or Nature."

Spinoza, like most pantheists, undercuts his phenomenal beginnings;[18] Burke, however, never forgets the phenomenal character of his. Whereas Spinoza describes the finite in terms of the infinite, Burke describes the infinite in terms of the finite; whereas Spinoza's metaphysical propositions assume the character of assertions about external reality, Burke's metabiological ones are projections of the internal. His infinite NATURE that contains the principle of speech is an extension of the finite body that is genetically endowed with the ability to learn language. Our phenomenologically limited view of Being is of human being writ large.

Burke defends this anthropomorphism as more than a mere projection. The point of view from which we approach NATURE is itself a part of NATURE (*Permanence*, 256).[19] "Our calling has its roots in the biological, and our biological demands are clearly implicit in the universal texture," he says. A biologically rooted point of view is the most undeniable we can possibly have, as near rock bottom as human thought can get (*Permanence*, 261). A grasshopper will find a universe different from ours because it approaches the universe from a point of view rooted in a different biology. What we can know of NATURE is determined by our own nature. What we do know is that *the biological and linguistic attributes of human being must also be attributes of that universal being from which we spring, or else we could not spring from It*. To deny those attributes of NATURE is to deny them of ourselves, for NATURE is (at least) our larger self.

Burke asks us to revere this all-inclusive NATURE as a parent out of which the biological and the linguistic are undeniably born. Far from being barred by some impenetrable barrier, as its children we are bound to and can know NATURE as intimately as our very bodies and minds. Thus out of Burke's pantheism grows a concern for ecology—a deep ecology.[20]

Ecology and Recalcitrance

NATURE is not a machine whose power modern science would have us exploit, but an organism whose life Burke would have us love and care for as we would care for ourselves. In 1937 he called us to the practice of ecology. He warned the world that "the total economy of this planet cannot be guided by an efficient rationale of exploitation alone, but that the exploiting part must itself eventually suffer if it too greatly disturbs the balance of the whole" (*Attitudes*, 150, note).[21] Normally ecology is defined as the science that treats of the "interrelationship of organisms and their environments" (*Webster's Ninth*).[22] But ecology carries an additional connotation for Burke: NATURE as a living organism manifests a level of organization above that on which separate organisms interact. Ecology means for Burke, and has come to mean for us, "the totality or patterns of relations" (*Webster's Ninth*).[23] For organismic biologists, says Beckner, "the concept of organization is correlative to the concept of whole." Parts constitute wholes "by virtue of the organizing relations between parts" (Beckner, *The Biological Way*, 5). The relationship NATURE bears to its parts parallels the relationship we as organisms bear to ours. Just as our parts must function cooperatively for us to stay healthy, so too must NATURE's.

The principle of cooperation in NATURE is of course complicated by the presence of competition. Still, says Burke, "big beasts would starve, if they succeeded in catching all the little beasts that are their prey." Their lack of efficiency in exploiting their ability as hunters acts as efficiency on a higher level, "where considerations of balance count for more than considerations of one-tracked purposiveness" (*Attitudes*, 150, note).

But modern science denied the higher level at which conflict could be resolved and made a battlefield of Nature. "The keystone of *vis a tergo* causality," says Burke, "was an evolutionary relationship between organism and environment" in which "the organism was considered a separate unit more or less at odds with its environmental context—and to this context it sought with varying degrees of success to adapt itself" (*Permanence*, 232).

> Darwin himself had specifically recognized that the struggle for life gives rise to cooperative attitudes, that tenderness, charity, good humor are as truly factors in the survival of man as was any primitive ability to track and slay animals in the jungle. But this aspect of his doctrine was generally ignored—and the struggle for life was usually interpreted in a bluntly militaristic sense. As a result, the world seemed to be composed simply of harsh antitheses, impossible choices, like the choice between conquest and surrender. (*Permanence*, 174)[24]

Confronted with "discordancies between himself and his environment," man refused to surrender to the environment oppressing him and set out to conquer it instead. Reason as the guide of conduct gave way to intelligence, "which was a mere implement of will." This attitude, says Burke, "amounted to a simple declaration of war" (*Permanence*, 172–73).[25]

Competition is a biological fact of life, but not the only or the ultimate; cooperation is what life depends on most (*Permanence*, 235–36, 266). Overly competitive attitudes wreak havoc on the human and the natural world, affronting biological norms (*Permanence*, 271). A sound system of communication, such as lies at the roots of civilization, must be built on cooperative enterprise, says Burke. No sound system can be built on a structure of economic warfare. "The whole idea of progress," he says, "seems to have cloaked one long hysterical attempt to escape from a grossly mismanaged present" (*Attitudes*, 150, note). Now "the laws of ecology have begun avenging themselves against restricted human concepts of profit by countering deforestation and deep plowing with floods, droughts, dust storms, and aggravated soil erosion" (*Permanence*, 163).

The scientific orientation, like all orientations, contains within itself the germs of its own dissolution (*Permanence*, 169). Historic institutions result from externalizing nonhistoric, biologic patterns. Externalizing these patterns brings forth by-products that eventually attain proportions that frustrate the same biologic need satisfied at an earlier stage or other biologic needs equally important (e.g., the need for locomotion interferes with the need to breathe—smog) (*Permanence*, 228–29). Any orientation seeking to be externalized discloses "significant respects in which the material of externalization is recalcitrant" (*Permanence*, 257). In response to increasing recalcitrance new patterns are externalized and embodied in new institutions; in turn, they bring forth new by-products, new orders of recalcitrance, new patterns, and so on. Burke seeks to escape the cycle of orientations by grounding his proposed poetic orientation in the recalcitrance of biology and ecology.

Burke believes that "the ultimate metaphor for discussing the universe and man's relations to it must be the poetic or dramatic metaphor" (*Permanence*, 263). The mechanistic metaphor "leaves too much out of the account," says Burke; it is truncated as the poetic, buttressed by the concept of recalcitrance, is not (*Permanence*, 261). At the same time, the poetic orientation must show some affinity with the religious orientation that "focused its purposes upon the controlling of human forces (the organic productive forces of the mind-and-body itself)" (*Permanence*, 65).

Conclusion

Burke claims in *Counter-Statement* that "in so far as an age is bent, a writer establishes equilibrium by leaning," either as his age leans or in the opposite direction (vii).[26] Burke of course opts for the opposite. Throughout his life he sought to persuade us that we have strayed far from our biologic sources; he struggled through his writing to return us to the basic biologic patterns of the "good life." Burke the metabiologist would be a physician too, examining and healing both humanity and the NATURE it has harmed. Whatever the ultimate ground of all possibility may be, he prescribes:

> the proper study of mankind is man's tendency to misjudge reality as inspirited by the troublous genius of symbolism. But if we were trained, for generation after generation, from our first emergence out of infancy, and in ways ranging from the simplest to the most complex, depending upon our stage of development, to collaborate in spying upon ourselves with pious yet sportive fearfulness, and thus helping to free one another from the false ambitions that symbolism so readily encourages, we might yet contrive to keep from wholly ruining this handsome planet and its plenitude. ("The Poetic Motive," 162)[27]

A modern Hippocrates, Burke practices a sacred craft: he seeks to comprehend our nature so that a balance lost can be refound and health can be restored,[28] both ours and earth's.

Notes

1. Not until the *Grammar* does Burke make a careful distinction between purposes intrinsic to the nature of biological organisms and human purpose— probably after reading more Aristotle and thinking more deeply about the differences among growth/development, animal appetite, and human action. As Marjorie Grene notes (135), the transformations observed in growth and development are *directive*, not *purposive*. Purposive action involves deliberation and choice; but nature does not deliberate or choose. "Human, purposive action," says Grene, "is but a limited case of such forward-directedness, with the superadded qualification of knowledge and deliberate choice." Nature's directedness "is the intrinsic directedness of organic development, not itself thinking or planned by thought, but like thought, ordered and determinate and therefore an appropriate object for the thinker."

2. Spinoza may seem an extremely odd choice as a major influence on Burke. Marx and Freud are cited more often. But, as pointed out in notes 4, 9, and 10, an interest in Marx and Freud could lead quite naturally to an interest in Spinoza. See also Norris.

3. See also *Permanence*, 188, note 1.

4. In this regard, see Barnard, "Spinozism": "No other pre-Marxian philosopher, with the possible exception of Hegel, has received as much attention in the Soviet Union. . . . Following Marx and Engels, many Soviet writers credited Spinoza with having solved the fundamental ontological problem concerning the relation of consciousness to being, and of thought to things. Indeed, admiration for Spinoza prompted some to call him 'Marx without a beard.' Spinoza's rejection of an act of creation, his denial of a continuing intervention in the governance of the world by a supernatural being, his acceptance of nature as something ultimate, self-caused, and 'given,' without limits of time and space, were features not lost upon dialectical materialists." No less congenial "was Spinoza's determinism and naturalism. Most importantly, the allegedly passive role of thought in Spinoza's system was regarded as the most convincing proof of Spinoza's profound understanding of the historical process." See also Kline.

5. Against Occam's law Burke proposes a contrary according to which "entities should not be reduced beyond necessity." Burke has "no great respect for such tactics as those of the materialist who, after telling you, for instance, that 'everything is nothing but chemistry,' will at some strategic point advise, 'accordingly, let us do such-and-such.' We should consider this as evidence that the speaker had derived his position from an unhappy choice of [representative] anecdote, since one would not seek to affect the behavior of a chemical by an exhortation" (Burke, *Grammar*, 324).

6. Final cause covers directedness as well as human purpose.

7. Note the Marxist quality of this position. See note 9.

8. A philosophy of being, says Burke, is characterized by a "Spinozistic concern with man *sub specie aeternitatis.*" For Burke, "An ethics involves one ultimately in a philosophy of being, because it aims to consider the generic equipment of man as a social and biological organism. To this extent, any schema of the 'good life' tends to be anhistoric in quite the same way that an account of digestion or metabolism would be" (Burke, *Permanence*, 271).

9. Cf. Burke, "Permanence and Change: In Retrospective Prospect" (*Permanence*, 298). Burke himself notes that Marx begins *The German Ideology* with the claim that "The first premise of all human history is of course the existence of living human individuals. The first fact to be established is therefore the physical organization of these individuals and their consequent relation to the rest of nature. . . . All historical work must start on the basis of these natural conditions and their modifications in the course of history through the action of men."

10. Though Spinoza denies purpose, Burke argues that "purpose" is still implicit in much that he says, for example, the conatus (the drive toward self-preservation). The conatus has been interpreted as one ancestor of Freud's libido. There are other similarities worth noting: "The Spinozan thesis of confused ideas which men cite as reasons for what they seek and avoid, items which in fact are not the causes which move them, is the ancestor of the Freudian thesis of rationalization. . . . Spinoza also anticipated Freud in the view that to become aware of causes which move us is no longer to fall victim to them." See Barnard, "Spinoza, Benedict (Baruch)."

11. Other misinterpretations arise if both aspects are not stressed. Interpreters suspicious of metaphysics and science shift the emphasis and fail to notice that the scope of Burke's philosophy is in consequence considerably reduced. Overemphasize "meta" and epistemology appears to be Burke's prime concern; but emphasize "biology" equally and ontology emerges instead. Accent "meta" too much and "biology" too little and the mind–body split that Burke himself repeatedly denies is in effect assumed. Too often interpreters suppose that language for Burke is a barrier between man's mind and Nature. By such a division, study of the mind (agent) is assigned to dramatism and study of the body (scene) to science. The distinction between action and motion becomes in effect a distinction between action-minus-motion and motion itself. Thus dramatism is misinterpreted as idealism and science as materialism. When "biology" is given equal weight, the "materialistic" aspect of dramatism becomes more apparent.

12. An organism exhibiting *directedness* (entelechy) is born, develops, has appetites, reproduces, and dies, and therefore is not totally reducible to the motion characteristic of inorganic particles; but an organism lacking language cannot *act* with the *purpose* characteristic of an agent either—thus, an organism is equivalent to "agent-minus."

13. See "Counter-Gridlock." "Endocrinologists would tell me anything," says Burke. He was very much taken with the Nobel Prize-winning neuro-

physiologist Charles Scott Sherrington, whose research he refers to throughout his corpus.

14. See Burke, *Permanence*, 93–94, 232. Also Woodger.

15. See also Beckner, "Organismic Biology," and Goudge.

16. See Burke, "(Nonsymbolic) Motion/(Symbolic) Action." See also Burke, *Permanence*, 296–98.

17. Rather than print out the full phrase "nature containing the principle of speech," the shorter NATURE is used. NATURE is the expression of choice over "nature" to make clear the distinction between the "nature" is normally thought of as material nature (nonverbal or less-than-verbal nature) and the more inclusive "nature containing the principle of speech" (growing out of the phenomenological view of the "body genetically endowed with the ability to learn speech"), which is similar to Spinoza's "God or Nature."

18. See Farrer, 20.

19. Burke says that an orientation corrective of the scientific must "move in the direction of the anthropomorphic or humanistic or poetic" (*Permanence*, 65).

20. See Scarce, 35–36. According to Scarce, "two core values guide deep ecology praxis." (1) *Self-realization*—the extension of "the environmentally conscious individual's perception beyond the traditionally accepted aspects of the 'self' . . . to the environment as a whole." There is an experience of unity with all else, "a release of the small, individual self to the larger Self through heightened environmental consciousness." And (2) *Ecocentricism*—"the ethical stance that everything in nature [living and nonliving] possesses inherent or intrinsic worth or value." Human-centered ("anthropocentric") worldviews grant a privileged status to human being. Deep ecology "teaches that no individual or species warrants such a special status. For ethical purposes ecocentricism places humans on par with trees, blades of grass, mountain lions, and roaches." Burke's pantheism is consistent with "self-realization." See, for example, Deleuze (back cover): "Recent attention has been drawn to Spinoza by deep ecologists such as Arne Naess, the Norwegian philosopher; and this new reading of Spinoza by Deleuze lends itself to a radical ecological ethic." But the phenomenological basis for that pantheism as well as Burke's stance on the inevitability of hierarchy would appear to be inconsistent with "ecocentricism." See also Devall and Sessions.

Somewhat akin to deep ecology is *eco-feminism*, which could be characterized as agreeing with deep ecology's first core value but not its second. According to Scarce, deep ecologists and eco-feminists are sharply divided on "the root cause of humanity's subjugation of nature—human-centeredness versus male-centeredness," anthropocentricism versus androcentrism. Gender-neutral deep ecology is supposed to have overlooked the masculine worldview responsible for the domination of Nature, women, and other minorities. "Eco-feminists believe that industrial societies, like others dating back thousands of years, are male-dominated hierarchies embracing androcentric values instead of more 'feminine' values like egalitarianism, connectedness, and non-aggression. They note that men, driven by rationalism, domination, competitiveness, individualism, and a need to control, are most often the culprits in the exploitation of animals and the environment" (Scarce, 39–40). Burke, too, would appear to disagree with eco-feminists on the root cause, being gender-neutral like the deep ecologists. The modern world's orientation originates in the Renaissance attitude of competition with Nature, when human beings, confronted with discordancies between themselves and an environment oppressing them, refused to surrender and set out to conquer instead—an attitude that "amounted to a simple declaration of war" (*Permanence*, 1 72–73). Burke would also disagree with eco-feminists on the nature of hierarchy. Burke and eco-feminists would agree, however, on an *organic* orientation. On this question, see Capra, 37–38: medieval science's "main goal was to understand the meaning and significance of things, rather than production and control. Medieval scientists, looking for the purpose underlying various natural phenomena, considered questions relating to God, the human soul, and ethics to be of the highest significance. The Medieval outlook changed radically in the 16th and 17th centuries. The notion of an organic, living, and spiritual universe was replaced by that of the world as a machine." Also Capra and Spretnak, xxiv: the Green movement describes itself as "an ecological, holistic, and feminist movement. . . . It emphasizes the interconnectedness of all phenomena, as well as the embeddedness of individuals and societies in the cyclical processes of nature [i.e., organicism]. It addresses the unjust and destructive nature of patriarchy."

21. The Greek root of both "economy" and "ecology" is *oikos*, "house."

22. See also "oecology," and (in the Supplement) "ecology," *The Compact Edition of the Oxford English Dictionary.*

23. Burke would no doubt feel comfortable with the "Gaia hypothesis."

24. See also Burke, "Communication."

25. Instead of dominance Burke would emphasize ingratiation and inducement (*Permanence*, 63), that is, "persuasion" classified in most cases "as the very antithesis of war" ("Communication,"144). "Social life, like art, is a problem of appeal," says Burke. The poetic metaphor gives us "invaluable hints for describing modes of practical action" measured too often "by simple tests of utility and too seldom with reference to the communicative, sympathetic, propitiatory factors" present in formal art and the informal arts of living (*Permanence*, 264).

26. "*Permanence and Change* in effect takes up where *Counter-Statement* left off" (*Permanence*, 302–3).

27. Rueckert (162) identifies this passage as the original ending of the "Symbolic of Motives."

28. In ancient medicine, health was associated with balance and disease with imbalance. Burke, like Aristotle, appears quite taken with medicine. For both, drama is medicinal, a cathartic or drastic (from the same root as *drama*), that is, a powerful laxative, for purging the social body of tensions that upset the equilibrium. For Burke, catharsis is central to the entire system, since speech is cathartic. Given the medical origin of the idea of catharsis, it is no wonder that Burke discovers a physical dimension that bothers most people, for whom the idea has been thoroughly aestheticized.

References

Barnard, Frederick M. "Spinoza, Benedict (Baruch)." In *The Encyclopedia of Philosophy*. Edited by Paul Edwards. New York: Macmillan, 1967.
———. "Spinozism." In *The Encyclopedia of Philosophy*. Edited by Paul Edwards. New York: Macmillan, 1967.
Beckner, Morton O. "Organismic Biology." In *The Encyclopedia of Philosophy*. Edited by Paul Edwards. New York: Macmillan, 1967.
———. *The Biological Way of Thought*. Berkeley: University of California Press, 1968.
Burke, Kenneth. *Attitudes Toward History*. 3rd ed. Berkeley: University of California Press, 1984.
———. "Communication and the Human Condition." *Communication* 1 (1974): 135–52.
———. "Counter-Gridlock: An Interview with Kenneth Burke." *All Area* 2 (1983): 6–33.
———. *Counter-Statement*. 2nd ed. Berkeley: University of California Press, 1968.
———. *A Grammar of Motives*. Berkeley: University of California Press, 1969.
———. "(Nonsymbolic) Motion/(Symbolic) Action." *Critical Inquiry* 4 (1978): 811–12.
———. *Permanence and Change: An Anatomy of Purpose*. 3rd ed. Berkeley: University of California Press, 1984.
———. Personal interview. November 5, 1987.
———. "The Poetic Motive." *Hudson Review* 40 (1958): 59–60.
———. *A Rhetoric of Motives*. Berkeley: University of California Press, 1969.
———. *The Rhetoric of Religion: Studies in Logology*. Berkeley: University of California Press, 1970.
The Compact Edition of the Oxford English Dictionary. Edited by Burchfield, R. W. New York: Oxford University Press, 1968 ed.
Capra, Fritjof. *The Turning Point*. London: Fontana Flamingo Series, 1983.
Capra, Fritjof, and Charlene Spretnak. *Green Politics*. Santa Fe, N.M.: Bear, 1986.
Deleuze, Gilles. *Spinoza: Practical Philosophy*. Translated by Robert Hurley. San Francisco, Calif.: City Lights, 1988.
Devall, Bill, and George Sessions. *Deep Ecology: Living as If Nature Mattered*. Salt Lake City, Utah: Peregrine Smith, 1985.
Farrer, Austin. *Finite and Infinite: A Philosophical Essay*. 2nd ed. Westminster: Dacre, 1959.
Goudge, T. A. "Woodger, Joseph Henry." In *The Encyclopedia of Philosophy*. Edited by Paul Edwards. New York: Macmillan, 1967.
Grene, Marjorie. *A Portrait of Aristotle*. Chicago: University of Chicago Press, 1963.
Kline, G. L., ed. *Spinoza in Soviet Philosophy*. New York: The Humanities Press, 1952.

34   Richard H. Thames

Norris, Christopher. *Spinoza and the Origins of Modern Critical Theory.*
Cambridge, Mass.: Basil Blackwell, 1991.
Rueckert, William H. *Kenneth Burke and the Drama of Human Relations.*
Minneapolis: University of Minnesota Press, 1963.
Scarce, Rik. *Eco-Warriors: Understanding the Radical Environmental Move-
ment.* Chicago: Noble, 1990.
Woodger, J. H. *Biological Principles.* New York: Harcourt, Brace, 1929.

2

Toward an Ecology of Language

Star A. Muir

The theme of "balance" has frequently danced through Kenneth Burke's work and the work of those who seek to extend and apply his system. Offering his critical observations as a response to the excesses of human victimage, social and otherwise, Burke has long emphasized an awareness of organic context within which human symbolic and instrumental capacity is inextricably woven. It is therefore fitting and appropriate, in probing the evolution and application of his system as we move into the twenty-first century, that we look more closely at some potential imbalances in his own critical corpus, and begin to explore how his system offers a way of both seeing and of not seeing significant forces shaping the human condition.

Burke, as has been noted with increasing frequency,[1] devotes considerable attention to the instrumental and technological implications of human symbolic capacity. Burke's dramatism, and indeed the whole of his epistemological and ontological system, can be described as a reaction to what he views as a pervasive and pernicious scientism, an improper attitude that extends scientific methods to all aspects of life, that truncates human purpose, uses language as a means of mystification, and dominates Nature to the point of ecological imbalance. Scientism, not to be confused with the poetry of science itself, is extended and manifested in a monolithic conception of how humans know about themselves and about the world around them. This reductive perspective is also apparent in the ascendance of technologism, or the unremitting and unquestioned use of technology as an instrument of progress.

Burke offers critics a vocabulary of Counter-Nature, a terminological development that incorporates a view of the distinction between the principle of personality and the principle of instrumentality, a critical but not completely Marxist perspective on the Cult of Commodities, and an understanding of the perfecting nature of human symbolism in an entelechial striving for fulfillment. His idea of entelechy, the tracking down of implications within a particular vocabulary, is the principle that undergirds a fundamental part of his definition of human: the motivation for fulfillment that makes humans "rotten with perfection." Entelechy is illustrated, for Burke, in the scientific "perfection" of the vocabularies of genetic manipulation, and in the creative clutter of technology that now threatens our existence.

In discussing the ubiquity of the technological "empire," Burke is seemingly resigned to the advance of Counter-Nature. There is no political system, he maintains, capable of controlling the forces of our symbol-guided inventions ("Methodological Repression," 412). It further becomes evident in his vocabulary of Counter-Nature that the drive for fulfillment of our symbol-systems, the rottenness of our entelechial motivations, brings the symbol-using animal closer and closer to an eschatological "perfection." Where, then, in Burke's frame of acceptance is hope for the future? What corrective does he offer to counter his seemingly tragic view of technology? How can critics meaningfully cope with the implications of his system without losing the vitality and wisdom of his perspective?

Addressing some of these concerns, this essay explores the possibility of an "ecology" of language and offers some means by which an assessment of the power of human symbolism can perhaps reassert a balance of technique and vision. The development of this ecology of language touches on four areas: a general perspective on ecology in Burke's writing; an exploration of Burke's own sense of piety, merging organic and mechanical metaphors of being; a discussion of the tensions within the logological impulse to perfection, developing criticism as more than just a species of technology; and a brief inquiry into Burke's Neo-Stoic conception of duty, including the "bridging" function of the office of the teacher/critic. In his discussion of "toward" in Burke's titles, Rueckert argues that it is an entelechial word, reflective of the directional, process-oriented, and meliorative nature of Burke's work (278–79). It is in this sense that this essay hopes to move toward an ecology of language.

Ecology as a Critical Perspective

Burke, as noted previously, has long been concerned with the problem of ecology.[2] Credited by Bowen as being among the first to recognize the importance of ecology among the sciences, Burke draws attention to the Neo-Malthusian proliferation of habits, rather than of people. The imbalance resulting from the overemphasis on efficiency is a "bureaucratization" of purpose as one aspect of wastage (inefficient farming, for example) is reduced only to increase wastage in another area (chemicals), which thereby approaches a limit of ecological capacity (*Attitudes*, 298–303). Burke applies the concept of a "bottleneck" to describe the limitations of this efficiency and the societal concept of "progress" that surrounds industrial innovation. There are inherent limitations, he notes, in the growth of industrial "by-products" and the capacity of the environment to endure such trespasses without breaking down.

Burke has a deep and abiding concern with the general nature of such an "ecological" balance. Burke's own fictional Herone Liddell (little hero) is "haunted by ecology" and dismayed by the twistings and intensity of the human symbolism that he revels in (*Complete White Oxen*, 294). More than a passing fancy, Burke's preoccupation with technology and the accelerating imbalance of society resonates with his ideas about the central role of language in shaping human reality. Burke uses a sense of ecology that is both environmental and symbolic, including perspectives on the "by-products" of industrial production and on the excesses of bureaucratization (*Attitudes*, 411).

At an organic level, if we somehow manage to avoid the alienation and international victimage and conflict magnified by increasing technological efficiency, Burke argues that humans are now continuously confronted with the problem of environmental balance:

> [E]ven if we contrive to postpone permanently an ultimate world-encompassing chemical, bacteriological, thermo-nuclear showdown, even in their peaceful exploitation of raw materials the side-effects of the new powers may fatally upset the balance of nature on which human existence ultimately depends. ("On 'Creativity,'" 71)

The science of ecology, Burke writes, involves the "kinds of balance that prevail among biological organisms, considered as members of a sub-verbal, extra-verbal, or non-verbal community" (*Permanence*, 275). This literal perspective focuses on human interaction with the realm of motion, or the biological context.

As important as this aspect is, symbolic conceptions of ecology and balance are also significant for Burke, given the close tie between symbolism and technological creativity. Ecology, at both levels, involves a proportion between individual motivation and contextual constraints. Once the shift is made to the realm of action, or human symbolism, ecology becomes a much richer form of technology's "self-criticism"

(*Attitudes*, 412), involving a balance among *terms* for technology and criticism as well. The symbolic organism is necessarily both an animal and a symbol-user, and Burke's treatment of the comic corrective illustrates the need for a symbolic "balance" to prevent the ascendance of linguistic efficiency:

> The metaphorical migration of a term from some restricted field of action into the naming of acts in other fields is a kind of "perspective by incongruity" that we merely propose to make more "efficient" by proposing a methodology for encouraging still further metaphorical migrations. And this efficiency, while open to distrust, is to be tested in turn by tests of "ecological balance," as we extend the orthodox range of a term by the perspective of a totality. (*Attitudes*, 173)

Conceiving ecology in reference to symbolic manipulations, a symbol-smith move if there ever was one, is consonant with Burke's ongoing concern with avoiding absolutism in his critical philosophy. In detailing the resources of language, he is ever reluctant to aspire to any absolute grounding, except perhaps in his insistence that dramatism is not a metaphor. In his dramatism and logology, Burke ascribes to a balance of perspective, a reciprocity between critical modes of being and understanding. His penchant overall for a dialectical suspension of principles, coupled with a mediating principle that bridges the dialectic, might be termed the critical "ecology" of his system.

Such a critical ecology is well represented in the writings of those who respond to and extend Burke's system. Bertelsen, for example, develops a transformational principle operant in human versions of reality by exploring the inherent tensions between the biological and the social. Recognizing these tensions, Bertelsen argues, the critic is sensitive to an imbalance between social and biological representations of particular rhetorical situations. Brock, in noting a shift away from Burke's early dualistic perspective, views the dialectic among Burke's later ontology and epistemology as a more unified system in which "the human process of symbol using integrates, shapes and controls both external and internal realities simultaneously" (310). Again, it is the tension, or the balance, between these co-present elements that constitutes the force of Burke's system.

The theme of balance is therefore a significant one for Burke and for critics seeking to understand and to apply his concepts. Balance in this context reflects his distress at industrial "habits" exceeding the limits of ecological capacity, and it also reflects Burke's concern with the rigidity of linguistic and philosophical perspectives that cannot mediate between realms, or even recognize the vitality of ambiguity in human symbolism. The notion of balance here is a fruitful one, with the interplay of differing conceptions of the term. Identified by the *Oxford English Dictionary* as a condition in which two (or more) forces hold each other in equilibrium, "balance" also embraces two further contradictory meanings: "subjective uncertainty, hesitation, wavering, doubt," and the "power to decide or determine; authoritative control" (158). An ecology of language, then, incorporates an awareness of the basic uncertainty and subjectivity of language, and plays that off against the entelechial qualities of control and determination. The basic move of this essay, in keeping with the reflective nature of Burke's system, is to investigate the concept of balance more closely across a range of his ideas, and perhaps to foster an ecology of language with a view toward implications for an ecology of life.

Piety and the Organic Metaphor

In the twists and turns of Burke's own critical system, the role of irony as a master trope has gained considerable attention. His "frame of acceptance," the comic view, reasserts awareness of the ambiguity of life and language, even as it entertains the variety of "terms" that compete in the dialectic of irony. What has not gained as much attention is Burke's loyalty to an organic sense of being, to the metaphor, or perspective, of human existence and interaction as an organism.[3] While it is tempting to describe Burke as an organicist, this misses the varying ways in which the machine metaphor is also a perspective taken by this vehemently anti-industrial critic. In examining Burke's sense of piety, the loyalty to the sources of his own being, the proposition advanced is that tension exists in the metaphorical perspectives that Burke brings to bear, and that the conditions for transformation of human attitudes revolve in many ways around this tension.

Burke identifies the notion of piety as a "system-builder," a schema of orientation (*Permanence*, 71–83). It is an organism's sense of what properly goes with what, and it is for Burke not just a religious concept, but an affinity for the proper order of things, an order often acquired in childhood. This "loyalty to the sources of our being," in Santayana's words, is often painfully counteracted by the pragmatic necessity of utilitarian actions. What "needs" to be done, or the immediate and rational expediency, can counter the deep-seated feelings of propriety. Burke's understanding of *im*piety, then, is revolutionary in seeking to replace an entire orientation, one often rooted in childhood experiences and in the strength of emotional experience.

The Organic Metaphor

To understand Burke, and his own sense of placement, the organic metaphor is a fruitful one, a perspective Burke often contrasts with the machine metaphor. The organic metaphor, which features interaction with the environment (an open system), fertility (creativity), and purposive movement (teleology), is apparent in much of Burke's perspective on the duality of the symbol-using animal. Floyd Matson's treatment of the dichotomy between mechanistic and organismic views of man is sympathetic in many ways with Burke's own view of behaviorism and Cartesianism. In his description of the "biological freedom" that is helping remove vestiges of the reductive mechanistic scientific approach to human nature, Matson considers the wholeness of the organic system, its pattern and form, and its purpose, as central characteristics of an organism. Matson argues that human consciousness, or insight into *self* as organism, is the key to the reassertion of individuality and the proper placement of scientific ways of knowing:

> Both the actual processes of organic life and our knowledge about them operate on two complementary levels. One level is that of mechanism-mechanical in process and mechanistic (physicochemical) in analysis. The other level is free from mechanism, both in process and in observation. On either description, then—that of organic processes or of our knowledge about them—mechanism is only half the story, in the deepest sense a half-truth. (151)

The organic "counter" to the alienation of a pervasive "mechano-morphization" is clearly demonstrated in Burke's approach to the problem of scientism. Burke is not as sanguine as Matson about the capacity of the uncertainty of physics, the emergence of purpose in biology, and the evolution of psychology to overcome the bureaucratization implicit in the hierarchical psychosis. Burke does exemplify, however, at least a partial integration of these competing metaphors.

Burke's organism, he is quick to point out, is not the scientist's organism (the biologist will stress the scenic qualities of the organism—an "agent-minus"), but is instead endowed with the capacity for self-movement. When biologists encounter aspects of such self-movement, they "make claims" covered by Burke's term *agent* (*Grammar*, 157). Burke's organism is purposive; it takes action, and is not merely acted on. This purposive capacity is drawn in contrast to the sterility of mechanical movement; indeed, Burke's organic frame often surfaces largely as a reaction to the machine metaphor, a mechanistic and rational perspective on human interaction. The variety of ways Burke derides the mechanical perspective comprise, in large part, his own organic frame.

At the base of his distinction between action and motion, of course, is the biologically individuated human, the discrete organism. Burke's conception of self is grounded in this duality of action and motion ("(Nonsymbolic) Motion," 813), and his argument about the body–mind distinction is that they are not truly split, but that there is a continuum in the body ("In Haste," 330–31). At a fundamental level, Burke is commenting on his own biological nature, his own genius being grounded on a continuum of consciousness and reflexivity that springs from the bone and tissue of his existence.

Outside his system, there is ample evidence of his adherence to an organic perspective, since his own life establishes a concern with holistic interactions with the environment, sexual fertility, and a degree of purposive movement. Living in Andover, with the garden, the bees, and the wrens, having no electricity or running water for years, and raising his five children, no one can doubt Burke's closeness to his own biological nature. Blankenship, discussing his ecological perspective, notes Burke's strong sense of place, his close connection to the "eco" (the Greek *oikos*, or "house") in ecology (253). This "placement" is the organic perspective taken in relation to the "web" of Burke's own life. His poetry, and his reflections on his home in Andover, orient him as part of a larger whole, part of an interconnectedness between and among all natural things ("In New Jersey," 98). Yet even in his participation in this great whole, Burke senses his own difference, his own distinctness, from the web of nature. He displays a sadness about his own "counter-natural" existence, and the lost opportunities symbolism imposes on the biological animal. In a poem entitled "Night Piece," Burke expresses his own longing:

> O pulsant autumnal jungle
> Restore me to thy rhythm
> Teach me the knack.

> I have stood on the edge of the jumping-off place
> Waiting.

> Have looked down
> To see still stars at the bottom of a lake;
> Looked out
> Upon dark riddle within.

O mad dreaming absolute City
O Nature's Babylon
Make me   of thy rhythm
Make me   of thy pageantry.
(*Collected Poems*, 29)

Even as he might long for a simpler existence, Burke, firmly
grounded in the organic metaphor that frames his lifestyle, nonetheless
recognizes the totality of the "fall" into symbolism. His system strives,
however, to take as its root the biological nature of the symbol-user. He
discusses the integrative nature of such a perspective:

> Essentially, it involves the selection of a purposive or teleo-
> logical metaphor (the metaphor of human action or poetry) as
> distinct from a mechanistic metaphor (the vis a tergo causality
> of machinery) for the shaping of our attitude toward the
> universe and history. And it bases this choice upon the most
> undeniable point of reference we could possibly have: the
> biological. It aims less at a metaphysic than at a metabiology.
> And a point of view biologically rooted seems to be as near to
> "rock bottom" as human thought could take us. (*Permanence*,
> 260–61)

In his deliberations on a metabiology, Burke questions the positivist's
causal scheme whereby the organism is caused, *vis a tergo*, by the
environment. Yet Burke's metabiology, spanning rational and irrational
conceptions of human thought, is purposively methodical (from the
Greek *met-hodos*, or "way after") (*Permanence*, 234). The method
proceeds in accordance with an implicit view as to the basic purpose of
the human genus. Burke takes care to reassert the rationality, the
methodology, of the biological perspective. Accepting the notion of life
as a method suggests, for Burke, that "all the universe could likewise be
designated as a method or aggregate of methods-in which case the
selection of the biologic metaphor should not necessarily interrupt our
rational investigations" (*Permanence*, 261).

Mechanistic By-products

This brings us in a roundabout way to some tensions in Burke
between the mechanical and the organic, even as he and others laud the
biological foundation for his system. In his admitted ontology of dramatism, and certainly in his epistemological logology, the "aggregate" of his

methods, Burke's dialectic evinces some "mechanical" inclinations. There is an interaction between poet and critic, where the poet is "synthetic" (putting things together in symbolic mergers), and the critic is "analytic" (reassembling in a new way what is first taken apart). The vast instruments of Counter-Nature, Burke argues, have overemphasized the analytic. This opens up a variety of critical resources (science, technology, philosophy), but it also engenders an analytic approach to the problem of overemphasis. For Burke, "technology itself has produced an analytic world—hence, no other instrument but analysis can confront it with the necessary precision" (*Attitudes*, 215). That he takes this premise seriously is evident in the complexity of his "bureaucratized" system. Here lies part of the dialectical tension between his vision and his systematic pursuit of that vision.

The five (no, innovation leads to six!) terms of the pentad are a complex, an amalgam, whose entirety is necessary for a full account of human motivation in a particular situation. The assessment of ratios allows a more sensitive analysis, a "fine-tuning" of the instrument. One by-product of this system, which Burke develops as a partial antidote to the extremity of various philosophical schools that emphasize one term at the expense of the others, is the mechanical utility of his "formula." As any teacher of rhetorical criticism soon discovers, the pentad contains the seeds of facile and mechanical use. Overcoming this tendency is one of the most continually challenging features of Burkean pedagogy. While not reflecting an inherent mechanical inclination of Burke's system, this "cookie-cutter" trap illustrates that his system contains an instrumental and mechanistic flavor, and can commonly foster a rote approach to criticism.

Burke's early *Counter-Statement* offers a "Program" to counter the effects of industrialism and mechanization, an aesthetic means of "reclamation." The preface to the first edition describes the central chapter of the book as an instrument designed for criticism. This reflective description of "Lexicon Rhetoricae" fits much of Burke's work from that point:

> It is a kind of judgment machine, designed to serve as an instrument for clarifying critical issues (not so much for settling issues as for making the nature of a controversy more definite). It seeks to perform this function by working out a set of "pivotal" or "key" terms for discussing the processes of literary appeal. It should be a critical nomenclature for paralleling in analytic terms what a work of art itself performs in terms of the "creative," the "imaginative." (*Counter-Statement*, ix)

Burke specifies that it is a machine for criticism, and not for poetry (which, he notes, is "always beyond the last formula" [ix]). His frank intentions in this instance, where he is describing the varieties of form, the psychology of information, and the nature of aesthetics, are significant in the context of his larger system. Burke is ever working out a set of terms or schematizing critical concepts that are floating about. This "methodical" approach, with its instrumental implications, is likewise illustrated in the essentializing move of his logology.

The Impulse to Perfection

Given the specific human proclivity to track down the implications of their terminology, an entelechial motivation to "perfect" our symbol-systems, the question remains: How can the symbol-using animal mute the eschatological implications of this "progress"? There is evidently no other means than by self-reflection that humans can avoid the entelechy "trap," and yet the resources of symbolism are themselves being "perfected" in this critical process of self-reflection. Burke has commented on this embodiment of the principle of perfection in his own system of logology:

> Incidentally . . . I do not judge my position as outside the technological orbit. In fact, I take it that Logology's wan methodological analogue of HOPE, its involvement with "the tracking down of implications," is at every point following implications that Technology itself brings to the fore. . . . Logology is vigilant with admonitions (and corresponding perspectives) that the resources of Technology have brought into being by exactly those conditions—hence a whole new set of moot questions arises. ("Variations," 171)

Whereas technology promises us a pill for everything, logology (a "dreary substitute") offers a futuristic possibility of tracking down the implications of human symbols, of shifting from "know thyself" to "spy on thyself" (165). That having been said, it is useful from an ecological point of view to investigate in greater depth the means (or agencies) by which such tracking down occurs, and to briefly explore the role, or "office," of the critic in such a perspective. In other words, what is the nature of logology as a tool, and is the critic in that regard an engineer, or, more generally, a technocrat? The answer to that question has significant implications for a balanced view of language, and for the interaction between agent and scene.

The Logological Instrument

Burke's theory of language has been loosely differentiated between two terms: dramatism and logology. Burke argues that dramatism is his ontology, stressing what humans *are*, and that logology is his epistemology, rooted in the symbolic means by which humans come to *know*.[4] Burke's larger view of logology is intertwined with his views of Counter-Nature: both are concerned with the inception of symbolism, and the creativity and motivations that are implied by variations of symbol usage. Logology presumes a kind of analogical extension between the realm of Nature and the "duplicates" of a verbal medium, and is thus grounded in the basic dualities of human existence: between symbolism and nonsymbolic motion, and between the positive realm of Nature and the negative that arises symbolically. The function of this duality (or polarity) is clearly central to a logological view of human activity. In contrast to the monadism of behaviorism, Burke puts "primary stress upon DUPLICATION, POLARITY, NEGATION (and countless variations of such) as the very soul of logological inquiry" ("Theology and Logology," 175). These variations are featured by logology in a set of possible relationships that provide a basic grounding for the critic.

Burke invokes a process whereby such nontemporal principles are translated into narrative terms, a mythologizing operation that he terms the "temporizing of essence."[5] In his discussion of "King Lear," Burke first summarizes the plot in narrative terms; it is about an old king who is forced to foolishly abdicate his throne (10). In logological terms, Burke analyzes the principle of abdication, which leads him in turn to the psychosis of authority in general, implying a "paradox of substance" whereby personal identity is interwoven with the situations and events one is identified with. Burke's essential move, toward which he mobilizes his critical system, is to lay out, or "essentialize," the temporal sequences he analyzes. The equations, implications and transformations are enumerated in sufficient depth to return to the first principles from which the narrative originally flowed.

"Implications"

Two observations can be made about the nature of this logological "machine" and about the role of the critic concerned with the linguistic impulse to perfection. Perhaps the most obvious implication is that logology forsakes a "proportionalizing" move.[6] In "essentializing" the narrative, logology takes the equations, implications, and transformations out of time, out of imagery, and out of personality. Burke's analytic motivation in making this move is enhanced by his own observation that conflict is involved in the interrelationship of concepts only insofar as the narrative is introduced. As he explains in his "Words Anent Logology,"

> So far as terms merely imply one another, they are in a state of directionless "interpenetration," the Logological analogue of "eternity" and "infinity." . . . But so far [as] any such terms attain quasi-temporalized counterparts in the form of narrative or dramatic personalities or personal motives, the "heavenly" peacefulness of their relationship to one another is disturbed by such accentuating of their possible division from one another as gets its fullest or most characteristic dramatic expression in terms of revolt or combat. The term "Disobedience" doesn't "rebel against" the term "Command," but a dramatized representation of their relationship in terms of personalities does involve such destruction of the terms' mutuality, or angelic "interpenetration." (78)

What is somewhat disconcerting here, even in its role as an instrument of understanding, is the eclipsing of the principle of personality. Burke is excising that element that sparks conflict—the human personality. He analytically distills relevant linguistic and grammatical relationships, he purifies the implicit nature of the implication (which personality renders problematic), but he does not offer a "downward way," a proportionalizing function that would operate dialectically with his essentializing move.

In his discussion of a Platonist dialectic, Burke notes that terms from the supernatural are borrowed from the empirical realm (the upward way), and then are analogized back to the empirical (the downward way) (*Rhetoric of Religion*, 37). Thus nature, the sociopolitical order, and symbolism are sources of analogy for constructing the supernatural order, which is then itself a source of analogy for infusing secular and empirical terms. Burke analytically dissects the operations whereby essences are distilled (the upward way of logology), but his analogical extension is systemically limited in grounding and reinfusing human narrative with the principles of his secular "God-principles." Recall the problems Burke outlines with regard to the ascendance of the instrumental principle, including the imbalance inherent in the instrumental magnification of power, the "hyper"-rationality of the Dynamo, and the bureaucratization of the imaginative implicit in the creativity of Counter-Nature.[7] The subjugation of the principle of personality, a process Burke views with serious misgivings, is seemingly at the core of his own methodological prescription. It is, of course, more complicated than that, since his logological critiques contain the essentially personalistic as they address words about the supernatural and about God. But the analytic technique he offers is quite clear on trimming away the narrative account (like Melia's algebra equation "trims away" the story problem [65–67]), and it is the account that gives the personality depth and the power to resist the transcending force of the instrumental principle. Lentricchia observes in Burke the two strategies of "essentializing" and "proportionalizing," but his reading is that essentializing moves toward one motive from which all others spring, while proportionalizing "rests with complex interrelations of motives" (124). This notion of proportionalizing operates at the level of the principle, however, and the interrelated motives are still abstracted from the realm of conflict. Frank's reiteration that there is a translation back and forth between the two realms is unclear (137), especially since Burke's own critical applications stress the extraction and juxtaposition of motivational principles, without a concomitant development of critical strategies for reinsertion.

Burke could "recover" from his move by providing some means to reassert the story of his insights, by critically attending to the proportionality of his distillation vis-à-vis the larger context of the narrative. In practice, he does relate the "new" sense in which the story conveys meaning, and he does move back and forth between logical and temporal schemes of priority. But the central tendency here, in the evolution of Burke's corpus, is an essentializing inclination, a privileging of the space metaphor (involving atemporal relations) over the time metaphor (the narrative account). In the context of an ecology of language, both the upward way (abstraction) and the downward way (grounding) are critical to a balanced perspective on the range of linguistic transformations. Burke's anecdotes about the "natives," or the "man he once knew," serve this function to a degree, but they seem scarcer once he moves into his extended treatment of logology. Those concerned with the machinations of the human symbolic need pay close attention here, as the lure of such essentialization could well be endemic to the critical enterprise.

A second implication, closely related to the first, is that logology, in its titular analogy, is itself an embodiment of the entelechial motivation. Burke founds his logological perspective on six analogies, starting with the analogy between "words" and "The Word," and concluding on the close likeness of the design of the Trinity and the form of the linguistic situation.[8] The fourth analogy, the "titular" analogy, involves the linguistic drive toward the Title of Titles; it is really the logic of perfection that at other points Burke labels the entelechial principle. This analogy implies a movement "rising to ever and ever higher orders of generalization" (25). Titles sum up their subject matter, or in another view, the variations of the subject matter "radiate" from the titles. The point being made here is that logology itself, embracing this titular analogy, thereby embraces this perfecting movement—it is "rotten with perfection."

Burke identifies the problem with this purifying and distilling analogy when he discusses the possibilities for avoiding the symmetry that implies the destruction of civilization:

> The dreary likelihood is that, if we do avoid the holocaust, we shall do so mainly by bits of political patchwork here and there, with alliances falling sufficiently on the bias across one another, and thus getting sufficiently in one another's road, so that there's not enough "symmetrical perfection" among the contestants to set up the "right" alignment and touch it off. (*Language*, 20)

Elsewhere, citing the vast and hazardous implications of the terminologies of biology and physics, Burke explains that "there is no inner check to stop these things," and that the "only way they get checked is by their checking one another" (Woodcock, 713). Exploring the principle of perfection as groundwork for his logological perspective, Burke echoes the necessity for this "conflict" to overcome the liabilities of such motivation:

> In more restricted ways, the tracking down of implications towards various perfections manifests itself in our many technological nomenclatures, each of which suggests to its particular votaries further steps in that same direction. Such expansionist ambitions are near-infinite in their purely visionary scope; but though they have no inner principle of self-limitation, their range of ideal development is restricted by the ways in which they interfere with one another, including academic problems to do with the allocation of funds among the various departments. ("Theology and Logology," 154–55)

What is apparent in the analogic extension toward a Title of Titles, and in the logological privileging of essences, is the effort to obviate this overlap, or conflict. Burke argues that it is only with the introduction of narrative that the terms (implications) of a cycle come into conflict; the logological stress is on detemporalizing these conflicts into an ever-present set of principles (titles of titles). The Title of Titles would be logology itself, since "Logology could properly be called central, and all other studies could be said to 'radiate' from it, in the sense that all -ologies and -ographies are guided by the verbal" (*Rhetoric of Religion*, 26). Burke immediately qualifies this, noting that such centrality is "ideal" and not literal, and that logology is but one specialized form of study among others. Burke's ideal, however, is instructive in its summarizing attitude, and it embodies the systemic tendency that counters the "pandemonium" that keeps us from the Final Word.

Logology is thus problematic not only because it ostensibly prioritizes the instrumental over the personal, but because at its core it is a vehicle for purifying the biases that cross human purposes and prevent the symmetrical perfection of Burke's eschatological conclusion. Certainly Burke is referring to political biases, and to academic conflicts, but he insists that human symbolism is central to those endeavors, and a critical "machine" to distill linguistic relations in the sociopolitical realm must also have "implications" in empirical terms. Perhaps it is unfair to characterize the purification of essences as the removal of biases—after all, the purified essences are still held in dialectical suspension as equations, cycles of implications, and transformations. But the move away from narrative and toward a logological conception, Burke insists, is a move away from conflict, since it is the entrance of narrative that gives rise to a personified conflict between principles. Tracing the relationship between logology and myth, Burke parenthetically notes that while "'polar' terms such as 'order' and 'disorder' imply each other without strife, they imply much conflict when reduced to terms of irreversible story" ("(Nonsymbolic)," 820). The move away from myth thereby removes the "conflict" implied by the temporal realm, and risks what Burke would term the elimination of pandemonium and the symmetrical perfection of a sterile world. While Burke cautions us against an "overly 'universalizing' view of myth and its 'archetypes'" ("Doing and Saying," 111), the analogous point needs to be made about Burke's own universalizing move in the titular analogy adopted by Logology. As early as *Counter-Statement*, Burke argues that "'inefficiency' is required as the counter-principle to prevent the machine from becoming too imperious" (*Counter-Statement*, 120–21).

Visual Perfection

Of interest here is a real world analog of the essentializing move. In a recent article in the *Wild Earth*, a compilation of writings by members of the radical environmental group Earth First!, one writer objected to the prevalance of what they termed "eco-porn," or the perfected visual representation of Nature scenes (Knighton, 76–78). Via calendars, magazines, pictures, and framed photographs, such perfected natural beauty (visualize the Grand Tetons with snow-capped peaks and scudding clouds, or the majestic full-antlered moose captured in mid-bellow, or the breaching whale frozen in a spray of jubilant exodus) has become symbolic of our natural landscape. As with logology, such representations are abstracted from the temporal and imperfect realities of the wild. Gone from these pictures are the mosquitoes, the dirt, the varying temperature, and the lack of facilities. Gone are the impurities that characterize the biological, that make Nature truly "wild."

The problem here, in the perfection of the landscape, and even of the wildlife that is captured with magnificent clarity, is the difficulty of reinsertion into the natural context once such an image is solidified in our minds. Nature, like the airbrushed and perfected human bodies shown in the nude, is idealized and objectified. There is, of course, the initial problem of expectation, the anticipation of perfection that is inevitably short of experience. The letdown that accompanies the actual encounter may draw the individual further into the safe and civilized cocoon of mediated reality. In symbolic terms, an expectation of such an idealized abstraction may also come to characterize the critical essentializing of temporal texts, as we search for harmonized relationships among key terms. Committing to a critical typology, at times a comforting theoretical alignment, can itself engender a most obstructive form of "not-seeing." The arduous task of bringing oneself out of a perspective once such an alignment of terms has occurred can simply overwhelm the critical effort altogether.

A further difficulty illustrated by this idea of "eco-pornography" is the carelessness with which Nature can now be handled. An objectified image, as with displays of the human body, can be treated with disrespect. The beauty of an "object," human or otherwise, does not necessarily imply respect for it. Quite the opposite is true, in fact, when the readily available perfected image is distanced from the tangibility of the particular. The implication for critical practice, then, may be the continued viability of a respectful treatment of the individual work. There is more than a little concern in the commentary on Burke's work that privileging such a Christian system of guilt and redemption—the abstracted cycle of terms—may powerfully name some operant human motivations, but may also shape a way of not seeing for many critics as well.[9]

If there is a cautionary note to be sounded here, in resisting the impulse to perfection, it is that the instruments of critical analysis themselves must be scrutinized and proportionalized within a larger context of human experience. As a rationalistic endeavor, critical understanding operates through the instrumentalities of a particular frame of acceptance or rejection. The truism that all observation is theory-bound finds its measure here in the "means" by which text and context are related and understood. Burke's logology does provide some stunning possibilities in the derivation of suspended atemporal relations among human motivations. But as an analytic instrument, it likewise privileges its own nature as "instrumentality" in reaching some undestanding about these motivations. What might be a generic cautionary view of critical schemes as a whole is here magnified in the quintessential suspension of personality.

Dancing around and about the tension between his vision of our collective entelechial "destination" and the systematic and methodical tendencies of his own system, Burke negotiates his way into the realm of attitude. Conceived of originally as suspended action, attitude mediates between the inevitable catastrophic side effects of technologism and hopelessness at the inherent symbolic motivations driving technological perfection.

Duty, Attitude, and "Bodies That Learn Language"

Burke has named his own stance, in a variety of contexts, as one of "Neo-Stoic resignation." Describing in his *Grammar of Motives* the moralistic reasons for his project involving the grammar, the rhetoric, and the symbolic, Burke explains the attitude that undergirds his effort to cope with industrial expansion:

> To an extent, perhaps, it will be like an attitude of hypo-chondriasis: the attitude of a patient who makes peace with his symptoms by becoming interested in them. Yes, on the negative side, the "Neo-Stoicism" we advocate would be an attitude of hypochondriasis. But on the positive side it would be an attitude of appreciation. And as regards our particular project, it would seek delight in meditating upon some of the many ingenuities of speech. (443)

Burke's view of himself as a "Neo-Stoic" draws on a long history of Stoic thought. The Stoics, beginning about 300 B.C., developed a philosophy of Nature as determined according to a rational design, the Logos, or reason, of the mind of God.[10] Everything proceeds according to this schema of natural law, the Stoics held, and individuals should not aspire to a destiny outside the process. The movement, originally founded by Zeno of Citium and by Cleanthes, grew to prominence in the Roman

Empire, and later was influential in the Renaissance. Following the path of reason and the pursuit of virtue, the Stoic is indifferent to joy, grief, pleasure, and pain. Since providence determines our fate, the question of evil arises only in regard to human attitudes and intentions, rather than behavior. The proper moral stance for the Stoic is an understanding of and acquiescence to the cosmic pattern through the development of logos, or reason. Moral choice is not simply a response to the environment, but the maturation of rational thought based generally on the inherent human tendency to act in accord with Nature (an attraction toward things that promote well-being, for example).

This postulate of individual intention as the key to moral good erects in turn the question of duty in the ordained cosmic order of Nature. As Edel explains,

> A duty-like concept makes its appearance in that one should do what the divine has ordered or arranged, but the order comes in the assignment of role, or what befits one's place. Particular decisions are thus expressive of the jobs or offices in which one finds oneself. (176)

While rationality is universal, the order of experience and attitude is reflected in the merely generic office or role of the individual. The relationship between the universal and the generic is apparent in the Stoic concern with another aspect of *logos*—the grammar of human speech. Recognized as among the first to elaborate a speech theory of parts (noun, verb, conjunction, and article), the Stoics sought knowledge of the means by which humans grasp connections in Nature, and their concern with grammar reflected a belief that true statements are the symbolic expressions of such connections (Ellegard, 664).

Burke, characterizing himself as a Neo-Stoic, resonates in various ways with these precepts. The nature of human reality is determined by the interaction of the active principle (symbolic action) and the passive principle (animality/biology/Nature). The "tension" within the "symbol-using animal" frames Burke's view of human ethics; even as it implies the subjugation of Nature through instruments of our own making, it offers the *possibility* of a humanistic perspective.[11] In his assessment of symbolic fulfillment, the entelechial principle, Burke seems to locate a grand human design not in rationality per se, but in the motivations residing within symbol-systems, within the *logos* of logology. Burke is hardly indifferent to pain, or pleasure, or grief, or joy, but he does accept the inexorable advance of technology.

In his discussion of the Stoics in the *Grammar of Motives*, Burke is intent on his overall purpose of identifying impurities in philosophies that privilege one term of the pentad. The Stoic "pre-agentification" of scene is instrumental, he notes, in arriving at a variety of moral utilitarianism, where what is created with God's purpose must have some *use* (161). The rationality of the Stoics is translated in political and social terms as a duty to serve other humans, making allowance for the use of the nonrational (nonhuman) in the service of virtue. Burke thus broaches the rhetoric of hierarchy, and the means by which such utilitarianism, while not at that time embracing the full scope of business use (or of scientific and technological use), bridges the gap between providence and pragmatism.

"Perfect Freedom"

Striking a cautionary note about melding agent and scene, Burke nonetheless posits a design, in his own way, for the unfolding of the symbolic universe: the fulfillment of our symbolic implications implied by the entelechial principle. Tracking down the variations on the theme of providence, Burke differentiates design by rationality and design by entelechy:

> Each specialized nomenclature, with its corresponding modes of attention and suggestion, is the technical equivalent of a vision, and thus goads to further unfoldings, each tentative effort being like an answer to a call. . . . The Logological concept of our species as the "symbol-using animal" is not identical with the concept, *homo sapiens*, the "rational" animal—for whereas we are the "symbol-using animal" all the time, we are nonrational and even irrational some of the time. ("Variations," 182)

Rationality, or the hyperrationality embodied in technologism, as Burke suggests throughout his work on the Helhaven satire,[12] is the source of environmental and social imbalances that threaten our existence. Burke will not accept the totality of the rational frame, especially in the emotional "moments" of his poetry, but he does privilege the analytic mode of the critic, and he posits a design for human reality, an entelechial design of advancing human symbolic fulfillment, in resigning himself to the problems of Counter-Nature. In his discussion of Goethe's *Faust*, he remarks that this "tracking down of implications" contains an element of ultimate freedom:

This "entelechial" motive is the poetic equivalent of what, in the moral realm, is called "justice." It is equatable with both necessity and freedom in the sense that the consistent rounding out of a terminology is the very opposite of frustration. Necessary movement toward perfect symmetry is thus free. (*Language*, 155)

Or, as Burke comments in his Psychological Fable, in the "devotion to such formal unfolding there are the makings of perfect freedom" ("A (Psychological) Fable," 206). This notion of freedom, which might be taken as problematic for a philosophy that centers on the concept of act, is consistent with Burke's location of freedom in the realm of symbolic action, in the Spinozistic "adequate ideas" that allow us to accurately name our condition (*Dramatism*, 31–32).

The resurrection of attitude thus becomes central to Burke's Stoicism, in light of this paradoxical "perfect freedom" that we "enjoy," and he speaks of an attitude of delight, even appreciation, toward the dilemmas of modern times. It is hard to conceive of such an attitude as being sincere when Burke is so emphatic in loathing the excesses of environmental victimage. But Burke has apparently "fulfilled" his symbolic nomenclature and has painted himself into a corner—he really has no choice but to embrace such an attitude of hypochondriasis. In his discussion of the problems of creativity, he touches on the "civilizing virtues of Imagination":

There is a great "enrichment" of our lives to be derived from the human pursuit of the humanities. Appreciation is a form of thanksgiving—and thanksgiving is among the most felicitous of attitudes (perhaps the best of all we can have, towards the opportunities that the need to have lived affords us). ("On Creativity," 79)

Burke is stoical in his resignation to the advance of Counter-Nature, and additionally posits species knowledge as the survival of the human race. His discussion of predestiny and providence underscores that the freedom to act is not possible without knowledge of the alternatives ("Variations," 177). Rueckert, grappling with the "tragedy" of the entelechial principle, perceives a mixture of rationality and irony in Burke's system:

When asked what we can do about this tragic drama, Burke tends to answer somewhat ironically that the only solution lies in our coming to understand the nature of the human dilemma.

Burke seems to be saying that species knowledge, and an ecological vision, rather than more technology, are what might save us (and our world) from ourselves before it is too late. There has always been a strain of salvationist fervor in Burke's belief that knowledge can save us, as well as a sense that, if knowledge can't save us, it can allow us to go down laughing ironically at our follies. (274)

Burke, rather than simply adhering to a rational knowledge of the unfolding design, conceives of attitudinizing as a means of mediating between the realms of action and motion-between symbol-use and biological organism. As he describes his revision of the original pentad into a hexad, an all-important function is implied:

[Attitude] designates the point of personal mediation between the realms of nonsymbolic motion and symbolic action. Its "how" refers to the role of the human individual as a physiological organism, with corresponding centrality of the nervous system, ATTITUDINIZING in the light of experience as marked by the powers of symbolicity (both in themselves and in the realm of the Counter-Nature that has developed as the results, intended and unintended, of those powers). Hence our notions of "reality" amount to a tendentious though unstable complex of "personal equations" that are implicit in such simultaneously unique and socially infused "orientation." (*Attitudes*, 394)

The end result is that while human symbolism "counters" the sheerly biological nature of the organism, there is possible an orientation by which imbalance between the realms can be minimized.

Offices of the Critic

Enter in this regard the duties of the individual and the roles assigned within the hierarchy of human social interaction. Following the Stoic lead of identifying offices and jobs that guide appropriate attitudes, Burke, in the appendix to *Attitudes Toward History*, lists the seven "offices" that comprise central tendencies in human motivation (353–75). Acknowledging overlap and incompleteness, Burke isolates these human motivations: to govern, serve (provide for materially), defend, teach, entertain, cure, and pontificate (minister in terms of a "beyond"). These offices, which Burke explicitly identifies from the point of view of a global, technological scene, are not related in any fixed way; they are not mutually exclusive, neither are they intended to be exhaustive. Governance, of course, includes rulers and kings, as well as managers and legislatures. Service, subsuming agriculture, industry, and transportation, encompasses clerical work and the means by which business covertly governs while overtly serving. The office of defense, the policing of order, permeates the duty of governance and informs the service of the public. Teaching includes education, journalism, and perhaps the efforts of advertising agencies, insofar as they "teach" the public what to want. Entertainment, including an array of social rituals, is now an industry unto itself, with a vast separation of participants and observers. Both entertainment and teaching share the capacity for "indirect governance" in the "shaping and intensifying of such attitudes as have their corresponding role in practical conduct" (362). Curing entails both medicinal treatment and mental therapy. Overlapping with entertainment is the kind of curative cleansing, or catharsis, that comes with watching tragedy. The last office, to pontificate, is essentially terministic, in treating humans in terms of a "beyond." Rejecting "consolation" as a title for this office, Burke assumes the solemnizing or formalizing functions of the priesthood under the interpretation and sanctioning implied by pontification. Pontification "bridges" the gap between the world as we experience it and the world beyond, between the temporal and the eternal, between Nature and the supernatural.

Burke offers these offices as a general set of motivational descriptors, under which all other motivations can be made to fit. He further observes, however, that they are names for acts, rather than motives, and that each individual will bring a range of personal motivations to the "office." These motivations move beyond a state of "natural motivation" with the advent of symbolic capacity. This realm of symbols "joins us with wordless nature while at the same time standing between us and wordless nature" (373). With the addition of words, human experience can no longer perceive the "Old Adam" sensations of pleasure, pain, hate, and fear. These motivations are transformed with the addition of human symbolism:

> You could state the matter bluntly thus: Pleasure and pain can no longer be exactly what they would be to us sheerly as animals, and similarly with love and hate (or fear), once we approach problems of "acceptance" and "rejection" through the genius of that specifically linguistic pair, "Yes" and "No" (to which we should add the strategic midway stage of "Maybe"). With the negative, "conscience" is born (as attested in the Biblical formula, "Thou shalt not . . . ," conscience being the

power to say no to the self, deep within the self, or equally deeply it may say no to the thou-shalt-not's of others). (*Attitudes*, 373–74)

It is this sense of conscience that returns Burke to the seven general offices of the symbol-using animal. Each of these offices, to govern, serve, defend, teach, entertain, cure, and pontificate, involves this "conscience" in the possibilities for abuse of the office. The ultimate perversion of the various offices, Burke notes, is made possible by the regularities of order, which necessarily implies hierarchy. The "hierarchical psychosis," or The Scramble, as he terms it, is "what the conditions of empire add up to, in their drearier manifestations" (374).

The "duty" of the Stoic, in this context, is transformed into an awareness of the possible perversions of the offices as they are enmeshed in a bureaucratized and industrialized society. Knowledge of the psychosis, and its effect on the generic motivations, or offices, of human action, is the reflective prerequisite for Burke's morality. Which brings us to Burke's "Neo-Stoic" motivation, the office of his own critical action. The function of the teacher, Burke posits as he concludes his discussion of the seven offices, is to communicate an awareness of self in relation to evolving Counter-Nature:

The basic educational problem at this stage of history would be: How best adapt the symbol-using animal to the conditions of world empire that are being forced upon us by the irresistible "progress" of technology? (Such would be the "global" aim of education.) (*Attitudes*, 375)

The point is clear enough: Burke's Neo-Stoicism is not sheerly contemplative; it is strongly pedagogical as well. Human conscience, in assuring the balance of ecology, is not a consistently mature motivation. It must be developed. Burke, even in the resigned contemplation of the advance of Counter-Nature, holds out the need for active participation in the maturation of human attitudes toward Nature. The critical examination of society's operating assumptions, a purely "theoretical" undertaking, is thus located in the office of teaching. Burke moves from his early characterization of humans as "symbol-using animals" to his more recent description of "Bodies That Learn Language."[13] This reconceptualization moves the focus from the use and abuse of language to the learning of language—a positive move accentuating the possibilities of teaching and learning for future action.

Learning for the Twenty-first Century

What, then, is to be taught? The ultimate source of perversion for these offices, Burke is quick to note, is the often psychotic motivations, *stemming from language*, to instill order and hierarchy in human relations. From this perspective, there are at least two major areas that can be addressed with regard to Burke's Neo-Stoic duty to teach.

First, the teacher must foster an attitude of appreciation as well as an understanding of the consequences of industrial development. Any other approach risks the very infection of what is to be "cured." Burke sees very little hope for the resurrection of attitude through the "direct indictment," the often boring recitation of statistics and studies cataloguing the avenues of impending doom from technological excess. He likewise foresees the folly of cleansing the self by victimizing technology and purging oneself of the ills of industrial innovation. Interest and appreciation, instrumental in deeper levels of attitude change, are also essential in avoiding the "pollution" of symbolic conflict with attendant possibilities for real conflict.

The tensions within Burke's own attitudes toward technology are illustrative of the problems associated with maintaining an attitude of appreciation. Burke, at one point, clearly advocates the biological frame as a corrective to the current overemphasis on mechanical rationality. This is a distinct approach, since it foregoes the integrative attitude by investing more directly in human animality:

> Today, it seems to me, our quandaries sum up as the need for a kind of Humanism that would be defined as antithetical to "Technologism." . . . Humanism, as so conceived, would look especially askance at the typical promoter's ideal of a constant rapid increase in the consumption of "energy" (though perhaps it is a trend that the whole "logic" of investment comes close to making imperative). An anti-Technologistic Humanism would be "animalistic" in the sense that, far from boasting of some privileged human status, it would never disregard our humble, and maybe even humiliating, place in the totality of the natural order. (*Dramatism*, 53–54)

Note that as Burke defines his humanism in opposition to technologism, he enjoins a dialectical relationship between the terms. This "dialectic" seems contrived, however, since in this case, Burke has previously determined the nature of the term that calls forth an interactive "counter." If Burke's humanism is always opposed to the use of more technology to solve the problems of society, then his perspective cannot reach beyond a mere diatribe on the nature of the beast. A true dialectical relationship between technique and body, between organism and machine, implies a degree of malleability not present in his dichotomy. If his humanism is always *anti*-technologistic, then it loses its flexibility to both contrast and contain its dialectical opposite. Positing his humanism in this way (this "method"), Burke solidifies the distinctions that the critic/poet is trying to overcome.

After this discussion of an anti-technologistic humanism, Burke does offer a more integrative possibility for using technology. Discussing humans' awareness of their biological state, Burke identifies a human capacity to use technology for "discrimination," or for finer perceptions and differentiations. A "well-rounded frame of acceptance," Burke observes, "involves constant discrimination" (*Attitudes*, 33). Likewise, the realm of motion knows constant discriminations, as when water "discriminates" to ice or steam. But in the realm of Counter-Nature, discriminations of a type previously unavailable to humankind have become commonplace. Discussing the clash between the personalistic and the instrumental principles, Burke identifies a peculiar capacity of technology, or instrumentation, to discriminate between these principles:

> To the extent that Technology succeeds in perfecting instruments of precision designed for the study of the body's behavior as an electro-chemical mechanism, scrupulously discriminating among the physiological processes that match corresponding stages of expression and communication in the realm of "symbolicity," to that extent the very documentation of the parallels between those two orders will accentuate our awareness of their difference. (379)

Burke, embracing a humanism that is "anti-technologistic," is now describing the possible benefits of using technology to enhance human awareness of the sheerly biological. Such discrimination, writes Burke in his more recent "In Haste" essay, allows us to expand our horizons, to increase the metaphorical borrowing between realms (334, 360). Technology thus becomes, in its capacity for "fine tuning" our perceptions, a heuristic, a means of merging epistemology and ontology, of conjoining the universe of discourse. Burke relates this to his own sense of piety, a heightening of his sense of his own place:

> What's going on in my body? And I think for the first time in the world's history, our technological machine has got the

resources to check on that. And what we have is a totally new
kind of disassociation. I am out there, recorded on a dial. Who
am I? Here I am, a person, and now that stuff! And I believe it
will give us an ultimate. I can even believe—the irony of this—I
suddenly get a little notion, all of a sudden, I can be pious
again. I can see beyond. There is something! There is something! ("Counter-Gridlock," 13)

The technological "fix," which Burke's anti-technologistic humanism
denigrates, is dialectically resurrected as a means of instilling appropriate
attitudes toward the organism, the functioning of its faculties, and the
interactive determination of what might be termed its environment.

The attitude of appreciation, as practiced in the office of teaching,
does not feature acquiescence, or acceptance of the inevitability of
entelechial "perfection," but rather allows us an ironic chuckle as we
reconceive our own place in an ecological balance, a balance read as
both "uncertainty" and "control." A very difficult lesson Burke offers us
in our efforts to impart our awareness to others.

Applying this to the context of critical practice, where critical
typologies and methods can themselves become purely instrumental, an
ecology of language would encourage critics to apply their methods to
overcome nonreflective acceptance of social meanings, but would also
encourage them to see themselves in the act of criticism and to retain a
sense of their own analytic essentialism. Burke prescribes critical analysis
as a means of countering the sheerly analytic powers of scientism and
technologism, but he recognizes and embraces the rhythm and pageantry
of his own natural experience.

The second major area concerns the role of learning in the assertion
of hierarchy and order. Burke's point about the Stoics was that their
offices were "moral utilitarianism," conceiving of human service in such
a way as to assure the subjugation of all nonhuman nature in this
service. Hence his indictment of the Stoics as ordaining the hierarchical
psychosis through the service of humanity. The teacher, uncovering an
awareness of ecological balance, must be especially careful in this regard.
Burke's system, predicated on distinguishing humans apart from Nature,
contains the seeds of this psychosis. For the human animal stands above
the other animals by virtue of its symbolicity, since it uniquely enjoys the
capacity to abstract words about words, to transform Nature with
language and its pragmatic extensions. Burke is quick to ground humans
as animals, but he will never relinquish their uniqueness as symbol-users.
This is problematic for teachers, since it requires them to highlight the

differences between humans and Nature, even as they empower a conception of human and Nature in balance.

Perhaps the saving grace of Burke's system, for pedagogical purposes, is the mediatory nature of language. Language, bridging the realms of action and motion, is poised midway between humans and wordless Nature. Knowledge of this "pontification," this bridging of realms, is one way to try and break the utilitarian attitude of use that characterizes human relations with Nature. Grounding humans as animals is one way of embedding humans in Nature—the teaching of motivations in language is another way of admonishing students about the consequences of our "fall" into symbolism. Asserting the uniqueness of human symbolism does not necessarily imply the superiority of *logos*, nor does it inherently invite the promissory stance toward human invention. What is needed from a pedagogical view is the development of larger perspectives on Bodies That Learn Language, including knowledge of the students' place in Nature as bodies and an appreciation of the potentially destructive powers unleashed by fulfilling the language they have learned. The being of students' Bodies should, for the teacher, remain in equilibrium with the learning of all the powers of language.

The increasing prevalance of environmental corporate appeals has been largely aimed at educating the public about which products or services can be purchased or used to minimize negative environmental impacts. The target audience for such appeals is varied, but has a large youth component. These appeals hierarchically "place" humans in relation to their environment by channeling human striving for ecological balance into a commodified economic context. This "green consumerism" has received considerable attention from critics of language strategies,[14] and operates through the offices of "service" and "entertainment" to bridge the gap between humans and the natural beyond. Rife with implications of both individual empowerment and imbalance, green consumerism offers a potentially rewarding study of the power of language and representations of the relationship between humans and their environment. The focus on deceptive practices, a common theme in critical assessments of corporate appeals, provides insight into one of the many perversions of powerful economic motives. It may also divert attention from the central move of these suasive appeals: the shift from identification with Nature to identification with a corporation that identifies with Nature. The hermetic nature of this relationship should continue to concern critics of the strategic alignment of environmental and economic motives. Burke's concept of the "bureaucratization of the imaginative" is relevant here in the institutionalized conception of ecological balance. Burke's "bureaucratization" names what happens when "men try to translate some pure aim or vision into terms of its corresponding material embodiment, thus necessarily involving elements alien to the original, 'spiritual' ('imaginative') motive" (*Attitudes*, introduction). In his discussion of the Protestant transition, Burke argues that "[b]ureaucratization equals the tendency to 'move in on' and 'cash in on'" (141). This relation to systems of production and distribution is clarified in his assessment of the concept as a "perspective by incongruity":

> An imaginative possibility (usually at the start Utopian) is bureaucratized when it is embodied in the realities of a social texture, in all the complexity of language and habits, in the property relationships, the methods of government, production and distribution, and in the development of rituals that reenforce the same emphasis. (225)

As a means of articulating the vision of ecological balance for mainstream America, green consumerism oversimplifies and perhaps even secularizes human interaction with the environment. Relating to the environment through biodegradable trash bags, "environmentally friendly" detergents, and recycled toilet paper seems disturbingly bureaucratized, another way of seeing and of *not* seeing an individual's relationship to the environment.

Bureaucratization is in this instance directly related to the question of balance in human ecology. In his new afterword to *Attitudes Toward History*, Burke invokes a symbiosis between the incongruous elements. "[W]hen on the subject of 'imagination' and its 'bureaucratic embodiment,'" he explains, "I figuratively idealize: 'A well balanced ecology requires the symbiosis of the two'" (411). The issue essentially becomes a question of transmission and balance:

> One tries to "bureaucratize" his own life—and even if he succeeds in part, the process is not alienation for him. It is the "comes after" that matches his own "goes before." It is the proper logical completion of his life (the imaginative being the seed, and the bureaucratization the fruit; they are two stages in the development of himself as an "entelechy"). But we hand on to others some measure of our own bureaucratization. And we thereby "dispossess" them by this inheritance, unless they find their own positive ways of "earning it anew." Bureaucratization equals sterility and death, except insofar as men make it the "goes before" for a new "comes after" of their own. (246)

If the corporate bureaucratization of this imaginative ecological vision allows us to actualize our own environmental consciousness, then we are not alienated. But if this modus operandi characterizes the individual relation to the environment, if the process shifts the relationship from self-to-environment to self-to-corporation-to-environment, then that is a disturbing feature of current trends.

Teachers must therefore pay close attention to the relationship between an environmental vision and the bureaucratization of that vision as it is translated into public policy. Even as the greening of American consumerism is a "comes after" to the unimpeded industrial exploitation of resources, so must careful attention be paid to its limitations as a "comes before" for the twenty-first century. The totality of that move needs to be countered, at some level, both by debunking efforts and by attempts to remove artificial layers isolating individuals from their ecological context. In this area, the pontification of the natural world extends to opening up individuals to temporalized, imperfect, and even risky interactions with the wild.

Critics drawing on the vast resources of Burke's system should also heed his cautionary note about transmitting a measure of his own bureaucratization. A common thread here, validated by Burke's concern over the imbalances within any entelechial symbol-system, is the dispossession of the imaginative seed. In the context of our industrial empire, Burke implies that all symbol-smiths are teachers, responsible for the resurrection of human attitudes toward Nature and language. The duty of Neo-Stoicism, in his view, entails both contemplation and transmission. To critically examine the assumptions of society, or to posit methods that allow us to grasp these assumptions, is but the first step of criticism. It would be a mistake, therefore, to read into Burke's resignation an attitude of quiescence. The discussion of the seven offices, offering the critic ample insight into the perversions of these offices in a bureaucratized society, is clear on that point when it ends on the grand and global aims of education. Burke's system can itself imply an instrumental psychosis, but pedagogy can and must reassert the connection between biology and symbolism, even as it explores the twists, turns, and resources of language.

Toward an Ecology of Language

In summarizing these perspectives on an ecology of language, Burke's Neo-Stoic resignation guides his conception of the duty of the critic—it is at once appreciative and pedagogical. It seeks to understand, to cherish, and to teach the qualities that make us a duality of symbolism and biology, with all of the implications and by-products that radiate from that duality. Burke expresses a preference for an organic frame of reference, yet the development of his schema of analysis is methodical and instrumental at points. The meeting point of these two formative principles is, for Burke, the bureaucratization of his own vision, and for the student of symbolism a vast corpus of insight. Burke's logology, emphasizing the removal of the temporal development of the personalistic principle, and perfecting and essentializing the relationships and terms of the human story, contains the seeds of the very entelechial imbalance that he identifies operating in mythic structures and in language in general. The challenge for criticism here is the establishment of balanced movement between realms of abstraction and tangibility.

Having noted this tension between Burke's sense of piety and placement and his analytical system, several points can be made about the simplicity and complexity of Burke's perspective of perspectives and the implications of his frame in broaching an ecology of language. At a basic level, Burke is aware of both perspectives, and argues for a pedagogy that asserts awareness of both aspects of human existence. That is, in describing the switching back and forth between critic and poet, Burke observes that humans can both act and observe their action, and can cooperatively assess needed areas of change. The analysis of technology is integrative, Burke explains, as in this formulation it "gives substance to a synthesizing attitude" (*Attitudes*, 215). Faced with the vast resources of scientific rationality, the critic/poet engages, analyzes, and engages again, adjusting as necessary to the recalcitrance of the natural and social world. Burke is willing to explore the possibilities whereby the mechanical and the biological are not competing perspectives (either/or), but are compatible (both/and).

Regarding the possibilities for control over the advance of technology, and the relentless "tracking down of terms," the implication is that a truncated perspective forsakes the insight of an "ecological" view. The corrective cannot be an extremist perspective, for as Burke has consistently pointed out, extremism is but one step removed from a victimizing stance. The mechanistic metaphor, so powerful in shaping conceptions of progress and causality, is fatally flawed in the very symmetry of its perfection. The organic metaphor, floundering in the undifferentiated "wholeness" of its view, is incapable of analytically grappling with the hyperrationality of a driving scientism. Our collective sense of place, our piety, is inspired in Burke's view not by the combative element of either metaphor, but by the interaction and the tension between the two. Vision, absent integration, is vacant; technique, absent the poetic, is hermetic, and even dangerous. Reflective of his concerns with the principle of instrumentality in human industry, this cautionary stricture applies likewise to the very instrumentality of Burke's own system.

In his discussion of metaphor as perspective, Burke observes that "characters possess degrees of being in proportion to the variety of perspectives from which they can with justice be perceived" (*Grammar*, 504). Burke's own "character," viewed from both organic and mechanical perspectives, is attitudinally predisposed toward viewing humans as organisms, but is rationally and systemically comprised of mechanical approaches to "charting" the human symbolic. The interplay of these perspectives has significant implications for tracing means by which the advance of Counter-Nature can be controlled. Pirsig's protagonist in *Zen and the Art of Motorcycle Maintenance* infuses the man–machine interaction with an aesthetic, reconciling rational and romantic tendencies in Western thought. The alternative "logic" of rationality, Phaedrus discovers, invites a descent into madness. Burke understands the human as constituted biologically and symbolically, yet his reaction to technologism attitudinally borders on the extremism that his system is dialectically designed to avoid. Rationally tracking down the implication of duality, Burke seems unable, or perhaps unwilling, to infuse the machine with an aesthetic.[15]

Though his humanistic perspective, as an anti-technologistic frame, strikes a faintly reductive note, Burke would foster an appreciation of both perspectives, or metaphors, in order to more fully appreciate the possibilities for human understanding and for human survival. A stunning set of possibilities, Burke's critical methodology is more than just a machine for criticism—it is a philosophy, a method, a perspective, and a vision rolled into one. The lesson for the critic, concerned with the power of human technological creativity, and with human survival in the twenty-first century and beyond, is to scrutinize the means by which critical vocabularies become purely instrumental, to avoid unreflective extremism where possible, and to utilize this and other radical extremes to illustrate and teach an appreciation for the range of possibilities of the human symbolic. An awareness of the juncture of the genius of symbolism and the marvel of organism must ever spring anew, keeping the admonition against the fulfillment of our symbolic perfection alive.

Notes

1. See for example, Rueckert, 281; Muir, "On Kenneth Burke"; Thompson and Palmeri.

2. For an excellent review of his key terms and perspectives in this area, see Blankenship.

3. This area is now receiving greater attention. For a developed perspective on biology and organic conceptions in Burke's writings, see Thames' work on metabiology.

4. See Burke's "Dramatism and Logology." Brock and others present an extended discussion of these issues.

5. See *Grammar*, 430–40, and "Theology and Logology," 183.

6. The author is here indebted to Trevor Melia for his insight that while Burke frequently mentions the essentializing of the temporal, he never discusses the temporizing of the essential. This observation, locating a fundamental asymmetry in Burke's logological move, was largely responsible for a focus on logology in the context of an ecology of language. Very instructive in this regard is Melia's discussion of logology as an algebraic formulation of a story problem. See his work on quasi-mathematical motifs in Burke.

7. See especially his "In Haste" essay.

8. This analysis is detailed in *Rhetoric of Religion*, 7–42. See also Rueckert's discussion of the analogies of logology, 246–60.

9. A very interesting reiteration is provided by Condit.

10. This discussion of Stoicism is informed by Long's summary in the *Dictionary of the History of Ideas*.

11. See, for example *Dramatism*, 53–54.

12. The Helhaven project, Burke's reflexive treatment of satire as a means of reasserting appropriate attitudes toward technology, epitomizes the perfecting motivation, as it satirically tracks the logical implications of technological innovation to the end of the line. Burke offers three works that address this project: "Towards Helhaven: Three Stages of a Vision," "Why Satire, With a Plan for Writing One," and "Towards Looking Back."

13. See both *Language*, 3–16, and Simons and Melia, 263.

14. For an extended discussion of the attitude:agency ratio, and related side effects on the unification of environmental and economic motivations, see Muir, "Shaping Patterns." A similar point has been made in different contexts by Paystrup, Panetta, and Salvador and Samosky.

15. For efforts to bridge this gap, and to meld the aesthetic and the mechanical, see Florman, Ferkiss, and even Schumacher.

References

Bertelsen, Dale. "Kenneth Burke's Conception of Reality: The Process of Transformation and Its Implications for Rhetorical Criticism." In *Extensions of the Burkeian System*. Edited by James W. Chesebro. Tuscaloosa: University of Alabama Press, 1993.

Blankenship, Jane. "Kenneth Burke on Ecology: A Synthesis." In *Extensions of the Burkeian System*. Edited by James W. Chesebro. Tuscaloosa: University of Alabama Pressress, 1993.

Bowen, William. "Our New Awareness of the Great Web." *Fortune*, February 1970, 198–99.

Brock, Bernard. "The Evolution of Kenneth Burke's Philosophy of Rhetoric: Dialectic between Epistemology and Ontology." In *Extensions of the Burkeian System*. Edited by James W. Chesebro. Tuscaloosa: University of Alabama Press, 1993.

———. "Epistemology and Ontology in Kenneth Burke's Dramatism." *Communication Quarterly* 33 (1985): 94–104.

Brock, Bernard, et al. "Dramatism as Ontology or Epistemology: A Symposium." *Communication Quarterly* 33 (1985): 17–33.

Burke, Kenneth. *Attitudes Toward History*. 3rd ed. Berkeley: University of California Press, 1984.

———. *Collected Poems, 1915–1967*. Berkeley: University of California Press, 1968.

———. *The Complete White Oxen*. Berkeley: University of California Press, 1968.

———. "Counter-Gridlock: An Interview with Kenneth Burke." *All-Area* 2 (1983): 4–32.

———. *Counter-Statement*. Berkeley: University of California Press, 1931.

———. "Doing and Saying: Thoughts on Myth, Cult, and Archetypes." *Salmagundi* 7 (1971): 100–119.

———. *Dramatism and Development*. Barre, Mass.: Clark University Press, 1972.

———. "Dramatism and Logology." *Communication Quarterly* 33 (1985): 89–93.

———. *A Grammar of Motives*. Berkeley: University of California Press, 1969 [1945].

———. "In Haste." *Pre/Text* 6 (1985): 329–77.

———. "In New Jersey, My Adopted, and I Hope, Adoptive, State." *New Jersey Monthly*, November 1981, 68+.

———. "King Lear: Its Form and Psychosis." *Shenandoah* 21 (1969): 3–18.

———. *Language as Symbolic Action: Essays on Life, Literature, and Method*. Berkeley: University of California Press, 1966.

———. "Methodological Repression and/or Strategies of Containment." *Critical Inquiry* 5 (1978): 401–22.

———. "(Nonsymbolic) Motion/(Symbolic) Action." *Critical Inquiry* 4 (1978): 809–38.

———. "On 'Creativity'—A Partial Retraction." In *Introspection: The Artist Looks at Himself*. Edited by Donald E. Hayden, University of Tulsa Monograph Series No. 12. Tulsa, Okla.: University of Tulsa, 1971. 63–81.

———. *Permanence and Change: An Anatomy of Purpose*. 3rd. ed. Berkeley: University of California Press, 1984.

———. "A (Psychological) Fable, with a (Logological) Moral." *American Imago* 35 (1978): 203–07.

———. *The Rhetoric of Religion: Studies in Logology.* Berkeley: University of California Press, 1970.

———. "Theology and Logology." *Kenyon Review* 1 (1979): 151–85.

———. "Towards Helhaven: Three Stages of a Vision." *Sewanee Review* 79 (1971): 11–25.

———. "Towards Looking Back." *Journal of General Education* 28 (1976): 167–89.

———. "Variations on 'Providence.'" *Notre Dame English Journal* 13 (1981): 155–83.

———. "Why Satire, With a Plan for Writing One." *Michigan Quarterly Review* 13 (1974): 307–37.

———. "Words Anent Logology." In *Perspectives in Literary Symbolism.* Edited by Joseph Strelka. University Park: Pennsylvania State University Press, 1968.

Condit, Celeste. "Post-Burke: Transcending the Sub-Stance of Dramatism." *Quarterly Journal of Speech* 78 (1992): 349–55.

Edel, Abraham. "Right and Good." In *Dictionary of the History of Ideas.* 4 vols. Edited by Philip P. Wiener. New York: Charles Scribner's Sons, 1973. 4:173–87.

Ellegard, Alvar. "Study of Language." In *Dictionary of the History of Ideas.* 4 vols. Edited by Philip P. Wiener. New York: Charles Scribner's Sons, 1973. 2:659–73.

Ferkiss, Victor. *Technological Man: The Myth and the Reality.* New York: George Braziller, 1969.

Florman, Samuel C. *The Existential Pressleasure of Engineering.* New York: St. Martin's, 1976.

Frank, Armin Paul. *Kenneth Burke.* New York: Twayne, 1969.

Knighton, Jose. "EcoPorn and the Manipulation of Desire." *Wild Earth* 3 (1993): 76–78.

Lentricchia, Frank. "Reading History with Kenneth Burke." In *Representing Kenneth Burke.* Edited by Hayden White and Margaret Brose. Baltimore, Md.: Johns Hopkins University Press, 1982.

Long, Anthony. "Ethics of Stoicism." In *Dictionary of the History of Ideas.* 4 vols. Edited by Philip P. Wiener. New York: Charles Scribner's Sons, 1973. 4:319–22.

Matson, Floyd W. *The Broken Image: Man, Science and Society.* Garden City, New York: Anchor, 1966.

Melia, Trevor. "Scientism and Dramatism: Some Quasi-Mathematical Motifs in the Work of Kenneth Burke." In *The Legacy of Kenneth Burke.* Edited by Herbert W. Simons and Trevor Melia. Madison: University of Wisconsin Press, 1989.

Muir, Star. "Shaping Patterns of Environmental Interaction." In *The Conference on the Discourse of Environmental Advocacy.* Edited by Christine Oravec and James Cantrill. Salt Lake City: University of Utah Humanities Center, 1992.

———. "On Kenneth Burke on Technology." Diss. University of Pittsburgh, 1990.

Oxford English Dictionary. Compact edition. Oxford: Oxford University Press, 1971.

Panetta, Edward M. "The Status of Humanity in 'The Modern Crisis.'" In *Argument in Controversy: Proceedings of the Seventh SCA/AFA Conference on Argumentation*. Edited by Donn W. Parson. Annandale, Va.: Speech Communication Association, 1992.

Paystrup, Patricia. "Marketing 'Green' Claims: Environmental Salvation and Mortification." *The Conference on the Discourse of Environmental Advocacy*. Edited by Christine Oravec and James Cantrill. Salt Lake City: University of Utah Humanities Center, 1992.

Pirsig, Robert M. *Zen and the Art of Motorcycle Maintenance*. New York: Bantam Books, 1974.

Rueckert, William H. *Kenneth Burke and the Drama of Human Relations*. 2nd ed. Berkeley: University of California Press, 1982.

Salvador, Michael and Jack Samosky. "Is Doing Something Better Than Doing Nothing?: Environmentalism and the Paradox of Green Consumerism." In *Argument in Controversy: Proceedings of the Seventh SCA/AFA Conference on Argumentation*. Edited by Donn W. Parson. Annandale, Va.: Speech Communication Association, 1992.

Schumacher, E. F. *Small Is Beautiful: Economics as If People Mattered*. New York: Harper & Row, 1973.

Simons, Herbert W., and Trevor Melia, eds. *The Legacy of Kenneth Burke*. Madison: University of Wisconsin Press, 1989.

Thames, Richard. "The Body Learns Language: Biology and Entelechy in Kenneth Burke." Paper presented at the Annual Meeting of the Speech Communication Association, San Francisco, Calif., November 1989.

———. "Nature's Physician: The Metabiology of Kenneth Burke." Paper presented at the Annual Meeting of the Speech Communication Association, New Orleans, La., November 1988.

Thompson, Timothy and Anthony Palmeri. "Attitudes Toward Counternature (With Notes on Nurturing a Poetic Psychosis." In *Extensions of the Burkeian System*. Edited by James W. Chesebro. Tuscaloosa: University of Alabama Press, 1993.

Woodcock, John. "An Interview with Kenneth Burke." *Sewanee Review* 55 (1977): 704–18.

3

Kenneth Burke's Pragmatism— Old and New

David Blakesley

The pragmatist says simply: "The universe is." And, the universe being, it does—so the pragmatist will situate his knowledge, not in *what* the universe is, but in *how* it works. He will seek to understand operations, to find in what order things generally precede and follow one another. He will also consider himself as involved in the process, will recognize that one discovers "reality" in accordance with one's terminology, that a shift in the vocabulary of approach will entail new classifications for the same events.

—Burke, "Intelligence as a Good"

Burke has Dewey in mind, but the above remarks describe equally well his own efforts to characterize how *language* works, especially how it works rhetorically in science, philosophy, religion, art—in essentially all forms of speculation. In Burke's view, pragmatists investigate how interpretive frames exploit the resources of terminology to direct the attention and form the attitudes that motivate action. Resigned to the entelechial nature of any terminology, he nevertheless argues throughout his work that resourceful critics and artists can and should cultivate alternative perspectives by shifting the "vocabulary of approach." He pursues this goal himself in *Permanence and Change* and *Attitudes Toward History* via "perspective by incongruity," a method of verbal "atom-cracking" (*Attitudes*, 308). In *A Grammar of Motives*, under the heading "dramatism," he seeks to "study and clarify the *resources* of ambiguity" (*Grammar*, xix). Ever-mindful of the human desire for "totality," Burke admits as early as 1935 that the "only thing that all

71

this seems to make for is a reinforcement of the *interpretative attitude itself"* (*Permanence*, 118).

As we near the close of the twentieth century, the blindnesses and insights—to use Paul de Man's phrase—of critical inquiry have already received exhaustive scrutiny across the disciplines. (The "linguistic" or "rhetorical" turn in critical theory has, ironically perhaps, revealed our logocentric past beyond the shadow of a doubt.) Not surprisingly, critics like Richard Rorty, Giles Gunn, and Frank Lentricchia have recognized in these developments a return to the pragmatist's concern for agency, complicated now by the realization that systematic inquiry must account for the "problem" of language. This "new pragmatism" has spread its influence across the disciplines of philosophy, literary theory, and rhetoric. Gunn in *The Culture of Criticism and the Criticism of Culture* and Lentricchia in *Criticism and Social Change* (and elsewhere), already place Burke firmly in the history of this new movement, but their identifications rely heavily on secondary sources and a limited number of instances when Burke behaves like a pragmatist. Neither Lentricchia nor Gunn links Burke explicitly to the intellectual tradition of pragmatism. Extending Burke into this ongoing conversation requires, I think, a more thorough account of his perspectives on pragmatism (old and new), its rhetorical (and comedic) function in his own work, and, finally, how Burkean pragmatism can inform poststructuralist theory, which, in the opinion of many, is distinctly *not* pragmatic.

In mapping this reorientation, I place Burke at the juncture between the traditional pragmatists—Peirce, James, and Dewey—and the new pragmatists. Burke bridges the abyss between old and new in three key ways. First, by recognizing the rhetorical implications of traditional pragmatism, he anticipates the new pragmatists' view that the speaking subject, the philosopher, is always already encrypted by history and culture. Second, Burke's insight that philosophies may "work" in spite of inherent structural or conceptual contradictions provides the new pragmatists the will to believe despite the acknowledged absence of transcendental signifieds and metaphysical presence. Third, and perhaps most important, Burke develops our concept of rhetoric well beyond its traditional scope, creating space for the intellectual free play so distinctive in his own writing and, to some, so infuriating in postmodern literary theory. Burke includes within the range of rhetoric an "area of expression that is not wholly deliberate, yet not wholly unconscious. It lies midway between aimless utterance and speech directly purposive" (*Rhetoric of Motives*, xiii). As Lentricchia points out, Burke has in mind here a form of critical inquiry that falls midway between "a subject apparently in full possession of itself and in full intentional control of its expression, and a subject whose relation to 'its' expression is very problematic" (*Criticism*, 161). Both Lentricchia and Gunn argue that Burke's seriocomic version of pragmatism distinguishes him from those who view rational inquiry as the assertion of the will and those post-structuralists who view it as a self-devouring practice.

This latter positioning of Burke will serve as the organizing principle behind my discussion of Burke's pragmatism. Burke's comic perspective—the view that all of us are necessarily mistaken—and cultivation of perspective by incongruity make him an enigma in the historical development of both pragmatism and, more generally, critical theory. For even as Burke considers the implications of a given terminology (writes from within its implicit structure), he does not resist the impulse, as he says in the epigraph, to "consider himself involved in the process." That involvement and the understanding that it generates require, for Burke, tracking down "the kinds of observations implicit in the terminology you have chosen, whether your choice of terms was deliberate or spontaneous" (*Language*, 47). Burke's well-known penchant for "Joycings," perspective by incongruity, representative anecdotes, irony, puns, and thinly disguised autobiographical digressions makes him seem too unsystematic even to those who value systematic pluralism. Burke grants himself comic license so spontaneously that he rarely ends up where we expect his terminology to lead him.

In this regard, Burke has much in common with critics like Derrida, who has described the movements of deconstruction as "inhabiting" a structure (or terminology) not simply to map its boundaries but to decenter its presence. In other words,

> Operating necessarily from the inside, borrowing all the strate-
> gic and economic resources of subversion from the old structure,
> borrowing them structurally, that is to say without being able to
> isolate their elements and atoms, the enterprise of deconstruc-
> tion always in a certain way falls prey to its own work. (24)

Of course, Burke can "operate" within a given terminology without subverting it. But because of the provisional nature of the sign, he very often whimsically introduces distinctions or incongruous terminology that "violate" the integrity of the structure. (His motto, "When in Rome, do as the Greeks," is meant quite seriously.) At play in his writing is a tenuous dialectic between purposeful, directed discourse and an unconscious, spontaneous free play of signifiers. Burke, however, does not fall prey to his own work because ultimately he tracks both the boundaries of a given terminology and the self. As he says in "Intelligence as a

Good," "[T]he pragmatist is strongest when he is more like the artist than like the metaphysician" (*Philosophy*, 388).

I begin "Old and New Pragmatism" by briefly defining the meaning of the term *pragmatism* in the traditional sense. I then summarize the work of the new pragmatists and their efforts to ally themselves with Burke. The section concludes by returning to the origins of pragmatism in Charles Sanders Peirce and William James. I have resisted presenting in chronological order the historical and intellectual developments in pragmatism to highlight the position that Burke assumes in relation to both new and old pragmatism. The new pragmatists notably ignore Burke's own efforts to situate his brand of pragmatism in relation to that of James and Dewey. So in "Burke's Pragmatism," I identify Burke's early conceptions and applications of pragmatism, found primarily in *Counter-Statement* but extended in *Permanence and Change*. His exploration of piety and perspective by incongruity in this latter book builds the case for viewing Burke's pragmatism as seriocomic or—when viewed from the utilitarian perspective of positivist theory—"piously vulgar." This section concludes by noting Burke's critique of pragmatism in *A Grammar of Motives*, where he dissociates pragmatism from its "operationalist" or positivist applications in the later Dewey and others. "Burke's Pragmatic Rhetoric" presents a detailed discussion of the pragmatic aspects of Burke's rhetorical inquiry and its links to the concerns of Rorty, Lentricchia, and Gunn. Ultimately, I argue that Burke's pragmatism diverges from the positions mapped out by these theorists because he conceives of his own text as heterogeneous, as literary. As evidence, I briefly analyze one of Burke's most frequently quoted passages, his analogy of history as an "unending conversation" (*Philosophy*, 110). With its puns and layers of meaning, this passage exhibits an attitude toward the critical text that would later become a fundamental premise of poststructuralist theory, namely, the idea that "discourse is always already caught up in the warring forces within our own critical text, the play of differences *within* the critical text that both allows us to write and guarantees its deconstructibility" (Anderson, 150–51). In keeping with the pragmatist's aim, I hope to coach shifts in our understanding of Burke's pragmatism that will lead to "new classifications of the same events," thus refining our understanding of Burke's place in intellectual history, reconceptualizing contemporary pragmatism, and extending Burkean theory and criticism into the twenty-first century.

Old and New Pragmatism

The term *pragmatism* has a complex history of usage and thus a range of meanings before its emergence as the key term in the work of Rorty, Gunn, Lentricchia, and others. Peirce and James contribute the definitions cited most frequently by the new pragmatists and by Baldwin in his *Dictionary of Philosophy and Psychology* (1902, 1940) (a work that Burke himself quotes frequently in *A Grammar of Motives*). Peirce believed the problem of metaphysics could be cleared up by the application of this maxim: "Consider what effects, that might conceivably have practical bearings, we conceive the object of our conception to have. Then, our conception of these effects is the whole of our conception of the object" (Baldwin, 321). There is a positivist strain in Peirce's maxim in that it "is intended to lead toward (though not necessarily to attain) true opinion and thus a knowledge of reality" (Harris, 300). James' conception of pragmatism differed considerably from Peirce's, emphasizing that it was a method for investigating the practical consequences of a particular conception (or, in Burkean terms, a terminology): "In methodology it is certain that to trace and compare their respective consequences is an admirable way of establishing the differing meanings of different conceptions" (Baldwin, 321). While Peirce saw pragmatism as a method of *understanding*, James saw it as a method of *justification* (Williams, 202). Both Peirce and James believed pragmatism was the means of validating metaphysical "systems" (and their corresponding values) by equating their practical effects with their "truth content." In James, the truth of an idea was its "practical cash-value," and it was useful to the extent it indicated "ways in which existing realities may be *changed*" (46).

The new pragmatists, chief among them Richard Rorty, argue that pragmatism is both a method of understanding and justification, but deny the possibility of grounding any proposition in reality or an absolute principle of value (Harris, 299). Rorty, for example, shares James' view that the aim of philosophy should be to use theories as *"instruments, not answers to enigmas"* (32). Rorty argues in *Philosophy and the Mirror of Nature* that "pragmatic philosophers are skeptical primarily *about systematic philosophy*, about the whole project of universal commensuration" (368). Rorty diverges from Peirce and James, however, in his refusal to make the test of "what works" the means for validating philosophical reasoning. Echoing Peirce, Rorty stresses the difficulties of discovering truth in language, which makes all totalizing claims for knowledge problematic. His intellectual ancestors are Dewey, Wittgenstein, and Heidegger, philosophers who

> make fun of the classic picture of man, the picture which contains systematic philosophy, the search for universal commensuration in a final vocabulary. They hammer away at the holistic point that words take their meaning from other words rather than by virtue of their representative character, and the corollary that vocabularies acquire their privileges from the men who use them rather than from their transparency to the real. (368)

Rorty's program for philosophy would instead view the conversation initiated by philosophy as the object of inquiry, the aim being to characterize fully the agency of interpretation and its consequences. As Gunn puts it, Rorty proposes a "hermeneutic model of critical inquiry as a form of conversation or dialogue" (65).

Frank Lentricchia, in *Criticism and Social Change*, and Giles Gunn, in *The Culture of Criticism and the Criticism of Culture*, align the work of the new pragmatists with Burke in ways suggestive for our effort to characterize the pragmatic method in his critical theory. Lentricchia's appreciation and critique of Burke is so well known that I want to focus here on Gunn's critique of Rorty and Lentricchia, and his subsequent reassessment of Burke as a critical pragmatist. Gunn argues that positions like Rorty's abandon philosophical questioning as such because it is ultimately self-interested and solipsistic, due in part to its refusal to acknowledge the language problematic. Gunn agrees that "all the questions we put to culture, like the answers we are prepared to accept, may carry with them an inevitable prejudice, both epistemological and moral, in our own favor" (xiii). Nevertheless, he continues, there may "be real (i.e. measurable) differences between conceptions of what constitutes our, or anyone else's, best interests" (xiii). Pragmatism is the theory of these differences and the suasive tactics that disclose them (xiii). While Rorty would abandon all metaphysical disputation, Gunn believes doing so diverts attention from the consequences of our ideas, which are real even if the ideas that spurn them have no universal basis. To further his case for critical, culturally informed pragmatism, Gunn allies himself with Burke, whose "critical method is designed explicitly to take account of those conditions that are material to, in the sense of being constitutive of, whatever is constructed or produced culturally" (78). And while Burke acknowledges the political nature of all cultural forms, he "resists the essentializing tendencies in every theoretical attempt to make thinking more systematic, including his own" (75).

Lentricchia also appreciates Burke's effort to reinscribe critical inquiry in social practice, but ultimately he believes Burke essentializes his method by postulating a universal grammar (the pentad) in and with which critical inquiry functions to generate well-rounded statements about motives themselves. At the same time, Lentricchia sees Burke's analogy of history as an unending conversation in *The Philosophy of Literary Form* as the hermeneutic for understanding critical inquiry as the history/rhetoric dialectic (*Criticism*, 162). (In the third section, I show how Burke's analogy also deconstructs this hermeneutic with its self-referential dialectic, its free play of signifiers.) Gunn challenges Lentricchia on these two key points and thus reveals important differences between their respective conceptions of contemporary pragmatism. First, Burke explicitly states in the opening lines of the *Grammar* that he wants to answer the question, "What is involved, *when we say* what people are doing and why they are doing it?" (*Grammar*, xv; my emphasis). As Gunn points out, Burke restricts his interest to the terms that exploit ambiguities and not to their potential for making actual statements about motives themselves (76). Burke wants to identify how any theory of action uses ambiguities of *substance* to attribute motives. Gunn also challenges Lentricchia for his own essentialist position, which he shares with other Marxists, the idea that material conditions determine cultural practice (77–78), or, as Marx put it in *The German Ideology*, "Life is not determined by consciousness, but consciousness by life" (155). In sum, Lentricchia needs Burke to be essentialist only because it helps him echo Burke's idea of critical inquiry as a history/rhetoric dialectic. Gunn displays in his critique a fundamental principle of new pragmatism: understanding and justification are not only directed at the objects of inquiry, but also at the subject inquiring. In spite of Lentricchia's insufficient self-reflexivity, Gunn admires his effort to reinvest criticism with the power to foster social change. Essentialist or not, if criticism helps us, as James says, "get into satisfactory relations with other parts of our experience," then it "becomes true" (49).

The progenitor of new pragmatism is William James, whose particular version of pragmatism not only informs the newer version, but also Burke's conception of rhetoric as ideological inquiry (about which I will have more to say later). James, much like Burke, has returned to figure significantly in conversations about critical theory. (Lentricchia's 1986 article in *Cultural Criticism*, "The Return of William James," announces that he "is on his way back," under "the banner of a 'new pragmatism'" [5].) The pragmatic method in James was an attitude of orientation—one that Burke himself later identifies with art in "Literature as Equipment for Living." In that essay, Burke argues for a "sociological criticism" that "would seek to codify the various strategies which artists have developed with relation to the naming of situations" (*Philosophy*, 301). The Jamesian pragmatist views ideas situationally, as statements inscribed in or generating other statements that socialize perspectives and enable or restrict the range of possible identifications. New pragmatists like Lentricchia argue that this critical orientation politicizes the hermeneutic conversation:

> In the name of pragmatism and the American dream, James wanted to turn America against the self-pollution of its foreign policy at the end of the nineteenth century; in such an act of self-criticism, he thought, we would subvert the economic and political postures which, by treating all human subjects as if they were objects, for all practical purposes convert us into objects who suffer degradations that nonhuman commodities cannot suffer. So James's quasi-Cartesian postulate of an interior spontaneity is not ontological but thoroughly instrumental. It is his great heuristic principle, the energy of his criticism and the basis of his anti-imperialism. ("The Return of William James," 21–2)

Rather than viewing ideas as commodities, James treats them as strategies for naming and thus constituting experience. From this perspective, metaphysical quests are word-magic, so the pragmatist, he argues, should investigate the consequences of these acts, particularly as they reflect or constitute historical scenes. Self-criticism—or, in Burkean terms, the criticism of criticism—was a necessary means of adjusting to situations no longer accounted for by theory.

In "What Pragmatism Means" (1907) (the essay Burke refers to in the *Grammar*, 275–91), James provides two examples—an anecdote and an analogy—to explain how pragmatism functions as an interpretation of interpretations. The first goes like this. A group of campers, James among them, suppose a squirrel to be clinging to one side of a tree trunk, while a human observer stands on the opposite side of the tree. Attempting to get sight of the squirrel, the witness moves completely around the tree, but finds that the squirrel always keeps the tree between himself and the observer. The resultant metaphysical problem is this: "*Does the man go around the squirrel or not?*" (41). The observer circles the tree, of course, but does he go around the squirrel? As James describes it, "a ferocious metaphysical dispute" ensued among the campers in the "unlimited leisure of the wilderness" (41). Mindful that "whenever you meet a contradiction you must make a distinction" (41), James explains that which perspective is right depends "upon what you *practically mean* by 'going round' the squirrel" (42). In other words, if the frame of orientation is defined by the points on a compass, the observer does circle the squirrel. But if the frame of orientation is from the squirrel's perspective, to "go round" would mean being in front, to the side, and behind the squirrel. The metaphysical problem is terministic, dependent on one's conception of "going round." As James sees it, "make the distinction, and there is no occasion for farther dispute" (42). The following analogy, James' second example of how pragmatism works, is borrowed from Papini (and also quoted by Burke in the *Grammar*, 275–76):

> [Pragmatism] lies in the midst of our theories, like a corridor in a hotel. Innumerable chambers open out of it. In one you may find a man writing an atheistic volume; in the next someone on his knees praying for faith and strength; in a third a chemist investigating the body's properties. In a fourth a system of idealistic metaphysics is being excogitated; in a fifth the impossibility of metaphysics is being shown. But they all own the corridor, and all must pass through it if they want a practicable way of getting into or out of their respective rooms. (47)

In the first anecdote, pragmatism is "a method of settling metaphysical disputes that would otherwise be interminable" (42). ("Interminable" suggests here both "unending" and "inter*mi*nable"; that is, pragmatism makes the nature of controversy more precise by naming or renaming it.) James also alludes to the character of American philosophy after Emerson, the metaphysical dispute akin to what Geoffrey Hartman calls "criticism in the wilderness" in his book by that name. Not surprisingly, James identifies the disputants as "campers" with "unlimited leisure," a scene and circumstance distinctly apolitical. Lentricchia argues that while James admired Emerson's "transcendentalist commitment to a community of justice and dignity" ("The Return of William James," 18) and his image of the American scholar as "Man Thinking" (see "The American Scholar," *passim*), he believed "the interiorization of cultural power and the subjectification of freedom" in Man Thinking could translate into an attitude that could have pernicious social consequences.

The individual's appropriation or assimilation of history could lead to the reassertion of this will onto the sociopolitical world (19). Pragmatism mediates metaphysical disputes not simply by pointing out their inherent ambiguities but by demonstrating the "practical difference that must follow from one side or the other's being right" (James, 43). In the analogy, Papini's figure of the corridor suggests that the scene of pragmatism is language, the "corridor" that frames of orientation share. Jamesian pragmatism would demonstrate the possibilities for and character of conversations in the corridor. In James' conception, pragmatism privileges agency or means (as Burke points out in the *Grammar*) but not exclusively. Rather, the agency:purpose and agency:scene ratios figure prominently. The purpose of pragmatism, to create the possibilities for and extend ongoing philosophical conversation, is realized through agency; these means can foster attitudes that reconstitute the historical or philosophical scene.

Burke's Pragmatism

The pragmatism of William James was new to Burke in the 1920s and 1930s and during those years signified to him a capacity for generating pluralistic accounts of human relations. (I should note briefly here that pragmatism had not yet reached its purified state in "operationalism," the view that the meaning of a concept is synonymous with its corresponding set of operations [see the *Grammar*, 280].) Throughout my discussion of particular texts, I intend to focus on those features that demonstrate the influence of pragmatism on Burke's method, with special attention to the possible connection between this method and his desire to investigate the rhetorical dimensions of critical theory for its comic possibilities.

In Burke's early critical writings, pragmatism is a "spirit" or attitude that ought to accompany critical reflection. For example, in "Chicago and Our National Gesture" (1923), he derides those critics who proclaim "the doctrine of a national literature" (500). Such critics fail to "apply the spirit of pragmatism in forming judgment" (501). To Burke, this failure was "an exceptionally bewildering mistake on the part of the nationalists, since pragmatism has been so well nourished in America" (501). Attempts to silence alternative voices (literary, critical, philosophical) by proclaiming America's "massiveness" betray the spirit of pragmatism, a move that causes the individual to be seen as "the microcosm of this same massiveness" (501). Efforts to reify the critical terminology of Americanism were both antipragmatic and antidemocratic.

In *Counter-Statement* Burke initiates a dialectic whose hermeneutic principle is that our understanding and justification of art depends on our ability to make statements and counter-statements. He selects his title because "as regards its basic concerns and tenets—each principle it advocates is matched by an opposite principle flourishing and triumphant today" (vii). Burke's desire for extending critical dialogue is most explicit in the "Program" chapter, where the dialectical pairs "agrarian-industrial," "practical-aesthetic," "fascism-democracy," "unemployment-leisure," and "overproduction-underconsumption" generate his investigations of the resources of terminology exploited by each term. Each term (and the terminology it establishes) structures our conception of experience (or socializes perspectives), and Burke dissociates these perspectives in the interest of interfering with the efficiency with which they condition behavior. Burke does "side" with specific terms, such as "aesthetic" or "democracy," but in each case he redefines them. Democracy, for instance, becomes "organized distrust, 'protest made easy,' a babble of discordant voices, a colossal getting in one's own way—democracy, now endangered by the apostles of hope who would attack it for its 'inefficiency,' whereas inefficiency is the one thing it has in its favor" (114). While democracy ideally allows for the expression of individual will in building consensus, as Burke suggests, the apostles with the most rhetorical ammunition and power do everything possible to extinguish the democratic imperative that empowers others.

In *Counter-Statement*'s "Lexicon Rhetoricae," Burke adopts the method he praises in Walter Pater's fiction—his "resolution of an obscure idea into its component parts" (12); his search for "those changeless principles which might govern perpetual change"; his "predilection for the fluctuant"; his "drawing out the effects of his subject, aware that there was at least the indubitable and immediate certainty of his craft" (15). The method is pragmatic in the Jamesian sense; Burke wants to demonstrate *how* effects are produced, not "*what effects should be produced*" (123), and he initiates this inquiry by exploring the resources of *form*, which is the "fluctuant" and "obscure idea" that he divides into component parts, enabling further perspectives on the nature of appeals. Like "substance" in the *Grammar* and "identification" in the *Rhetoric of Motives*, form is "Lexicon Rhetoricae's" titular term.

Burke calls his theory of form "a kind of judgment machine, designed to serve as an instrument for clarifying critical issues (not so much for settling issues as for making the nature of a controversy more definite)" (ix). Here, he expresses the pragmatist's desire to make terministic distinctions to demonstrate the bases of metaphysical controversy. He "individuates" form into syllogistic, qualitative, repetitive, conventional, and minor types, but once he has done this he ranges farther, making such linkages as "form and information," "form and ideology," and "form and symbol." Rather than settling on a theory of form that could be used to create literary hierarchies or a universal aesthetic, Burke instead wants to reclassify our experience of texts and thus avoid the pitfalls of aesthetic standards, which inevitably rest on metaphysical grounds. The "form" itself of "Lexicon Rhetoricae"—unfolding as a series of stops and starts, restatements, shadings, recontextualizations—is like a fugue, a dialectic of many voices on a repeated theme.

The pragmatic method of "Lexicon Rhetoricae" privileges agency, but the agency:scene ratio also structures Burke's inquiry in *Counter-Statement* as a whole. This book initiates his attempts in the 1930s to mediate the formalist/Marxist controversy that then fueled literary thought. The formalist-aesthetic position held that critics needed to refine principles of aesthetic judgment, while Marxist critics countered that texts were social artifacts revealing class differences and the harmful effects of capitalism. Burke discusses form as both an aesthetic feature of texts *and* as an appeal to desire, which gave form both a psychological and a social function.[1] In a typically Burkean move, he rejects the "either/or" stance in favor of the pragmatic "both/and."

Burke begins *Permanence and Change* by noting that criticism is an orientation and that given present conditions we need to reclassify experience: "the very power of criticism has enabled men to build up cultural structures so complex that still greater powers of criticism are needed" (5). Criticism not only increases the range of solutions, but also the range of problems; hence, we need to interpret our interpretations to avoid the solipsism of "trained incapacity" (7). In Part II, "Perspective by Incongruity," Burke associates orientation with piety, "*the sense of what properly goes with what*" (180). A pious person brings "all the significant details of the day into coordination, relating them integrally with one another by a complex interpretive network" (75). Theologically, piety would be allegiance to the Divine Logos—the paradigm that leads the congregation of disciplined or trained devotees to spiritual transcendence. To preserve this motivational emphasis, the pious person divides the world of action into polarities (e.g., moral/immoral) and then coordinates the symbolic activities prescribed by the religion into a unified whole. Criticism functions similarly, Burke argues, and thus we should ask these questions: How, given our piety, do we discover new meanings? How do we account for contrary information? How do we avoid following the flock when our judgment tells us it is headed in the wrong direction?

Burke displays his comic and pragmatic skepticism when he answers that we should be purposely impious, which requires persistent reorientation and, as Nietzsche would have it, "the transvaluation of all values" (87). The Nietzschean method, characterized by a "dartlike" quality, utilizes the concept of "perspective by incongruity." Burke calls the method a "cult of perspectives" because it extends "the use of a term by taking it from the context in which it was habitually used and applying it to another" (89). (Burke's extension of piety to the secular is an example.) Perspective by incongruity works like metaphor, "revealing unsuspected connectives" and "exemplifying relationships between objects which our customary rational vocabulary has ignored" (90). The customary rational vocabulary Burke speaks of is what a particular philosophical system generates, the system regulating both the selection and application of terminology, the agencies of production, and the body of knowledge that unifies the system itself. Perspective by incongruity is pragmatic because it cracks disciplinary codes and helps us construct new patterns of experience and new ways of relating to them.

It can be comic as well. To develop the idea of "secular piety," Burke cites examples of piety for the judgments of our childhood (leading to patriarchy), the antithetical pieties of utilitarian and artistic responses, the pieties that Darwin disrupted, the pieties of ball games, and so on (71–76). Near the end of this discussion, he gives us a veiled autobiographical account of a lonely man who gradually links the ringing of a neighbor's doorbell, then any doorbell, with his distress (referring perhaps to Burke's early days in Greenwich Village). Then he announces, "We are now prepared to carry our term to its limits" (77). He imagines Matthew Arnold "loafing on the corner with the gashouse gang," and promptly realizes how "undiscriminating he would prove himself" (77). Arnold would soon discover that "vulgarity is pious" (77).

These final two extensions of piety reveal Burke's great personal stake in the method and idea of perspective by incongruity as well as his willingness to let his investigation of a terminology slip into alien, often subjective, territory. When we think in general terms of Burke's position in relation to mainstream critical theory, we see him as himself providing perspective by incongruity. The well-known picture of Burke wearing mock professorial regalia on the cover of *The Legacy of Kenneth Burke*, his counter-statements, Vincent Leitch's treatment of Burke as a strange but "exemplary case" because of his "inversion" of New Critical taboos (41)—all demonstrate Burke positioned (and positioning himself) on the periphery of critical theory for the sake of perspective by incongruity.

Since our training incapacitates us, we must introduce not only our ideas as distinctions, but ourselves as well. Burke creates occasions for reigniting the unending conversation when the hour grows late.

Burke's most explicit critique of pragmatism begins in his review of Dewey's *The Quest for Certainty* and continues in the *Grammar*, culminating in the scientism/dramatism (motion/action) dialectic that structures thought on human relations in general. Burke wholeheartedly endorses the purpose of Dewey's pragmatism, which aimed to connect this theory of knowledge with "an empirically verifiable theory of behavior" (*Human Nature and Conduct*, 125). While theological or metaphysical systems attain certainty "by affirming dogmatically how things *are*, how they *must be*" ("Intelligence as a Good"; rpt. in *Philosophy*, 384), Dewey's pragmatic knowledge

> is erected out of doubt, questioning, experimentation. It has no vested interests; to have one of its beliefs undermined is a gain, an aid in the better understanding of processes. It defines as truth *what works*. Possessing no certainties in itself, it has undeniably increased the certainties of living.

According to Dewey, rationalist philosophy had failed to secure a set of values that could both transform social life and "focus reflection upon needs congruous to present life" (*The Quest for Certainty*, 313). It did, however, impose a totalizing system on experience, and therein lay its weakness. Rather than constructing a system through the experimental method, by taking as true "what works," rationalist philosophy mistook logically consistent theory for reality itself. Dewey's rhetorical move, and the one Burke criticizes, is to consider values as processes grounded "not upon the authority of antecedent Being, but in accordance with their workings" (Burke, *Philosophy*, 385). Rather than posit some "key value" from which others follow, Dewey "praises intelligence, tact, taste in the formation of judgments" (386). Intelligence becomes the means for judging values, and as such it is a "good." Burke argues that defining intelligence strictly in terms of its processes overprivileges agency as the motivating principle. Intelligence is also an act motivated by purposes that can be linked to values. Dewey subtly extends scientific method, and its corresponding emphasis on motion, to a dimension of human experience that because it is directed by and through language, is symbolic *action* (*processes* being akin to unmotivated motion). While Burke appreciates the attitude accompanying Dewey's pragmatism, he doubts whether it is possible to erect new values by experimental methods that reduce human actions (e.g., the use of intelligence) to motions.

Burke extends this critique of pragmatism in the *Grammar*, and while his conclusions about the error of defining a thing by its processes stands, he still finds room for a form of rhetorical (and pragmatic) analysis that would help us mitigate the effects of scientistic thought, which, as Trevor Melia points out, may seek to "expunge the ideological component from social science" but "more often succeeds in hiding it" (70). In the *Grammar*, Burke argues that pragmatist philosophies "are generated by the featuring of the term, Agency" (275) and are thus philosophies of means (275). He qualifies this categorization when he points out that all philosophies announce "some view of human ends" and thus "require a corresponding doctrine of means" (275). Nevertheless, Burke believes the proliferation of agencies in modern science raises agency "to first place among our five terms," and consequently the philosophy of means is not the "rounded statement about motives" (xv) that his dramatism aims for.

Burke criticizes the positivist strain in pragmatism throughout Part IV of the *Grammar* ("Agency and Purpose"), tracing its origin back to James, who "classed his pragmatism with nominalism in its appeal to particulars, with utilitarianism in its emphasis upon the practical, and with positivism in its 'disdain for verbal solutions, useless questions and metaphysical abstractions'" (275; Burke quotes here from James' "What Pragmatism Means," 47). Pragmatism reaches its purified state in P. W. Bridgeman's "operationalism," the view that the meaning of a concept is "synonymous with the corresponding set of operations" (or agencies) (280). (For instance, "a concept of temperature would thus be equated with the actual operations by which one recorded temperature" [280].) Though this positivist strain in pragmatism was certainly prevalent by 1945, Burke recognizes that viewing pragmatism primarily in terms of means, as a method only, is reductive. As he puts it, the pragmatist might better see "instruments themselves as merely one aspect of a dialectic, one voice among the several voices whose competitive cooperation is necessary for the development of mature meanings" (280). While Burke explicitly critiques the "purification" of pragmatism that followed James' formulation, James himself resisted such a reification of method. In James, however, the "disdain for verbal solutions" was not an exclusive disdain for the nature of solutions; James instead tried to challenge the assumption that one could logically derive a full description of reality through language, which made claims to the contrary metaphysical. His significant point is that there lurks in such verbal solutions a rhetorical

slant, one hidden from view because of a failure to address the "solution" as one dictated by the selection of terminology.

In his critique of applied science's instrumentalism, Burke argues
that "Rhetorical and Symbolic factors can surreptitiously re-enforce the
appeal of Agency" (286), but the power of applied science derives from
its elimination of purpose, a move that suppresses the rhetorical nature
of all discourse. (Recall that the *Rhetoric of Motives* begins with Burke's
choice of "Identification" as the "instrument" for marking off areas of
rhetoric, by showing that "a rhetorical motive is often present where it is
not usually recognized, or thought to belong" [xiii].) Burke sees in
scientism the desire to reduce human action to motion, thus denying the
role of identification as a key motive:

> Since agents act through the medium of motion, the reduction
> of action to motion can be treated as reduction to Agency,
> Pragmatism having the advantage over Materialism that *tools*
> are more "purposive" than *impersonal backgrounds* are, so
> that the Pragmatist emphasis can more conveniently straddle
> the action-motion ambiguity. (286)

The reduction of ambiguity initiated by the privileging of motion side-
steps the problem Burke sees as fundamental: words are symbolic acts
that both transform the objects of thought and subsequently act to
reclassify them, making experience itself mutable and thus subject to
rhetorical manipulation. Put another way, while pure pragmatism would
hold that words are signs of things, Burke wants to show, as he does
later in *Language as Symbolic Action*, that things are also signs of words
(see "What Are the Signs of What," *passim* 359–79).

Burke's critique of the extremes of an emphasis on method should
not be construed as an absolute denial of the utility of systematic inquiry.
In fact, as Melia has argued, Burke distinguishes between rhetoric as a
call to arms and rhetoric as a mode of analysis:

> A rhetorical *analysis*, perhaps of social data, certainly of texts
> about those data, far from adding to the ideological element,
> should, by throwing it into sharp relief, somewhat mitigate its
> effect. It is precisely the virtue of Burke's mathematical attitude
> that it tends toward the detachment that has traditionally dis-
> tinguished the scientist from the engineer—even as it acknowl-
> edges that we are not objects in motion but human beings in
> *action*. (70)

The pragmatic aspect of Burke's rhetoric is most pronounced in the *Rhetoric of Motives*, where he analyzes the range of rhetoric as agency by elaborating the scene:agency, act:agency, agent:agency, and purpose:agency ratios. That is, all symbolic acts are situated rhetorical means of transformation and, hence, ideological; for example, the representation of history as materialist exploits the ambiguity of the scene-agency ratio in the interest of identifying the agent with means of production.

The pragmatic nature of Burke's rhetorical analyses has created and re-created perspectives that modern critical theorists continue to grapple with in their efforts to demonstrate the ideological bases of criticism itself. Burke's frequently repeated pronouncement that "[e]ven if any given terminology is a *reflection* of reality, by its very nature as a terminology it must be a *selection* of reality; and to this extent it must function also as a *deflection* of reality" (*Language*, 45; see also *Grammar*, 59), prompts us to examine the nature of symbolic action as ideological "deflection"; herein is the rhetorical imperative Burke establishes throughout his work and that critics have seized upon when demonstrating pragmatism's relevance for contemporary theory.

Burke's Pragmatic Rhetoric

Burkean critics have for some time called him a pragmatist, even if there has not been much consideration of all that this designation means for extensions of the Burkean system or of how this assessment might color attempts to reread and thus reconsider the pragmatic aspects of his rhetoric. Critics have hesitated to call Burke's rhetoric "systematic" because systematic implies practical—hence utilitarian—and his persistent criticism of criticism favors reflection over efficient action. As John D. O'Banion, Melia, Gunn, and others have demonstrated, however, there is more "system" in Burke than even Burke himself admits.[2] My discussion of Burke's relevance for extending the conversation on the new pragmatism is intended to outline rather than finalize possible applications of Burkean terminology.

Burke's much quoted analogy of history as an unending conversation in *The Philosophy of Literary Form* (110–11) conveys his conception of rhetoricians as social actors, not simply in their use of suasive tactics, but also in their role as producers and critics of orientations. Rhetoric in Burke is both *rhetorica utens*, the use of persuasive resources, and *rhetorica docens*, the study of persuasive resources. Echoing his call for the pragmatist to view instruments as one dimension of a larger dialectic, he describes the rhetorician in "Rhetoric—Old and New" as "one voice in a dialogue": "Put several such voices together, with each voicing its own special assertion, let them act upon one another in co-operative competition, and you get a dialectic that, properly developed, can lead to views transcending the limitations of each" (63). Burke's dramatization of philosophical schools in the *Grammar* can be read as his attempt to create such a dialectic among competing rhetorics. The ideal Burkean rhetorician has not one voice, but many, acting dialecti-cally to form rounded accounts of human subjectivity.

New pragmatists like Rorty, Lentricchia, and Gunn seize upon the metaphor of philosophical inquiry as conversation in their attempts to sketch a program for a critical hermeneutics. Rorty, though he doesn't mention Burke specifically in *Philosophy and the Mirror of Nature*, concludes that "[t]o see keeping a conversation going as a sufficient aim of philosophy, to see wisdom as consisting in the ability to sustain a conversation, is to see human beings as generators of new descriptions rather than beings one hopes to be able to describe accurately" (378). In application, a rhetorical terminology such as Burke offers would view social life as a problem of appeal and would supply us with terms for "keeping a conversation going." In *Permanence and Change*, for example, he argues for extending the poetic metaphor (with "borrowings from the terminology of rhetoric" [266]) to all symbolic acts, not merely those traditionally labeled "artistic." Burke would have us translate the terminology of rhetoric into social equivalents, which "could lessen sectarian divisions by prompting a man to remember that his assertions are necessarily *socialized by revision*, an attitude which might make for greater patience" (265). Philosophy, as Rorty sees it, ought to socialize concepts of truth, which would lead to the view that human beings are not merely objects of contemplation, but *subjects* contemplating, or to borrow terms from Sartre, as both existing *pour-soi* (being-for-myself) and *en-soi* (being-in-itself), as both "described objects and describing subjects" (378). Rorty shares Burke's distrust of totalizing metaphysics and opts for a method whose aim is to generate alternative perspectives while resisting the impulse to settle on one system of absolute commensurability.

In *Criticism and Social Change* Lentricchia is prepared, with Rorty, "to set aside the classical claim of philosophy for representational authority" but, unlike Rorty, he urges a materialist view that "theory does its representing with a purpose" (12). Lentricchia borrows from Burke the idea that history is not simply an unending conversation, but that it is also charged rhetorically; historical conditions have been such that theory both constitutes and is constituted by ideological forces whose roots are in materialism. Lentricchia's aim is to rewrite history from this perspective, redescribing the cluster of conditions that inscribe critical inquiry. Thus, in *Criticism and Social Change* he uses as representative anecdote Burke's speech to the First American Writers' Congress to show the denial of the rhetorical nature of theory by Marxists in the 1930s, evident in their refusal to accept that theirs was not merely a social problem, but a rhetorical one as well. To cite a case less familiar to Burkeans, in "The Return of William James" Lentricchia rewrites the history that inscribed James' adoption and application of pragmatism, showing that shifts in theory result from changing social circumstances and not necessarily from the refinement of understanding. "The lesson of James," says Lentricchia, "is that theory is a phenomenon of everyday life in history and society, a phenomenon of all of society's institutions, and the name of a disposition whose consequences are revealed in oppression" (29). James' participation in the New England Anti-Imperialist League at the end of the nineteenth century, activism motivated by U.S. imperialist ventures in Cuba and the Philippines, helped him experience "a direct and co-determinative connection between his philosophical principles and his political life" (12). Imperialism, for James, was the nefarious application of a theory to a social situation for which it was not designed, the imposition of a patriarchal attitude in the interest of, in Lentricchia's words, "curing the world of diversity" (12). Pragmatism was James' response to the "theory-desire" (the desire for refinement) of classical philosophy, which too easily becomes the "*will to refine*" in the hands of imperialist governments (13). James' concern for the consequences of theory were profound; his adoption and reformulation of pragmatism were his way of creating an orientation he could live with.

Lentricchia's historically situated understanding of Jamesian pragmatism demonstrates the striking similarities between James' and Burke's efforts to carve a philosophical orientation that could help them "muddle through," as Burke might put it. Recall, for instance, Burke's observation in *Permanence and Change* that the book itself is his personal cure, "a kind of transformation-at-one-remove, got by inquiry into the process of transformation itself" (xlvii). Pragmatism was for James not just a method, but the philosophical attitude necessary for adjusting to social conditions. As Burke saw it, this Jamesian attitude was a frame of acceptance, a will to believe, "the more or less organized system of meanings by which a thinking man gauges the historical situation and adopts a role with relation to it" (*Attitudes*, 5). The importance for Burke of creating this organized system of meanings is profound. He wants his own art/criticism to forge this frame of acceptance, to establish equilibrium. And beginning with *Counter-Statement*, the attitude guides his understanding of all art, "the varied ways in which men seek by symbolic means to make themselves at home in social tensions" (xi).

In *The Culture of Criticism and the Criticism of Culture*, Gunn presents a critique of poststructuralism that both derives from and guides his interpretation of Burke's pragmatism. Gunn's conclusion is that Burke's rhetorical (or metacritical) "system" avoids the cynicism of poststructuralism and Rorty's new pragmatism because of his "comic realism, which has taught him that every perspective is limited, every position vulnerable to attack and revision" (84), including his own. Poststructuralists have ably demonstrated that all cultural forms are "more or less arbitrary constructions that bear little or no intrinsic relation to the things to which they refer, thus making of culture itself, and all talk about it, a web of artificial and largely self-serving constructs" (41). These "grammars" are not merely unstable fictions but "purposeful deceptions that need to be perceived as inherently hegemonic" (42). Given the proliferation of poststructuralism and what has now become the truism that perspectives are "privileged epistemic standpoints," Gunn cites the need to further investigate what differences they can or should make for the world of experience, since some perspectives are more persuasive than others and thus do their work in the world regardless of the contradictions inherent in them. Burke concedes that human beings are enmeshed in language, that they view everything through a "fog of words" ("Rhetoric—Old and New," 61). Yet methods like Burke's dramatism help us "see that while the fog is ubiquitous, it is not wholly blinding; the treachery of the fog is not due to its own opacity but to our all-too-willing disposition to make ourselves and our world over in the image of its distortion" (Gunn, 87). In Burke's adoption of the comic perspective and terminology of rhetoric, Gunn sees the critical antidote to the nihilism of poststructuralism. He admires in Burke the same qualities that Burke himself admired in James: "James's constant bursting into metaphor was not a mere trick of embellishment for popular consumption. It arose from the fact that he lived very close to an awareness of the emotional overtones associated with his ideas" (*Attitudes*, 11). James' writing, Burke says further, "arose from his unusual artistic sensitivity, forcing him to a concern with wayward manifestations that are, in their extreme aspects, called 'mystical'" (11). Gunn sees in Burke a verbal artist attempting through puns, perspective by incongruity, the proverbial, to "outmaneuver language" so that his terministic screens "do not become the prison-house of thought" (Gunn, 85).

The comic frame of acceptance plays itself out in Burke's work as the quest for more comprehensive systems and the continual effort to accept his own critical calculus as necessarily mistaken. Herein also is Burke's pragmatism (or "pragmatic wariness," to use Gunn's words). Burke acknowledges that any terminology is doomed to be self-contradictory in some respects; rather than resign himself to avoiding contradiction at all costs or adopting a form of pure relativism, he converts this realization into an asset. The poetic or dramatic metaphor called for in *Permanence and Change* and elaborated throughout the rest of his work helps Burke find a way out of the relativist's dilemma, not by simply refuting it with some theory more grand in scope, but by substituting a heightened sense of the ironic aspect of human behavior and the necessity of pragmatic skepticism for its attitude of resignation. Burke's choice of comedy as the healthiest of the poetic metaphors is unequivocal:

> The progress of humane enlightenment can go no further than in picturing people not as *vicious*, but as *mistaken*. When you add that people are *necessarily* mistaken, that *all* people are exposed to situations in which they must act as fools, that *every* insight contains its own special kind of blindness, you complete the comic circle, returning again to the lesson of humility that underlies great tragedy. (*Attitudes*, 41)

The comic frame views ambivalence as charitable—it is neither "wholly euphemistic, nor wholly debunking" (166). Rather than being strictly "sour grapes," the comic frame should say "sour grapes plus" (337). The attitude is manifest in one's willingness to accept that acts can dialectically contain conflicting motives—transcendental or material, imaginative or bureaucratic (167). Burke's pragmatism aims to divide, then reunite, the component parts of all such dialectics.

Burke's addition of a sixth term to his pentad, *attitude*, gives us an additional term with which to understand the influence of pragmatism on his attributing of motives. He views pragmatism as privileging agency in the *Grammar*, but the attitude that accompanied Jamesian pragmatism also appealed to him. Ideas for James are "true" in so far as they help us get into satisfactory relation with other parts of our experience. As an incipient act, attitude for Burke is the *desire* to get into satisfactory *symbolic* relation with aspects of our experience; attitude and identification shade into one another. We also read in Burke that identification

may be a deliberate device of the rhetorician, but that it can also be an
end, the appeal of which may or may not be conscious,

> as when people earnestly yearn to identify themselves with
> some group or other. Here they are not necessarily being acted
> upon by a conscious external agent, but may be acting upon
> themselves to this end. In such identification there is a partially
> dreamlike, idealistic motive, somewhat compensatory to real
> differences or divisions, which the rhetoric of identification
> would transcend. ("Rhetoric—Old and New," 63)

One way of extending the Burkean system would be to return to its
historical scene, in the interest of elaborating the range of Burke's own
identifications.

Burke describes everyone's scene in the famous history/conversation
analogy in *The Philosophy of Literary Form* that both Gunn and
Lentricchia view as the central metaphor for Burke's work. Not only does
he view the analogy as explaining the artist's situation, but also the
critic's. The analogy also shows Burke viewing his own work as self-
referential, and thus, deconstructible. The artist's drama, he says, gets its
materials from the unending conversation of history, which as Burke
envisions it, takes place in "a parlor." The discussion is heated. You listen
for a while until you catch the tenor of the argument, then you put in
your "oar." People respond to your argument, but ultimately the
discussion is "interminable." You depart "with the discussion still vigorously in progress" (110–11). I want to outline here four complementary
ways to read this analogy. Each shows Burke layering his text, shifting the
references from "other" to "self" to the "text itself."

Before I identify each of these readings, however, I should note
several of Burke's puns. *Parlor*, of course, refers to a room, but he also
has in mind the French *parler*, "to speak," which also forms the roots of
English *parliament, parlance, parlay,* and *parley* (pahr-lee), which is a
discussion among enemies. To enter a parlor, then, is to enter speech or a
language, so, "to speak." *Oar* can also be read as *or*, meaning that the
critic/artist puts in an "or," or makes a counter-statement. Finally, as in
James' squirrel anecdote, the discussion is in-*term*-inable, that is, cannot
be put into adequate terms.

The most common way to read the analogy is as a stylized account
of the social and rhetorical dynamics of constructing and reconstructing
knowledge. We enter a parlor (a language) and through dialogue, the
parameters of the dialogue take shape. But the analogy also describes the

individual's effort to interiorize the unending conversation as a form of reflection. We are born in history, learn to speak *to* and *with* others, becoming speaking subjects as we internalize the social conversation— the language of the other. Individual identity is but a composite of the many voices that populate a language. The parlor can also be viewed as "text," as agon. That is, art and criticism can be seen agonistically, as an assemblage of competing and cooperative idioms. The agon, says Burke, is a total drama "analytically subdivided into competing principles, of protagonist and antagonist" (*Philosophy*, 76). Our text, our parlor, is peopled with competing principles. Finally, we can also see the parlor as Burke's particular historical and intellectual scene, an agon of the self displacing and displaced by the tenor of the "argument" that Burke catches, the voices that provide the water for Burke's "or." Reading Burke pragmatically and as a pragmatist involves rereading and reevaluating his work in the context of those voices that affected him most profoundly: Aristotle, Shakespeare, Kant, Marx, Flaubert, Pater, Emerson, Freud, James, de Gourmont—and the list goes on. Since Burke perceives his own work as a dialectic of many voices, it may be worthwhile for us to do so as well. Burke's work demonstrates the poststructuralist notion that the warring forces within our own texts, the play of differences, can and should be subjects for direct contemplation and extension. In the end, such extensions may well be "dramatic."

Notes

1. For a provocative discussion of the pragmatic character of Burke's "negative hermeneutics" and dismantling of the dogmatism of aesthetic and Marxist approaches, see Timothy Crusius, "Kenneth Burke's *Auscultation*: A 'De-struction' of Marxist Dialectic and Rhetoric," *Rhetorica* 6, no. 4 (1988): 355–79.

2. See, for instance, John D. O'Banion, *Reorienting Rhetoric: The Dialectic of List and Story* (University Park: University of Pennsylvania Press, 1992); Melia, "Scientism and Dramatism"; and Gunn, *Culture of Criticism.*

References

Anderson, Danny J. "Deconstruction: Critical Strategy/Strategic Criticism." In *Contemporary Literary Theory*. Edited by G. Douglas Atkins and Laura Morrow. Amherst: University of Massachusetts Press, 1989.

Baldwin, James Mark, ed. *Dictionary of Philosophy and Psychology*. 3 vols. New York: Peter Smith, 1940.

Burke, Kenneth. *Attitudes Toward History*. Berkeley: University of California Press, 1984 [1937].

———. "Chicago and Our National Gesture." *The Bookman* 7 (1923): 497–501.

———. *Counter-Statement*. Berkeley: University of California Press, 1968 [1931].

———. *A Grammar of Motives*. Berkeley: University of California Press, 1969 [1945].

———. "Intelligence as a Good." Review of John Dewey's *The Quest for Certainty*. 1930. Rpt. in *The Philosophy of Literary Form*. Berkeley: University of California Press, 1973 [1941].

———. *Language as Symbolic Action: Essays on Life, Literature, and Method*. Berkeley: University of California Press, 1966.

———. *Permanence and Change: An Anatomy of Purpose*. Berkeley: University of California Press, 1984 [1935].

———. *The Philosophy of Literary Form: Studies in Symbolic Action*. Berkeley: University of California Press, 1973 [1941].

———. *A Rhetoric of Motives*. Berkeley: University of California Press, 1969 [1950].

———. "Rhetoric—Old and New." In *New Rhetorics*. Edited by Martin Steinmann Jr. New York: Scribners, 1967.

Crusius, Timothy. "Kenneth Burke's *Auscultation*: A 'De-struction' of Marxist Dialectic and Rhetoric." *Rhetorica* 6, no. 4 (1988): 355–79.

de Man, Paul. *Blindness and Insight: Essays in the Rhetoric of Contemporary Criticism*. New York: Oxford University Press, 1971.

Derrida, Jacques. *Of Grammatology*. Translated by Gayatri Chakravorty Spivak. Baltimore, Md.: Johns Hopkins University Press, 1976.

Dewey, John. *Human Nature and Conduct*. Rpt. Edited by Jo Ann Boydston. Carbondale: Southern Illinois University Press, 1988.

———. *The Quest for Certainty*. New York: Minton, Balch, 1929.

Emerson, Ralph Waldo. "The American Scholar." Rpt. in *Selected Writings of Emerson*. Edited by Donald McQuade. New York: Random House, 1981 [1837].

Gunn, Giles. *The Culture of Criticism and the Criticism of Culture*. New York: Oxford University Press, 1987.

Harris, Wendell V. *Dictionary of Concepts in Literary Criticism and Theory*. New York: Greenwood, 1992.

Hartman, Geoffrey H. *Criticism in the Wilderness: The Study of Literature Today*. New Haven, Conn.: Yale University Press, 1980.

James, William. "What Pragmatism Means." In *Pragmatism*. Rpt. Cleveland, Ohio: World, 1963 [1907].

Leitch, Vincent B. *American Literary Criticism from the Thirties to the Eighties*. New York: Columbia University Press, 1988.

Lentricchia, Frank. *Criticism and Social Change*. Chicago: University of Chicago Press, 1982.

————. "The Return of William James." *Cultural Critique* 4 (1986): 5–31.

Marx, Karl. *The Marx–Engels Reader*. 2nd ed. Edited by Robert C. Tucker. New York: Norton, 1978.

Melia, Trevor. "Scientism and Dramatism: Some Quasi-Mathematical Motifs in the Work of Kenneth Burke." In *The Legacy of Kenneth Burke*. Edited by Herbert W. Simons and Trevor Melia. Madison: University of Wisconsin Press, 1989.

Rorty, Richard. *Philosophy and the Mirror of Nature*. Princeton, N.J.: Princeton University Press, 1979.

Williams, Raymond. *Keywords: A Vocabulary of Culture and Society*. London: Croom Helm, 1976.

Part II

Burke and Feminism

4

"Being" and the Promise of Trinity

A Feminist Addition to Burke's Theory of Dramatism

Karen A. Foss and Cindy L. White

Kenneth Burke might be called the ultimate trinitarian because of his capacity to conceptualize the world in triadic cycles and components. While he labels himself a "confirmed trinitarian" (*Language*, 340) specifically when discussing the scatological triad of the fecal, urinary, and genital, such trinities are essential to his theory of human symbol use. The conscious, preconscious, and unconscious reveal the ways in which the body expresses itself through words that may lie beyond awareness (*Language*, 333). Furthermore, rebirth itself is a threefold process of pollution, purification, and redemption for Burke (*Rhetoric of Religion*, 314). In addition, the very foundation of his theory—the action-motion distinction—also admits a third possibility, in which symbolic action can influence the physical or biological: "If man is the symbol-using animal, some motives must derive from his animality, some from his symbolicity, and some from mixtures of the two" (*Language*, 62).

Despite his triadic preferences, however, Burke never satisfactorily names the midpoint of the action-motion continuum that is critical to his theory of human symbol use. He hints at what such a space entails when speaking of the necessary interplay between biology and symbolicity, by which the symbol realm depends on but also influences the animal realm: "It is a realm of 'essence' such that, without the warm blood of live bodies to feed it, it cannot truly 'exist.' The 'spirit' of all symbol systems could be said to 'transcend the body' in this sense" (*Language*, 342). Another way Burke conceptualizes this midpoint is as moments that "'just are'"—a standing still between the ontological realm of motion and the epistemological realm of symbols, or an "'external present' that has wound up the past and has the future wound up" (*Symbols*, 245).

Burke continues to talk around a middle point between biologic motion and symbolic action in his dialogue between the Lord and Satan that concludes *The Rhetoric of Religion*. He hints here at a "perfected" form of expression that might characterize the "communicative" possibilities of an in-between realm that is of but also transcends both biology and language. The language he envisions to express these "moments" is "intuitive . . . a dialogue between two persons that are somehow fused with each other in a communicative bond whereby each question is its own answer, or is answered even without being asked" (273).

Our aim in this essay is to provide the third concept missing from Burke's fundamental action-motion continuum by drawing on contemporary work in feminist scholarship. Such an effort not only enables us to better understand the full spectrum of human possibilities suggested by Burke's schema but also suggests the value of incorporating feminist perspectives into communication theories. We will: (1) describe Burke's motion-action continuum; (2) show how *being* is a suitable label for the intermediate position at which Burke hints; and (3) suggest the implications of this addition for rhetorical theory generally.

Realms of Human Activity:
The Motion-Action Continuum

Burke's distinction between motion and action divides human activity into two separate but not unrelated realms—the biological and the symbolic. The former is that realm in which humans are defined by and function according to their bodily processes. This is the realm of animality. While humans do have some rudimentary purposes in this realm—"desires for food, shelter, mates, rest, and the like"—those purposes are basic to their animality and do not elevate humans to the realm of action (*Language*, 28).

Action occurs only in the symbolic realm. In the realm of symbolic action, humans experience themselves apart from and as more than their animality. Symbolicity, the human capacity to acquire and use symbols, elevates humans above their animality, distinguishes them from other animals, and enables them to engage in action. Action, then, is the peculiar activity of the symbolic realm; it is not possible in the non-symbolic realm of "sheer motion" (*Language*, 54).

Although separate domains of human activity, action and motion are necessarily connected. Motion does not require action, and the realm of the nonsymbolic is quite possible without the symbolic realm. The reverse, however, is not possible. Action requires motion, and the symbolic realm is predicated upon the nonsymbolic realm. By providing the necessary material and biological conditions, the nonsymbolic realm makes the symbolic realm possible. At the same time, the symbolic often is used to affect and express the physical realm; one example of this is the process Burke calls "body-thinking" (*Language*, 341).

That Burke does not have a specific label for the in-between realm in which "the human process of symbol using integrates, shapes, and controls both external and internal realities simultaneously" (Brock, 310) means that the polarities of the motion-action distinction stand out. The action-motion distinction functions as a terministic screen, emphasizing the duality and limiting the conceptual grounds for communication.

A further consequence of Burke's not naming the ground between animality and symbolicity or action and motion is that a hierarchy is established that privileges the symbolic realm: the nonsymbolic realm supports the symbolic realm but remains beneath it—it is less noble, less complex, less interesting. The symbolic realm, poised above its counterpart, is the realm of thought, of language, of communication, of human motive, of humanity. Burke does not provide the terms to talk easily about possibilities of expression that do not involve the manipulation of symbols.

Finally, Burke's theory privileges communication as "doing"—as purposive and strategic. Human communication occurs in the realm of action and thus cannot be divorced from the sense of "doing" that pervades that realm. This focus on the strategic emerges in various vocabularies throughout Burke's writings. He refers to his theory of dramatism as a "theory of purpose based on the definition of man as the 'symbol-using animal'" (*Rhetoric of Religion*, 274) and speaks specifically of language as encompassing persuasion: "In the course of such uses, they will learn the arts of petition, exhortation [persuasion and dissuasion]. For language, as an instrument of guidance, is especially suited to persuade the language-using animal" (*Rhetoric of Religion*, 286–87). In another discussion, Burke admits that the concept of motivation itself—central to his theory of dramatism—is "directional" in that it involves movement of various kinds (Symbols, 245). By rooting communication in general, and persuasion in particular, in a sense of doing, Burke's motion-action distinction conceptualizes both enterprises as strategic activities. He suggests that his theory of motivation stresses not "'Who are you?' or 'Where are you from?' but 'Where are you going'?" (*Symbols*, 245).

We believe that the addition of a middle term—being—appropriately captures and locates the substantive ground between Burke's motion-action polarities and simultaneously shows what feminist theories can contribute to Burke's approach to communication. Many feminist theorists propose the notion of "being" as an alternative to traditional rhetorical strategies for accomplishing social change; thus it mediates between Burke's end point terms while also proposing a nonstrategic alternative for negotiating the symbolic realm. To explicate this theory of being, we will rely on the thinking of three feminist theorists—Sonia Johnson, Mary Daly, and Sally Miller Gearhart—whose work specifically addresses the possibility of "being" as a means of creating change.

The Nature of Being

"Being" is a state in which women simply experience life as freely, consciously, and fully as possible, realizing that this is not only the purpose of life but a genuine place from which change can occur. Sonia Johnson asks: "'Is there anything more important to do than to be aware of and enjoy being alive every moment'?" (175). The state of being Johnson envisions is one of true authenticity: "Only by being absolutely true to myself can I ever be true to anyone else. True is simply true, the same internal state whether I am alone or connecting with others. True is having integrity—wholeness, authenticity" (120). For her, it is captured in moments when she feels and experiences her energy, moments in which she describes herself as "a seething mass of unexpelled energy," and "incredibly alive, more awake than I had been for a long time, more aware of myself and therefore more aware of others" (21).

Sally Miller Gearhart also describes the sense of being in terms of energy; for her, it is an intrapersonal energy "generated from within the individual's own territory" ("Womanpower," 198). The notion of being Gearhart envisions accompanies a turning away from the patriarchy to an inward place in which a new kind of energy flourishes. The purpose of this inward turning is

> to find another source . . . a source deeper than the patriarchy and one that allows us to stand in the path of continuous and cosmic energy. That new source is discovered only by moving inward to the self, and it is being experienced most widely these days by women who are finding our individual or *intra*personal energy flow. ("Womanpower," 195)

Like Johnson, Gearhart's conceptualization of being points to an authentic self unfettered by patriarchal impositions that distract women's attention from the nourishing force of their own energy.

Mary Daly similarly conceptualizes being as energy, seeing it as the force that creates woman's most alive, genuine, and integrated self. Woman's energy "becomes unsplintered, unblocked," as she focuses her "dissociated energy," leading her to a place where she can "find her own Kind, unbind her mind" (375). It is an energy that is, like that Gearhart describes, a deeper, prior, grounded one, "rooted, as are animals and trees, winds and seas, in the Earth's substance. Our origins are in her elements. Thus, when true to our Originality, we are Elemental" (4–5).

The sense of being described by Johnson, Gearhart, and Daly contrasts with but also draws from both action and motion as Burke defines them. It is grounded in primary substances of nature, and in this sense, shares with Burke's notion some unconscious, fundamental processes that are necessary to life activity (Blankenship, 251–68). Johnson, Gearhart, and Daly suggest that women who choose to acknowledge "being" are indeed tapping into their elemental, connected natures that are always there and available to them. This state of awareness, then, incorporates notions of Burke's definition of action: to truly "be" is a highly conscious, fully aware state in which a woman remembers and acknowledges her true, connected self.

Symbolicity and choice are part of this state of being—dimensions that also distinguish Burke's notion of action—yet the focus is not on expressing oneself to others. What is most important is that a woman feels and experiences whatever is going on at the moment for herself, without needing to share that state with others. Johnson, in fact, suggests that interaction with others may dissipate the sense of power, connectedness, and aliveness that accompanies "being"; perhaps expressing feelings "can sometimes be a way of externalizing our energy and power and dissipating it. Perhaps we are trained to respond because response gives our power away" (Johnson, 21). Being, then, transcends symbol use because its essence, power, and fulfillment do not depend on sharing symbols: it simply *is*.

The Violence of Persuasion

The focus on being rather than on symbolic action is privileged by many feminist scholars who would disagree with Burke's insistence on language use and persuasion. The intention to change others is, in fact, considered an act of violence by these three theorists. Gearhart is most explicit in faulting rhetoric for "educating others to violence" with such audacity, and she does not excuse it for doing so "with language and metalanguage . . . instead of with whips or rifles" ("Womanization," 195). For Gearhart, there is an important difference between wanting things to change and wanting to change things. She acknowledges that change happens all the time: "To change other people or other entities is not in itself a violation. It is a fact of existence that we do so. The act of violence is in the *intention* to change another" ("Womanization," 196).

Daly also notes that violence as exercised among humans is opposed to the notion of Elemental female energy or being. She uses the analogy of the violence of a tornado to make her point; a tornado's energy simply is—a natural, wild part of nature:

> A tornado's violence is simply natural, Wild force. The movement of Elemental women also is forceful, in varying styles and velocities. . . . [O]ur Movement in its diversity is ultimately creative, as are the forces of nature. Elemental creativity is utterly Other than the acontextual and anti-contextual meddling with nature that characterizes phallic technocracy. (17)

Like the tornado, the energy of being may create change in others but that is not its purpose. Its purpose is to unlock the creative potential in the woman who has tapped its power. Daly, too, talks about women focusing on their own power as a process that results in change:

> The moments of averting, of wielding our Be-Witching Labryses as shields against nonbe-ing are magical magnetizing moments/ movements in Realms of Be-ing. . . .
> [Women] by this same movement attract others away from non-be-ing into the Centering Journey that is participation in Be-ing. Be-Witching women thus enchant others, chanting, calling, luring into Lust for transformation/transportation into Metabeing. Like Sirens singing the call of the Strange, Be-Witching women rearrange the shapes of our lives. (389)

For Daly, the transformative power of being rests in its capacity to attract rather than overcome. Change in others is accomplished as a consequence of their own desire to seek out their own examples of others who have connected to being. The creative energy of being in one person, then, may attract others who may change themselves by tapping their own energies.

Sonia Johnson similarly objects to efforts to change others, and shares her moment of recognition that trying to get her partner, Susan, to change was, in fact, abusive:

> "Force" is the pivotal word here. I tried every coercive trick I
> knew. After six months or so of this, I realized that my
> attempts to make her accompany me on my journey instead of
> accepting her autonomy and leaving her in peace to continue
> her own, . . . this was the stuff of abuse. (69)

Johnson came to understand that she could only change herself—but
that this was far more respectful and productive than were her efforts at
coercion:

> I knew that I couldn't change anybody but myself for the better.
> And I also trusted that other women were doing the best they
> could at the moment, as I was, and that, like me, all they
> needed from others in order to get on with their personal work
> was to be unconditionally accepted as the experts on their own
> lives. (162)

Gearhart, Daly, and Johnson envision being as the grounds for
authentic change that is freely chosen. The creative power of being
allows for the creation of an environment that is free from coercion and
the violence of intentionality. Being suggests a focus on the individual's
true self, a probing of her own desires and potentials rather than on
what others may want of her. Actions that arise out of being are those
that are truly embraced and thus energizing. As such they become a
powerful force for change in both the self and others who are motivated
to seek out their own energy.

Unlike Burke, then, many contemporary feminists eschew an auto-
matic connection between symbolic activity and persuasion. That
language use is possible does not mean it is the only form of influence
nor is it necessarily the most desirable. The perspectives of Daly,
Johnson, and Gearhart see persuasion as violence and seek alternative
conceptualizations of expression.

The Possibilities for Change

If being means making no effort to transform another and means
instead focusing on being the most centered, authentic, alive self a
woman can be, how is change possible? Is the answer simply sitting in
passivity, withdrawing, or waiting for miracles? The answer to this
dilemma, for Gearhart, Daly, and Johnson, is the creation of an environment in which others can change. Gearhart describes the process this
way:

> Communication can be a deliberate creation or co-creation of
> an atmosphere in which people or things, . . . may change
> themselves; it can be a milieu in which those who are ready to
> be persuaded may persuade themselves, may choose to hear or
> choose to learn. ("Womanization," 198)

Accompanied by a process of modeling, change can and does happen.
Gearhart elaborates:

> We know we can't change other women, that they must convert
> themselves. Our job is to continue in our own growth and thus
> to create the atmosphere (in this case supportive and exemp-
> lary) in which their internal bases for change can break
> through. ("Womanpower," 205)

Daly similarly describes a "free space" that promotes creative
pursuits and activities: women "strive to create an atmosphere in which
further creativity may flourish. . . . we become breathers/creators of free
space. We are windy, stirring the stagnant spaces with life" (18). Like
Gearhart, Daly suggests that the woman who is being fully herself is an
inspiring and motivating presence: "Actively potent, she makes sense of
things, inspiring her sisters to trust their own senses. Putting her
memories into words, she Nags others to find and weave their wholeness" (178).[1] Realizing her harmony with the elements, a woman
becomes more at home in her own integrated world, and this awareness
provides what is necessary to "Spin new/ancient gynergy patterns that
transform oppressive states. Sometimes this implies moving out of an old
environment physically; always it implies transforming the conditions
where/when one lives" (279).

Johnson's description of change begins with the acknowledgment
that being replaces doing and that being is enough:

> [T]he surest route to transformation is not what we *do* but how
> we *are*, that it's not doing but being that rearranges the stars of
> destiny. . . . [O]ut of who I *am*, out of who we *are*—not out of
> acts of desperation or resistance—is coming the new world.
> (210)

According to Johnson, the freedom women seek will not be achieved
through deliberate efforts to make others change, but in trusting the
capacities of others to know and do what they need to do to be free:
"Everything we want and need, and an abundance of it, depends on our

learning to let everyone and everything do only what they want to do, to go their own ways and be free. Doing this frees us as well" (190). Johnson realizes that the patriarchy has privileged efforts at persuasion as the source of change and that, in fact, just the opposite is true from her experience:

> Mensmachine has taken from us our knowledge that everything flows unobstructed and perfect when we are being whole and in our power. We have forgotten that actions arise organically out of who we are, and believe mistakenly that we must make them happen, we must organize people to do things. (322)

For these theorists, the gift-giving paradigm, frequently associated with women, is a metaphor for the process of change as they conceptualize it. When gifts are given freely, out of respect and affection for another and with no thought to what will be received in return, an atmosphere is created in which others can grow and change as they will. Gearhart contrasts this process with what occurs in traditional efforts at persuasion:

> Instead of probing or invading, our natural giving takes the path of wrapping around the givee, of being available to her/him without insisting; our giving is a *presence*, an *offering*, an *opening*, a *surrounding*, a *listening*, a *vulnerability*, a *trust*. ("Womanpower," 198)

Johnson also talks in gift-giving terms to contrast this approach with the exchange paradigm valued by the patriarchy:

> Like the woman who prepares food simply for the enjoyment of the act in the moment—not as means to some other end—I know now that when I touch for no ulterior reasons, when I refuse the linear-time lie, my touching is not a stimulus; it requires—it *desires*—no response. It is not in the reciprocal, exchange, adversarial, war paradigm at all, but is instead simply a gift, part of women's universal and beautiful non-exchange economy of abundance. (303)

Daly describes the process in slightly different terms—as wishing and encouraging in the context of Be-Friending and Be-Longing:

> Be-Friending is radically connected with Be-Longing. The latter
> is that which metapatriarchal women wish for each other and
> en-courage in each other, for only the longing/Lusting for be-
> ing can bring about Happiness. . . . As she is drawn into the
> Spiraling movement of Be-Friending, a woman becomes a
> friend to the be-ing in her Self, which is to say, her centering
> Self. The intensity of her desire focuses her energy, which
> becomes unsplintered, unblocked. (375)

The act of being, then, does allow change to occur, but it is change that stems from the "energy of receptivity, the energy of the listening ear, of the open meadow, of the expansive embrace" (Gearhart, "Woman-power," 198). Feminist theorists, with their notions of being, draw on both motion and action to suggest that any change that occurs is the result of a person being fully centered, connected, and present, and in that capacity of aliveness and awareness, facilitating the creation of an environment in which others also can change. Feminist theorists, then, are essentially labeling and elaborating on one possibility for Burke's middle realm between motion and action. Grounded in motion and symbolicity, being draws from both to synthesize a communicative possibility that transcends pure motion and pure action. It insists that there is a form of expression that is "essence" by which one simply seeks to fully acknowledge and realize the self and, in this process, model new possibilities for others.

Implications for Rhetorical Theory

The notion of being, as elaborated by Sally Miller Gearhart, Mary Daly, and Sonia Johnson, suggests some intriguing possibilities for the communication discipline. In charting a mode called "being," in which essence alone is sufficient, these feminist scholars ask us to explore the various ways in which humans make use of being rather than movement and motive to achieve expression. They suggest that we motivate not by persuasion but through modeling and the creation of an environment in which others can choose to change.

Such a focus should not be confounded with notions that eternalize differences between women and men while essentializing both. Feminists' treatments of being do not suggest a mystical attachment to women's biology, intuition, or the like. Nor do they pose a false duality between action and being that assumes eternal principles of femininity and mas-culinity. Rather, being arises from frameworks of thought and scholar-ship that rely on experiences that have been dismissed, marginalized, and obscured—women's experiences as communicators. Among others, attempts to account for, examine, and explain women's rhetorical experiences demonstrate the limitations of a canon that valorizes the activities of some and sacrifices those of others. In their articulation of being, Daly, Gearhart, and Johnson challenge the universality of traditional rhetorical perspectives and provide a critical means for overcoming the blindness of those perspectives to women's experiences and patterns of communication.

Burke's starting distinction between action and motion is critical to his theory of dramatism—a theory that helps us understand the complex processes and nuances that comprise the study of human symbol use. When feminist perspectives on being are added as a "stance" that also can form the substance of expression, a dimension of Burke's system is clarified and elaborated, opening up a new realm of possibilities for understanding human expression. While the motion-action distinction emphasizes a hierarchical duality that privileges persuasion, it obscures and distorts moments of communion in human interaction. Within the confines of the duality, communion becomes the result of persuasion. It is understood and treated as a potential end of various rhetorical processes, rather than as a rhetorical process. As an artifact of rhetorical processes, communion becomes the impetus for, rather than the focus of, rhetorical interest and study. In overcoming the duality between motion and action, being creates a range of terministic implications that emphasize the rhetorical essence of those moments that are characterized by harmony rather than strife. Moreover, in challenging the assumption that disagreement animates change while persuasion accomplishes it, being calls into question the consequent assumption that controversy is the most important and fruitful area of rhetorical study.

At the same time that the notion of being points up a limitation of Burke's work, it also reminds us of the acuity, value, and resiliency of his rhetorical insights. Burke's attention to terministic impulses and compulsions asks us to be ever vigilant of the power and implications of our terms. The feminist focus on being echoes the value of that admonition. The motion-action distinction results in a duality that neglects the middle realm and suggests a hierarchy that not only privileges symbolic action but, more important, treats persuasion as the pinnacle of that hierarchy. As Burke suggests, the "principle of hierarchy" carries with it "the entelechial tendency, the treatment of the 'top' or 'culminating' stage as the 'image' that best represents the entire 'idea'" (*Rhetoric of Motives*, 141). Thus, rhetoric is equated with persuasion at the top of the communication hierarchy.

Among the "mystifications" of such a hierarchy, however, is the possibility that change can be accomplished through processes and means that are creative and nonstrategic. Among the consequences of mystification is our own "trained incapacity" that blinds us to the discovery and examination of the rhetorical patterns of those whose "actions" are nonstrategic, or take place in contexts or moments when the need for persuasion is absent. Yet "the crumbling of hierarchies," Burke reminds us, "is as true a fact about them as their formation" (*Rhetoric of Motives*, 141). The notion of being unites the realms of motion and action, disrupts the polarity of the two, and transcends their implicit dualism. Its terministic promise is a window onto rhetorical forms, processes, contexts, and experiences that have hitherto been obscured. Even as being represents a means for demystifying his most fundamental distinction—hierarchy—we believe Burke anticipated and would applaud its crumbling.

Notes

1. Daly uses the word *nag* differently from its usual meaning. For her, it means "'to affect recurrent awareness, uncertainty, need for consideration, or concern'" (12). Nags, then, are noted for their constant awareness of the current state of affairs and for their efforts to nag themselves into a fully conscious state. Nagging others to change, then, is not part of Daly's definition.

Works Cited

Blankenship, Jane. "Kenneth Burke on Ecology: A Synthesis." In *Extensions of the Burkeian System*. Edited by James W. Chesebro. Tuscaloosa: University of Alabama Press, 1993.

Brock, Bernard L. "The Evolution of Kenneth Burke's Philosophy of Rhetoric: Dialectic Between Epistemology and Ontology." In *Extensions of the Burkeian System*. Edited by James W. Chesebro. Tuscaloosa: University of Alabama Press, 1993.

Burke, Kenneth. *Language as Symbolic Action: Essays on Life, Literature, and Method*. Berkeley: University of California Press, 1966.

———. *On Symbols and Society*. Edited by Joseph Gusfield. Chicago: University of Chicago Press, 1989.

———. *A Rhetoric of Motives*. Berkeley: University of California Press, 1969.

———. *The Rhetoric of Religion: Studies in Logology*. Berkeley: University of California Press, 1970.

Daly, Mary. *Pure Lust: Elemental Feminist Philosophy.* Boston, Mass.: Beacon, 1984.

Gearhart, Sally Miller. "The Womanization of Rhetoric." *Women's Studies International Quarterly* 2 (1979): 195–201.

———. "Womanpower: Energy Re-Sourcement." In *The Politics of Women's Spirituality: Essays on the Rise of Spiritual Power Within the Feminist Movement.* Edited by Charlene Spretnak. New York: Anchor, 1982.

Johnson, Sonia. *The Ship That Sailed into the Living Room: Sex and Intimacy Reconsidered.* Estancia, N.M.: Wildfire, 1991.

5

"Can This Marriage Be Saved?"

Reclaiming Burke for Feminist Scholarship

Phyllis M. Japp

For years, *Ladies' Home Journal* presented a monthly essay entitled "Can This Marriage Be Saved?" The title echoes concerns posed by many women scholars as they assess the relationship between the traditions of their disciplines and their experiences as women. Obviously, not all unions can be preserved. Some traditions may be so unusable for feminist scholarship (e.g., the elite public address focus on great speeches by great men) that divorce may be the only option. Yet others are so central to a domain of knowledge, so integrated into a community of scholarship, that separation would be traumatic to all concerned. Kenneth Burke's dramatistic perspective on communication seems an example of the latter. Burke has been a major influence on communication research in general and rhetorical theory and criticism in particular. Even scholars who do not explicitly cite Burke give evidence of how thoroughly his ideas about communication have permeated theory and research across various disciplines.

My conviction that Burke contains much that is relevant for feminist scholarship is shaped, in part, by personal experience. Certainly I encounter passages that seem alien to my experience of the world and engage concepts that fail to include my perspectives, yet I have found in Burke an indispensable array of guerrilla tactics for survival in a field of masculinist symbols. The comic frame, debunking, irony, transcendence, the ability to move between logical and temporal frames—these and other strategies have, over and over again, allowed me to explain, subvert, and even at times influence my world.

Although the relationship is fraught with problems, I believe the Burkean system represents what Rosemary Radford Ruether calls a "usable tradition" for feminist rhetorical scholarship. A tradition can be considered usable, Ruether argues, when it is possible to locate "intimations of alternatives" to dominant interpretations, when major concepts and constructs contain space for alternate meanings, when principles can function reflexively and self-critically so that the perspective can grow and change (21–22).

Recent Burkean scholarship acknowledges the need for reevaluation and reformulation of his system. Foss and Griffin argue that feminist scholars find Burke's concepts inadequate to their critical concerns and suggest limits be imposed on the utility of the system (343). Chesebro locates biases in the Burkean system, but calls for extension of the perspective rather than limiting application (84–88). Condit argues that the Burkean system is inadequately developed in the areas of sex/gender, class, and culture, and envisions a "post-Burkean" discourse (81–82). At issue in these and similar evaluations is the vitality of a now static perspective for an ever-changing cultural context. A stance of limitation or partial rejection considers the Burkean system closed, while one of extension defines it as an open system that can be reoriented to new sociopolitical environments.

Scholars disturbed by the inadequacies of the Burkean system but unwilling to reject it might well consider an alternative developed by feminist theologians, the critical reclamation of sacred texts. Reclamation is a strategy midway between acceptance and rejection, affirming the value of the text for a spiritual community while simultaneously reworking and reshaping that text and its accumulated contexts of interpretation to better serve all in the community. Feminist biblical reclamation, as described by Elizabeth Schlussler Fiorenza, acknowledges the androcentricity of the text and its role in perpetuating "misogynist mindsets and oppressive values" but at the same time recognizes that the text has also empowered women in their fight for equality (*Bread*, 153). Reclamation is not merely an alternate reading strategy, but a focus "on all the rhetorical dimensions and elements" generated by the text, a concern with the "politics of communication in past and present sociohistorical and ideological contexts" (*Bread*, 156).

While especially valuable for religious texts, the strategy is equally applicable to the influential texts of any cultural or scholarly community and certainly seems a useful option for those whose identity as scholars has been formulated within theoretical domains that have silenced, distorted, or negated aspects of their experience. Feminist scholars, for example, not only must address the inadequacy of extant concepts, models, and terminologies; they must expose how these have created misrepresentations that continue to devalue and distort their experience. Revered texts accrue layers of interpretative contexts, contexts developed in sociopolitical environments of reading. These layers of context serve, over time, to solidify some interpretations and silence others. Reclamation gives critical attention to this interaction of text and interpretive context as well as to the institutions, hierarchies, rituals, and norms that derive from accepted interpretations of text and context.

Reclamation seems an especially appropriate strategy for a feminist reading of Burke. As Foss and Griffin note, Burke's works are often treated as the "sacred texts" of the discipline (331). As with things sacred, however, the Burkean corpus is surrounded by a layer of other texts—works of adulation, explanation, exposition, interpretation, and application—that make it difficult to isolate Burke from the perceptual filters that dictate how he should be, must be, or must not be read. Encrusted in and stifled by this dogma (some of which Burke himself is responsible for), the Burkean perspective appears at first glance useless for emancipatory reading. Removed from this encrustation of affirmation and read afresh, however, I believe in its potential for feminist reclamation.

Feminist theologians who seek to reclaim sacred texts face two related problems: the virtual absence of women's voices and the systematic distortion of women's experience. Women's voices, missing in the central texts of the faith, have not been included in subsequent interpretations of those texts. Thus women remain silent and silenced within the tradition. As absences and silences are perpetuated over time, the tradition possesses no corrective for distortions and misrepresentations of women.

Feminist scholars clearly face these same problems when attempting to reclaim the rhetorical tradition. Because women (among others) are absent from that tradition, not only does it fail to reflect their experiences; its concepts and precepts often distort and devalue that experience (Foss and Foss, 1–2). As presently interpreted, Burke's vision of human symbol use presents the same challenge: it appears monolingual and thus silencing and limiting.

As one considers the possibility of reclaiming Burke, two questions immediately arise: (1) Can this process be undertaken without doing mortal damage to the integrity of the Burkean system? (2) How ought reclamation of a perspective such as Burke's proceed?

Burke himself provides a most positive response to the first question. Both his life and his writings exemplify the impetus for critical reevaluation. Burke often experienced life as one at odds with his world, chronically unable or unwilling to march in step with the academic drumbeats of any era, frequently challenging those comfortably empowered by prevailing intellectual hierarchies. While this experience does not make Burke a feminist in any sense of the word, it is a perspective with which feminists can partially identify and a stance from which his work can be reread. Moreover, because Burke was so often energized by the need to challenge and undermine the status quo of his time, his critical system was directed toward unsettling dominant and dominating structures and practices. The fact that patriarchal assumptions were not his target does not mean that his system could not be used against such, even those integrated into his own work.

Certainly Burke continued to extend and elaborate on his system throughout his life, often adjusting the meaning of his terms, realigning perspectives, and encouraging others to do so as well. While his life provides inspiration for continual revision, his writings are replete with strategies for revision and reclamation. For example, in *The Rhetoric of Religion*, Burke demonstrates how sacred texts can be resecularized. The language of theology, he argues, is a vocabulary drawn from, and therefore highly relevant to, secular concerns:

> Whether or not there is a realm of the "supernatural," there are *words* for it. And in this state of linguistic affairs there is a paradox. For whereas the words for the "supernatural" realm are necessarily borrowed from the realm of our everyday experiences, out of which our familiarity with language arises, once a terminology has been developed for special theological purposes the order can become reversed. We can borrow back the terms from the borrower, again secularizing to varying degrees the originally secular terms that had been given "supernatural" connotations. (7)

Burke here suggests a starting point for feminist reclamation. If the vocabulary for human communication encoded into our theoretical texts, Burke included, was borrowed from only part of human experience, that of elite males, feminist critics must demystify or resecularize the terms, borrowing them back for women by modifying them to include women's experience. Burke, we must remember, was adopted into, and therefore adapted to, a tradition of rhetorical theory and criticism at a time when there were few challenges to the masculinist assumptions inherent in the tradition. To now read Burke against that tradition is difficult, akin to reading the New Testament without the influence of centuries of Christian theology.

Burke provides additional resources for the reclamation process with his insights on the ideological dimensions of vocabularies of motive.

He argues that all vocabularies or terminologies "filter out" as well as "filter in" aspects of reality. Therefore, to understand the implications of any "terministic screen," we must consider not only what is explicitly stated in that terminology but must account for silences and absences as well (*Language*, 51). So far this is familiar territory, but what follows is not usually included in citations of Burke. He continues that in any vocabulary or terminology some potentialities are absent. Some are absent because they are deliberately repressed, but others are merely "remote," that is, not currently understood as falling within the range of that terminology:

> Why can there not also be ideas that are unclear simply because we have not yet become familiar enough with a situation to take them adequately into account? Thus, when we see an object at a distance, we do not ordinarily "repress" the knowledge of its identity. We don't recognize it simply because we must come closer, or use an instrument, before we can see it clearly enough to know precisely what it is. Would not a terminology that features the unconscious *repression* of ideas automatically deflect our attention from symbols that are not *repressed* but merely *remote*? (*Language*, 51)

These remote possibilities are not necessary antithetical to the vocabulary, but lay fallow, so to speak, as silent alternative meanings within the potential of that vocabulary, options not presently expressed in current interpretations (*Language*, 51).

If one applies this insight to Burke's own vocabulary of terms, it underscores the value of exploring that terminology for possible openings for feminist reclamation before declaring it unsalvageable. It suggests that while extant understandings of Burke's perspective have heretofore supported perceptions of rhetoric and rhetorical practice in ways that seem antithetical to women's experience, these readings do not necessarily exhaust the potential of his terminology nor should they discourage exploration of alternate, but currently implicit possibilities. I am not suggesting that there are inherent feminist tendencies hidden within the Burkean perspective—such is probably not the case. I do believe, however, that the full potential of Burke's critical system has not been realized, embedded as it has been in traditions that have constrained interpretations. If Burke can be reclaimed as a usable tradition for feminist scholars, we can recover alternative meanings within his system.

Although I will argue that Burke contains resources for his own reclamation, we first need a vision of how critical feminist reclamation proceeds. In reclamation, a critic works with a text much as a tailor works with a garment that does not fit, perhaps discarding some of the cloth, perhaps adding new material, rearranging, redesigning, and finally reassembling a wearable and functional new garment from elements of the old. Fiorenza's critical feminist approach to the reclamation of sacred texts, described below, is a rhetorical hermeneutic process that reworks text and interpretive contexts.[1]

A Critical Hermeneutics of Reclamation

Fiorenza's critical system consists of four interdependent strategies—a hermeneutic of suspicion, a hermeneutic of proclamation, a hermeneutic of remembrance, and a hermeneutic of creative actualization (*Bread*, 15–22). These strategies bear some relationship, I believe, to Burke's four master tropes—metaphor (perspective), metonymy (reduction), synecdoche (representation), and irony (dialectic)—likewise a set of interdependent strategies for interpreting vocabularies of motive (*Grammar*, 305–17). As with Fiorenza's strategies, Burke's master tropes work together to provide alternate routes into motives, such that wherever one starts, one will necessarily engage the other three. After describing Fiorenza's system, I will loosely pair her hermeneutic strategies with Burke's tropes—the hermeneutic of suspicion with irony/dialectic; the hermeneutics of remembrance with metonymy/reduction; the hermeneutics of proclamation with synecdoche/representation; and the trope of tropes, metaphor/perspective, with the overarching hermeneutic, creative actualization. By relating these two interpretive processes, my goal is not only to submit Burke to a process of critical feminist reclamation but to demonstrate that the Burkean system contains within itself the strategies by which it can be continually reshaped, redefined, and expanded.

The Critical Strategy of Suspicion

Fiorenza's first reclamation strategy, suspicion, is a process of reading sacred texts to discover "underlying presuppositions, androcentric models, and unarticulated interests" featured in both the text and contemporary interpretations (*Bread*, 15–17). This process is called into play by the dissonance between women's experience and the ideological dictates of a text. If a perspective does not provide room for women's experiences, Fiorenza argues, women have several choices of response. Historically, women have tended to react to sacred texts by either submission, muting those aspects of their experience that conflict with the text, or by rejecting entirely the authority of the text. In every era, however, there have been courageous women who have read sacred texts suspiciously. In nineteenth-century America, for example, the Grimke sisters, Elizabeth Cady Stanton, and others challenged Biblical interpretations that refused their right to a public voice.

It is this tradition that Fiorenza invokes, a stance that simultaneously affirms the value of a text to a rhetorical community and points out its inadequacies for some members of that community. It is important to see this process as more than oppositional reading, that is, it is not merely reading a text from an alternate ideological perspective, but allowing the text to cast a critical eye on a "reader's own practices and assumptions" as she encounters the text. As members of the rhetorical community for which the text has (or has the potential to have) value, one reads for both "liberating and oppressive values and vision" by considering the "dynamics of the text and its interpretations" as these operate both historically and in the present moment (*But She Said*, 57).

The tensions exposed are not only those between the readers and the texts but between the texts and reinforcing contexts of interpretation, both past and present. The purpose is not to rescue the text from erroneous interpretations and interpolations; there is no assumption of an initially pure version contaminated by subsequent interpretations. Instead the sacred text itself is viewed suspiciously, as a product of its own historical and ideological moments. A suspicious reading of the New Testament parable of Mary and Martha, for example, so often used to subtly denigrate women's caretaking activities, might inquire why the text foregrounds this particular episode in the complex, ongoing relationship between the sisters and the disciples (*But She Said*, 57). Why was the story originally constructed as it was and why, over time, have some interpretations been encouraged at the expense of others? Thus the strategy of suspicion attempts to discover a sacred text's inherent biases, as it peels away the layers of affirmation that have grown around the text. Suspicion interfaces with the other three strategies below, exposing opportunities for revision.

The Critical Strategy of Proclamation

Fiorenza's second hermeneutic strategy, proclamation, reads texts and accompanying traditions in the context of contemporary cultural politics; it is essentially a critical assessment of the texts in alternate contexts of reading. Proclamation not only points out the values embedded in the text but assesses the historical contextualizations that have reinforced those values. In this process of reading, proclamation

locates and articulates openings that can be exploited for new readings
(*Bread*, 18–19; *But She Said*, 68-73).

Proclamation is, in one sense, the counterpart of suspicion. As
suspicion undermines extant hierarchies to expose ideologies of dominance, proclamation simultaneously seeks to articulate the repressed
possibilities inherent in the text. Proclamation calls or cries forth the
nature of its encounter with the text. These proclamations may be cries
of frustration or pain, calls for revision or reconstruction. As noted, the
parable of Mary and Martha has traditionally been used to denigrate
women's caretaking activities. Proclamation of the contexts of interpretation can stress the political value of that particular reading for
generations of church "fathers," allowing women to be relegated to
activities of domestic service even as these are pronounced spiritually
inferior. Proclamation also must stress the pain inherent in this devaluation of women's work and the need for reinterpretation of these
traditions. As with suspicion, those who engage in proclamation refuse
to retreat in silence but insist their voices be part of the interpretive
community. Proclamation and suspicion interact to expose limitations,
biases, and contradictions as well as search for new interpretations for
contemporary readers.

The Critical Strategy of Remembrance

The third hermeneutic strategy proposed by Fiorenza, remembrance,
aids in constructing new meanings by recovering lost voices and silenced
traditions. Working from remnants and fragments of sacred texts,
remembrance reclaims traditions by emphasizing the experience of those
pushed aside in the hegemony of particular modes of thought. Remembrance recognizes the extant text as partial (in both senses of the term)
and thus seeks to reconstitute a more inclusive and unbiased vision.
While suspicion and proclamation engage the text itself, remembrance
moves beyond to the contexts of experience either unknown or discarded
as the text and its interpretations took ideological shape over time. It
asks whether the text adequately or accurately represents the rhetorical
community it purports to represent, if past and present interpretive
communities have limited access to the text, and inquires where, how,
and on what authority such exclusions are practiced. Remembrance not
only traces how exclusions become an accepted part of the text and its
interpretations, but attempts to recover alternate voices that might have
been, should have been included (*Bread*, 19–20; *But She Said*, 62–68).

In the example of the Mary/Martha parable, one might inquire what
voices were neglected when the story was first told (certainly the inter-

pretations of the sisters themselves), what contexts of reading were suppressed as it was retold to generations of women (certainly the reactions of women themselves), what challenges to the values encoded in dominant interpretations were suppressed. The recovery of such contexts allows expansion of the reductions that support patriarchy, suggesting these be read as markers in the struggle to achieve dominance, not as fundamental axioms of human practice. As with proclamation, remembrance is a move from text to context and back again. Here, however, the focus is on the recovery and revision of significant context for the text and accompanying traditions and interpretations. Remembrance feeds directly into the fourth strategic process, creative actualization.

The Critical Strategy of Creative Actualization

Creative actualization, Fiorenza's final strategy, requires moving beyond both the text and its interpretive contexts into new and imaginative worlds of possibility. This is the master strategy that incorporates the first three, for it allows women to read themselves into the text as they engage in the strategies of suspicion, proclamation, and remembrance. By "historical imagination, narrative amplifications, artistic recreations and liturgical celebrations," women expand, reconstitute, and appropriate the previously alienating text as their own (*Bread*, 20–22; *But She Said*, 73–76). This process releases the text from its previous uses and makes it accessible for new uses by heretofore alienated peoples. It provides room for the experiences, hopes, dreams, and insights of new readers and invites these to participate in the interpretative process. Major narratives are reworked to express the potentialities recovered in the previous strategies. This creative playing with "what if" moves readers into new areas of inquiry, into new ways of expressing their faith. In the case of Mary and Martha, Fiorenza suggests that women write their own creative story of the women and their experiences with Jesus and the apostles. In such revisions, qualities entrenched as oppositional, that is, Martha's concentration on housekeeping and Mary's on listening, can be re-created as necessary and compatible aspects of women's lives. These creative revisions, of course, must "always be submitted to a hermeneutics of suspicion," suspicion of one's own creations as well as of previous textual interpretations (*But She Said*, 73).

Burke's Master Tropes as Critical Reclamation Strategies

As noted above, in working Burke's tropes into alignment with the feminist critical strategies, I am not suggesting that one system is equivalent to, or a substitute for, the other. Each must be understood and appreciated on its own terms. My purpose is to establish that the Burkean system is open to and compatible with a project of feminist revision and then to employ a Burkean vocabulary for further reclamation.

Irony/Dialectic as Suspicion

Burke's trope of irony, renamed dialectic, seems the best fit with the strategy of suspicion; certainly irony implies a suspicious attitude toward closure, a rejection of superficial meanings. Irony, Burke explains,

> arises when one tries, by the interaction of terms upon one another, to produce a development which uses all the terms. Hence, from the standpoint of this total form (this "perspective of perspectives"), none of the participating "sub-perspectives" can be treated as either precisely right or precisely wrong. They are all voices, or personalities, or positions, integrally affecting one another. (*Grammar*, 512)

Burke's critical stance is inherently suspicious/ironic, as he struggles against the tyranny of symbolic forms. Who, he inquires, is doing what to whom and how is that power revealed and/or concealed in the language of the situation? Whose language, employing what powers of definition, tends to control the discourse? How can these terminologies be resisted, undermined, reconfigured, transformed?

As with suspicion, the critical challenge of Burkean irony is to resist affirmation, to locate alternate positions. As irony works to break down the assumptions encoded into terminologies, it requires the reader to challenge the exclusions practiced in the name of those terms, to expose the mystery of hierarchy and open the vocabulary to alternate interpretations. Irony forces elements of the human drama into tension, revealing the conflicts implicit or silenced in any given interpretation.

Feminists, for example, might well be suspicious of masculinist emphasis on verbosity in theories such as Burke's. Mary Daly argues that because women have been silenced, they have learned to communicate in "an underground language of silence." Indeed in masculinist theories, women's voices are often silent, for their speech falls outside the accepted parameters of logical and reasonable practice and thus is not officially "heard" (151–53). As Foss and Foss note, "much of the communication women produce is not only not in the form of speeches, but it often is not verbal" (17). To read Burke suspiciously, then, might be to critically appraise the mystery of verbosity in his system.

Synecdoche/Representation and Proclamation

Burke's trope of synecdoche/representation connects with Fiorenza's strategy of proclamation, for both seek to develop a more representative account of human experience. As Burke argues, an adequate representation must have both scope and reduction, but if an accepted anecdote's "scope and reduction become a deflection [of reality] then the given terminology, or calculus, is not suited to the subject matter which it is designed to calculate" (*Grammar*, 59). Certainly, feminist critics must challenge the adequacy of a reduction that presents a portion of human experience as an accurate representation of all human experience. Just as Burke worked against the behavioristic reduction of human action to stimulus/response and shaped a more adequate anecdote for humankind, feminist scholars can work with his anecdote of human drama and reshape it to represent a wider range of symbolic experience.

A feminist reclamation of drama, for example, might investigate more closely the possibilities of Burke's recent concept of STORY as less agonistic than drama. STORY appears to be grounded in bodily sensation and thus connects the physicality of experience to the symbolic. While STORY may include conflict, it seems more open to alternatives than Burke's fundamental formula that equates drama with conflict. STORY, Burke argues, "greatly expands the range of attitudes by which we relate to each other" (Attitudes, 382–85). Although Burke tends to cast STORIES as embodying competitive interests, the concept appears open to a dialogic, experiential vision of human experience.

Metonymy/Reduction and Remembrance

Burke's trope of metonymy/reduction joins the strategy of remembrance as both invite exploration of dimensions silenced in the reductions of the text. Metonymy, says Burke, is the process of conveying "some incorporeal or intangible state in terms of the corporeal or tangible" (*Grammar*, 506). He argues that terminologies are developed by borrowing back and forth across realms of experience, for example, by moving concepts and ideas from the material to the spiritual domains. With each borrowing, however, the term is subtly changed, becoming both less and more than it was before, as it loses some connotations and adds others.

Burke suggests a number of ways to expand and contract vocabularies of motive. One especially useful strategy is to move back and forth from the reductions of logic to the more open-ended narrative mode of expression (*Rhetoric of Religion*, 29–33). In sacred texts, human experiences are often condensed into terse axioms or commandments and these reductions accepted and passed on as representations of that experience. A move to narrative reopens and expands the reduction, as it invites multiple stories that illustrate the breadth of human experience. Narrativizing thus provides a process for recovering heretofore unheard voices. For example, as Ruether notes, the Gospels give us the apostles' version of the resurrection event, but not Mary Magdalene's (8–11). What might we understand about resurrection if her story had been written into the record now canonized as sacred text? Likewise, what might we understand about rhetoric if women's' stories had been written into our theories and practices? Certainly remembrance encourages the recovery of vital context, a reconstitution of what was abstracted, including women's voices and practices.

Metaphor/Perspective as Creative Actualization

Creative actualization, Fiorenza's culminating and overarching critical strategy, aligns best with Burke's master trope of metaphor or perspective. Metaphor, as Burke argues, "is a device for seeing something in terms of something else," telling "something about one character as considered from the point of view of another character," for it is by the "approach through a variety of perspectives that we establish a character's reality," as we "consider it in as many different terms as its nature permits" (*Grammar*, 503–4). Thus a new metaphor provides a new perspective by generating new terms or new meanings for old terms. Especially useful, says Burke, are those perspectives that are seemingly incongruous, for these open us to fresh possibilities about the phenomenon under scrutiny. A new perspective allows a redefinition of old terms as well as the addition of new terms as it plays with the potentialities suggested by the text. Burke suggests that metaphor is a means of "progressive encompassment," a "filling-out" of the potential of ideas in a way that is inclusive rather than exclusive. By this process of "saying all that one can say," one can integrate "wider areas of human relationship" (*Philosophy*, 144–45). Burke's metaphor of drama presents problems, as noted above, but the system seems open to the possibility of alternate metaphors of human symbol-using. We could explore the potential of such metaphors as dance, landscape, music, art, quilt-making, or other activities less focused on verbosity, hierarchy and conflict and thus not as closed to alternate experiences (see Foss and Foss).

Reclaiming Burke's Concept of Hierarchy

Extending the Burkean system with a feminist-friendly vocabulary is a long-term process that involves working through both Burkean texts and accompanying layers of interpretative context—concept by concept, precept by precept—to reclaim each to serve a broader constituency. To suggest how such a process might work, I briefly consider one of Burke's major concepts and tease out possibilities for reclaiming that term. Burke's conception of hierarchy, for example, is considered a major feature of his system, but the term as usually understood presents a major problem for feminist scholars, who tend to seek a more egalitarian vision of social action. Foss and Griffin note that hierarchy is "a central feature of Burke's rhetorical system," and argue that he sees this process as an inevitable concomitant of human symbol use (340).

The proposed reclamation of this concept is, at this point, an informal playing with potentialities, not an in-depth reworking of the term and its associations. Such would require an exhaustive consideration of Burke's treatment of hierarchy across his corpus, looking ironically at moments of choice and unchallenged assumptions, searching out unrecognized reductions, absences, and silences, pulling in alternate traditions, developing new metaphors for human orderliness. Here, I want only to suggest how we might use the four critical strategies to challenge and enlarge this term.

Suspicion/Dialectic/Irony

To reclaim hierarchy, the first challenge is to read Burke suspiciously/ironically, without the disciplinary baggage that features elite rhetorical subjects imposing ordered hierarchies on the world. Burke does indeed argue that humans are "goaded by a spirit of hierarchy," but immediately qualifies that statement by continuing, "if that sounds too weighted, we could settle for, 'Moved by a sense of order'" (*Language*, 15). On the surface, this would seem a substitution with great potential. Changing "goaded" to "moved" replaces the image of external challenge with one of internal emotional response, just as the move from "spirit" to "sense" creates an opening for intuition and sensibility. "Order" as a replacement for "hierarchy" suggests the possibility of pattern, flow, or rhythm as alternatives to evaluative, vertical ordering.

But the critic must remain suspicious; the fact that this substitution can be so easily entertained, without challenging any attendant concepts, suggests that "order" may serve only as a way of masking "hierarchy," rendering it less visible and thus even more dangerous. Indeed, in spite of Burke's implicit invitation to unweight the term, in most passages it seems a synonym for hierarchy. Elsewhere Burke posits "order" as a polar term, by definition in tension with its opposite, "disorder." Thus "order" is charged with the task of suppressing the unruly and the disruptive, requiring the imposition of control and thereby leading us back to "hierarchy." Moreover, Burke grounds his vision of order in terminology borrowed from the natural world, failing to stress (although he would undoubtedly agree) that humans have imposed their hierarchical notions of order on Nature, which they then affirm as essential and defining aspects of that world, to be borrowed back to support hierarchy in the social world as "natural" (*Rhetoric of Religion*, 183–96).

Proclamation/Representation/Synecdoche

However suspicious one might be, Burke's qualification does leave an opening for alternate possibilities. Feminist critics must proclaim their dissatisfaction with the explicit and implicit visions of human communication as a continual striving for mastery and dominance, a vision that permeates Burke. His metaphor of communication, the cocktail party or "unending conversation," is decidedly contentious:

> Imagine that you enter a parlor. You come late. When you arrive, others have long preceded you and they are engaged in a heated discussion, a discussion too heated for them to pause and tell you exactly what it is about. In fact, the discussion had already begun long before any of them got there, so that no one present is qualified to retrace for you all the steps that had gone before. You listen for a while, until you decide that you have caught the tenor of the argument; then you put in your oar. Someone answers; you answer him; another comes to your defense; another aligns himself against you, to either the embarrassment or gratification of your opponent, depending upon the quality of your ally's assistance. (*Philosophy*, 110–11)

Note that the discussion is "heated," those present are labeled either opponents or allies, the results are "embarrassment" if one is bested or "gratification" if one wins one's points. Participation appears limited to those who have been "invited," explanation offered to those "qualified," and only those who have an "oar," that is, a position to engage and the aggressiveness to "put it in," to insert themselves into the fray, will be heard.

"Communication as Argument" and "Order as Hierarchy" are mutually reinforcing metaphors drawn from the tradition of Western philosophy that has energized Burke's system. The sense of strife that permeates "order as hierarchy," the apparently locked-in progression of Burke's dramatistic process that links guilt and victimage to the need for order, may well be a vision that describes much of human history. Yet such agonistic definitions of human experience need to be challenged as unacceptable to those who have been excluded and/or repulsed by the practices of social hierarchy-making and -unmaking.

Remembrance/Reduction/Metonymy

Perhaps one might begin the reconstruction of this overly reductive image of human experience by interpreting Burke's comments on hierarchy descriptively, as comments on "what seems to be," as he reflects on the masculinist version of human history rather than as "what ought to be," that is, giving them moral authority. Few, least of all feminists, would disagree with the assertion that humans have misused their symbolic abilities in the interests of obtaining power over Nature and each other. This acknowledgment of how humans have used symbols imposes no necessary limits on either human or symbolic potentiality, other than Burke's observation that symbolic perspectives have an impulse to replicate themselves—again, an assertion that many feminists could echo. Hierarchy, in this view, would be an overly reductive anecdote that requires expansion.

If order is now to be substituted for hierarchy, as Burke suggests, can we create visions of order free from the constraints of hierarchy? One means of remembrance/reconstitution might be to retrace the "borrowings" from Nature, a Nature, as noted, already symbolically contaminated with human notions of hierarchy. Some feminists, for example, seek to recover a vision of Nature that is harmonious rather than hierarchical (Foss and Griffin, 337–45). Perhaps in remembering alternate ways of achieving security in human society, order can be reclaimed with meanings that do not lock humans into hierarchies, accompanied by continual strivings for power and status. Removed from the encrustation of accepted meanings, the belief that humans are "moved by a sense of order" can become a liberating rather than a constricting vision.

Creative Actualization/Perspective/Metaphor

Here the critic needs to envision new and creative paths to satisfy human desires for order and work these into Burke. If humans are indeed "moved by a sense of order," that is, seek the comfort of predictability in their experience, we can conceptualize order as the need for patterns that are stable enough to provide a sense of security and belonging, yet flowing, fluid, and open to change. Order then can be conceived, not as a grim struggle with disorder, but as continuously emerging from the processes of communication. Order can invite participation rather than support domination, can be envisioned as an inclusive web rather than an exclusive ladder. Do any of these conceptualizations of order destroy the essence of Burke's system? In fact, might they not be just as compatible with that system as the traditional interpretations of order as hierarchical?

Consider, for example, Burke's charting of terms for order in *Rhetoric of Religion* (184). If it suggests how ladder hierarchies are created, it also reveals how such hierarchies can be deconstructed, for within this weblike set of relationships, oppositions can be transformed into equations, reductions can be reconstituted, dialectics can be translated into metaphors. Opposites can open into circles, circles branch again into webs. Causes can become effects and effects causes and both restored into a circle, to become mutually reinforcing dimensions of a process. The constraints of logic can be transformed into the open-endedness of narrative as a way of including multiple voices and meanings. This stable yet flexible array of symbolic processes provides a much broader yet equally viable sense of order, a way of creating patterns that provide comfort and security while remaining open to an ever-changing range of possibilities.

Conclusion

While some concepts within the Burkean system may be reclaimed for women's experience, there may well be those that are not. Each concept must be critically assessed for its potential utility. For feminist scholars, the crucial question of whether "this marriage can be saved" may depend on whether we believe that Burke provides unique insights into human communication processes. If not, the reclamation project is hardly worth the effort it would entail and the hostility it might generate from Burkean fundamentalists. My own conviction that Burke can and should be reclaimed does not underestimate the degree of masculinist bias in his system or my own blind spots to that bias. Perspectives such as Burke's can be seductive, as Mary Daly warns, and the more familiar we are with them the more likely we may be to read affirmatively rather than critically. Daly is suspicious of philosophies that "use language that is not totally distorting, but which do not explicitly move out of patriarchal space." Yet she does acknowledge that some of these languages may be "still worth hearing," for when they have been reclaimed, what appear to be the "same sounds," will in reality be "new words, for the new context constitutes them as such" (189).

A culturally diverse readership must engage Burke differently but no less vigorously than did the behaviorists, New Critics, and Marxists of earlier eras. Burke never failed to learn from these engagements, moaning at times that he was misunderstood but ultimately using the encounters to refine and often reorient his work. Feminist critics, along with others, must reject closures, will insist upon redefinition of terms and restructuring of processes. But these critiques will keep the Burkean system alive and flourishing as they construct new visions and stories of the human drama. If Burke is to remain a "usable tradition" into the twenty-first century, his system must be continually reshaped to challenge the social and political terminologies that empower some people at the expense of others. And for feminist critics, as well as for others who refuse to disengage their intellectual lives from their social responsibilities, reclamation of Burke must not only provide strategies for personal survival; it must emphasize the power of Burke's system in the struggles for social change.

Note

1. Fiorenza introduces her critical hermeneutic strategies in *Bread Not Stone: The Challenge of Biblical Interpretation* and expands the system in *But She Said: Feminist Practices of Biblical Interpretation*. In the process of development, she makes minor changes in terminology. I have used the terms from *Bread*, but cite major discussions of the strategies in both works.

References

Burke, Kenneth. *Attitudes Toward History*. 3rd ed. Berkeley: University of California Press, 1984.
———. *A Grammar of Motives*. Berkeley: University of California Press, 1969.
———. *Language as Symbolic Action: Essays on Life, Literature, and Method.* Berkeley: University of California Press, 1969.
———. *Philosophy of Literary Form: Studies in Symbolic Action*. 3rd ed. Berkeley: University of California Press, 1973.
———. *Rhetoric of Religion: Studies in Logology*. Berkeley: University of California Press, 1970.
Chesebro, James. "Extending the Burkean System: A Response to Tompkins and Cheney." *Quarterly Journal of Speech* 80 (1994): 83–90.

Condit, Celeste. "Framing Kenneth Burke: Sad Tragedy or Comic Dance?" *Quarterly Journal of Speech* 80 (1994): 77–82.

Daly, Mary. *Beyond God the Father: Toward a Philosophy of Women's Liberation*. Boston, Mass.: Beacon, 1973.

Fiorenza, Elizabeth Schussler. *Bread Not Stone: The Challenge of Feminist Biblical Interpretation*. 2nd ed. Boston, Mass.: Beacon, 1995.

———. *But She Said: Feminist Practices of Biblical Interpretation*. Boston, Mass.: Beacon, 1992.

Foss, Karen A., and Sonja K. Foss. *Women Speak: The Eloquence of Women's Lives*. Prospect Heights: Waveland, 1991.

Foss, Sonja K., and Cindy Griffin. "A Feminist Perspective on Rhetorical Theory: Toward a Classification of Boundaries." *Western Journal of Communication* 56 (1992): 330–49.

Ruether, Rosemary Radford. *Sexism and God-Talk: Toward a Feminist Theology*. Boston, Mass.: Beacon, 1983.

Part III

Postmodernism and Multiculturalism

6

Kenneth Burke's Implicit
Theory of Power

George Cheney, Kathy Garvin-Doxas, and Kathleen Torrens

This essay is designed in part to respond to recent commentaries on the writings of Kenneth Burke that have noted the absence of a fully developed theory of power. Some of these criticisms have suggested that Burke is a "soft" critic in that his system does not allow for clear moral reckoning about brute instances of domination in the world and therefore also about the need for judgmental and certain responses to such forces. Fredric Jameson, the prominent Marxist literary critic, is perhaps most notable among such voices. Along with the charge, especially as Jameson articulates it, is the argument that Burke's framework for the analysis of human relations does not give sufficient attention to the realities of material history in the world and therefore contributes less than it could to the project of ideological critique (see also Condit, 349–55). Similarly, from the standpoint of ethics, Herbert Simons has argued that Burke's dramatism leaves us, as critics, little room for expressing moral outrage about instances of domination, oppression, or suppression (see discussions of this claim and the ensuing debate at the 1984 Burke conference in P. Tompkins).

In fact, the recent turn by rhetoricians and some communication theorists to diverse, yet broadly sociological European theorists such as Jürgen Habermas, Michel Foucault, and Anthony Giddens (see, e.g., the review by Whalen and Cheney) has gravitated to the explicit and systematic treatment of power as perhaps *the* central term for the analysis of human relations. And power has come to be a primary concept in every subfield of communication studies; it has even made its appearance in the psychologically biased and individually oriented area of interpersonal communication (see, e.g., Lannamann).

The criticism of Burke as being somewhat naive (or at least somewhat ignorant) with respect to power, along with related points about a presumed overemphasis on the rhetoric of cooperation, merits a considered rejoinder that is based empirically on the careful examination of Burke's words.

The other motivation for this study is our desire to shift the rhetorical stress on persuasion toward power—well, at least to move a bit in that direction—and to ask the question, What do the writings of the century's most important contributor to rhetorical thought "look like" when we scrutinize his work in an attempt to articulate his *implicit theory of power?* Acknowledging the importance of reflective analysis on a whole cluster of interrelated but distinct terms for how human beings affect one another—including, in addition to persuasion, power, authority, control, influence, domination, hierarchy, compliance, force, coercion, and so on—we wish to bring "power" into the foreground and explore the ways in which Burke characterizes power and situates it, both terminologically and conceptually. To do this, we use a bit of Burke's technique of "indexing" (see, e.g., Cheney and Tompkins). We surveyed these nine books: *Counter-Statement, Permanence and Change, Attitudes Toward History, The Philosophy of Literary Form, A Grammar of Motives, A Rhetoric of Motives, The Rhetoric of Religion, Language as Symbolic Action,* and *Dramatism and Development* (listed in the order in which they were originally published). Along the way through this essay, we contextualize the above-listed and other Burkean principles about power in terms of a number of contemporary social and political theorists, including Hannah Arendt, Michel Foucault, Steven Lukes, and Richard Sennett.

Power, in Burke's Terms

As we have already noted, "power" does not emerge as a predominant term in Burke's works, at least not in explicit formulations of its meaning, aspects, or roles in human affairs.

Burke offers perhaps his most explicit consideration of power as a term and as an empirical reality in the two forewords to *The Philosophy of Literary Form.* There he speaks of the reality of power as grounded in our nonsymbolic "motion"; he offers examples of the physicality of power and domination in such works as Richard Wright's *Native Son.* Burke identifies three important families of terms here: centering on "act," "order," and "power." (In his 1966 foreword to *Philosophy,* Burke regrets not having said more about each.) Burke describes briefly the "power family" or cluster of ideas, including social, sexual, physical, military, political, monetary, mental, moral, and stylistic power; powers of emancipation, liberalization, separation, fascination, "fascization" (or binding), wisdom, understanding, and knowledge. But while Burke sees all of these powers as in some way based in physicality, he emphasizes the ways in which humans necessarily endow them with symbolicity: for example, in the use of the metaphor of rape to describe one nation's invasion of another. For Burke, power (like order or act) *does actually exist* in the nonsymbolic realm of the empirical world; it can be *seen* in matters of separation or segregation, wholly nonverbal fistfights, and differences in abilities and strength of force. He would likely focus on power in terms of the rhetorical expression of human relations, the understanding of which is based in the symbolic use of language. However, Burke directs our attention not to the relative certainties of power as it exists, say in differential physical strength, but to the many meanings and ambiguities of power that symbols introduce into human experience. "Only by knowing wholly about our ways with symbols can we become piously equipped to ask, not only in wonder but in great fear, just what may be the inexorable laws of non-symbolic motion which our symbolizing so often 'transcends,' sometimes to our 'spiritual' gain and sometimes to our great detriment" (Burke, *Philosophy*, xvi). Through the study of the symbolic dimensions of power, then, we may actually come to understand better the range and limitations of purely non-symbolic power.

This brings Burke and us to an explicit consideration of language.

The Centrality of Language

In shifting the emphasis of a rhetorical consideration of Burke's works from persuasion to power, we do not need to assert for this audience that Burke's theory of human relations centers on language. In fact, the closest that Burke gets to some sort of essentialism in talking about human beings is saying, in the form of his "Definition of Man," that we are all symbol-users who also (at some point in our past) invented the negative ("This is not a pipe"; "Thou shalt not kill"). In fact, we can say in a summarizing statement that the essence of Burke's perspective on the world is that associations between and among terms reveal much about associations between and among people; this is perhaps the heart of Burke's theory of human communication (see, e.g., Cheney).

What remains to be discussed here, however, is how Burke's emphasis on language informs his implicit theory of power and how his implicit theory of power relies on certain concepts of language. Throughout his works, from *Counter-Statement* through *Dramatism and Development*, we find discussion of the integral relation of language to human relations. However, Burke has said in presentations and in conversation that his *Rhetoric of Religion* offers his best demonstration of the power of language. In his treatment of a variety of pieces of Judeo-Christian discourse, Burke reveals the full potency of linguistic magic—in words describing the supernatural, the transcendent, the ineffable, the realm beyond the material world. This category of terms is at the top of Burke's hierarchy, ranked above words for the natural (e.g., earth, fire, and water), words for the sociopolitical realm (e.g., democracy, capitalism, and socialism), and words for words (e.g., grammar, etymology, and philology). The realm of the supernatural is separate from these other realms because, according to Burke, "language by definition is not suited to the expression of the 'ineffable,' or super-natural" (*Rhetoric of Religion*, 15). Rather, these terms are borrowed from the other realms— meanings must evolve from the other order to the supernatural. Words for God and other supernatural things represent the full extent of our "linguistic reach": our ability to capture and inspire the imagination through reference to that which we cannot experience through the powers of the sensorium.

Burke begins with the Word = God equation, which appears in both the Old and New Testaments of the Bible. This equation provides Burke with one of the foundations for the explication by example of his epistemology, logology. In fact, Burke employs theology, or words about God, to illustrate his logology, or words about words. In the religious sense, God represents our attention to and movement toward the highest, most powerful, most omnipotent, most merciful, most just, most beautiful, most strong, and so on (as Burke describes in his treatment of Augustine's *Confessions* in *Rhetoric of Religion*). Burke writes, "Insofar as language is intrinsically horatory (a medium by which men can obtain the cooperation of one another), God perfectly embodies the petition" (*Language*, 20). "God-terms" represent our linguistic "drive" toward ultimate things, toward the spinning out of implications, toward the perfect name, toward the supreme title, toward the absolute, toward the completely generalizable, toward the full flowering of style, toward the superordinate purpose. In fact, the only strategy mentioned by Burke toward transcending guilt or blame that does *not* require the mortification of the self or the victimization of another is the *renaming of the situation* (see also *Rhetoric of Motives*).

Burke's implicit theory of power does not begin with language; nor does it end there—in the sense that we can never divorce our consideration of it from such things as physical capacities, physical relations, and physical arrangements (such as what Burke includes under the nonverbal heading of "administrative rhetoric" or the structuring of a situation; see his treatment of Machiavelli's *The Prince* in *Rhetoric of Motives* 158–66). However, Burke insists that we will best understand the power relations of a society (or how it is organized) by listening to what people say about their "place" in the social order. The term *order* (featured as one of the "families" of terms mentioned above and treated extensively in *Rhetoric of Motives* 183–333) itself becomes important here in the sense of how parts of the world and the people who inhabit it are associated (up, down, across, together, and apart) in language use. Some types of order exist in "Nature," that is, in the nonsymbolic realm. So, Burke is no nominalist who would argue that language brings all order (e.g., biological classification or human associational groupings) into being. Ordering exists in the forms of physical location, property relationships, and controls of various kinds (of both the self and the other). But, "the language factor thus shows in the ability to develop a complex human social order, in the corresponding ideas of status and property, and the thou-shalt-not's indigenous to such a structure, and in the various 'positives' that arise out of such negations" (Burke, *Language*, 443). Here we find a strong affinity between Burke's approach and that of anthropologist Mary Douglas, who seeks to illuminate the architectonic power of labels, titles and categories. As Douglas puts it, "An institution (such as a profession of an organization) provides the categories of (members') thought, sets the terms for self-knowledge, and fixes identities" (112). Both Burke and Douglas thus put a linguistic "spin" on the Durkheimian notion of the "social fact."

One of the most important and pervasive aspects of power is hierarchy: it is a social fact that manifests itself in numerous and complex ways, both physically and symbolically.

The (Nearly) Inescapable Nature of Hierarchy

The five clauses of Burke's "Definition of Man" (*Language*, 3–24)—one of Burke's clearest summarizing statements on the essence of his theories—have been widely discussed. The fourth clause, "goaded by the spirit of hierarchy," expresses succinctly Burke's perspective on categorization: that differences *do* exist in the world; that we seek to describe those differences with our terms; and that we are further led through our sheer use of language to create all sorts of other categories to describe physical, social, terminological, and supernatural relationships. Hierarchy, as it has been noted many times in the pages of our journals, begets mystery in that "king and peasant are 'mysteries' to each other"

(15). Such a situation—in politics, or the family, or the workplace—calls for identification between occupants of different social roles, however insincere that connection may be for either of the parties. This is one of the basic situations that calls for rhetorical exercise, in Burke's view.

Unfortunately, Burke has been read by some commentators to say that specific types of hierarchy—such as authoritarianism, or bureaucracy, or the dominance of one gender by the other—are inevitable. Such an interpretation overlooks Burke's careful choice of the term *goaded* and is the reason for our not-quite-committed use of the term *nearly inescapable*. As Torrens explains, based on her careful review of Burke's works for his notions of hierarchy, hierarchy in Burke's universe is something that can be minimized but not wholly eliminated.

One of the few published pieces to engage Burke's works in terms of an explicit consideration of power is the essay by Foss and Griffin, in which they contrast Burke's rhetorical theory with the implicit rhetoric of Starhawk, a witch and a prominent lecturer on personal and social development in the United States. We feel it important here to offer Foss and Griffin's argument as a different sort of counterpoint than that of Simons or Jameson in order to explain further what we find in Burke's words about hierarchy and power. Foss and Griffin argue that Burke's rhetoric is one of patriarchy and domination, representing "hierarchical, authoritarian systems that employ power-over" (343). Against such a presumably patriarchal and oppressive model, Foss and Griffin á la Starhawk, advance an alternative "ordering" of "the web or circle" (cf. Condit).

Our reading of Burke's books leads us to pronounce this dichotomy a basically false one. Burke's rhetoric distinguishes itself in part by deemphasizing the *agonistic* tendencies of ancient rhetoric and celebrating cooperation—not only as one "side" to rhetorical experience ("congregation" and "segregation" are our two basic social options, declares Burke; they are the grounds for rhetoric itself; see *Philosophy*). For Burke, both identification or connection and division or separation are primordial conditions, in the sense that both exist in our physical relations with one another, but he chooses to emphasize consensus, cooperation, and communion in the push for a big global "We" (see especially *Rhetoric of Motives*).

This is part of the reasoning behind Dilip Gaonkar's characterization of Burke's rhetoric as a "rescue operation": Burke seeks to elevate rhetoric in the study of human relations through emphasizing consensus and endowing it with a clear social conscience. In this respect, Burke's stress on the cooperative ideal is not unlike Habermas's ideals for speech communities; and both writers are therefore open to postmodernist critiques that would question the possibility for any authentic consensus. Writers on power such as Foucault would in fact have us fear any declarations of consensus, however circumscribed or universal they may appear to be, because of the necessary suppression of interests of those not at the "center" of control.

So, Foss and Griffin's indictment is surprising though somewhat understandable because of Burke's clever and ambiguous slogans such as *Ad Bellum Purificandum* ("Toward the Purification of War"). These critics seem to forget the ways in which Burke's notion of hierarchy is grounded not only in physical orderings but also in our inevitable drive toward categorization. Far from surrendering to sexism (though he indeed employed some of the sexist linguistic conventions of his day) or racism or even the "ladder" metaphor for corporate arrangements, Burke is simply saying how necessary *some* kind of hierarchical ordering is (Torrens). And these same critics seem to overlook also, that one of Burke's favorite metaphors for terms and for human experience is, in fact, the circle. That is what makes reading Burke so irritatingly difficult at first; it is also what reminds us of the many possibilities for connections between words and between people that exist outside of simple, linear arrangements (e.g., the model of the organization as concentric circles).

The whole matter of Burke's egalitarianism (or lack of it, from the point of view of the critics mentioned above) leads us toward a more developed consideration of power and (a)symmetry.

Asymmetrical versus Symmetrical Versions/Visions of Power

This is perhaps the most important theme in writings on power, as Steven Lukes' encyclopedic essay suggests. After surveying "the history of power," Lukes concludes that the view of power as *necessarily* asymmetrical has been predominant throughout the centuries. And such a view has been bolstered by some of the most famous and enduring writings on power, notably Machiavelli's *The Prince* and Hobbes' *Leviathan*. Lukes contrasts this prevailing perspective with one that is implicit and underdeveloped in the intellectual history of power: power as symmetrical.

Philosopher Hannah Arendt was notable in her celebration of the symmetrical view ("power with," as opposed to "power over"). Arendt argued strongly and articulately for a full consideration of the practical accomplishments of people working in concert in order to modify the widely used Weberian definition of power as the ability to act and achieve one's goal, even against the resistance of others. Arendt's "communicative" perspective on power would have us say that power is also *the ability of a group to act and achieve its goals, even against the resistance of the situation.* Such a perspective on power elevates cooperation over competition, the interests of the collective over those of the individual, and it requires an extraordinary degree of rhetorical success (to hold everyone and everything together). This is why Arendt appeals to the ideals of the ancient Greek *polis*, not as a certain place but as a political community of co-actors, a special kind of communication network. (In her popular book on power and gender, Riane Eisler goes back further in history to find her model for adaptation to the present: the goddess-centered, peaceful, and cooperative society of Minoan Crete; but she shares Arendt's impulse to put forth a cooperative vision of power.)

Burke, too, harks back to the *polis* in formulating his "new rhetoric," while reformulating rhetoric's purpose so as to confront the realities and dangers of division in the world (especially in the nuclear age), and in articulating the possibilities for power in collective action. Burke sees infinite possibilities in our arrangements of symbols. One such possibility, though not at all an easy one to achieve or maintain, is "Unity without Conformity," where "We the people" refers to the entire human race (*Rhetoric of Motives*). This is where Burke would have us direct our rhetorical energies: toward power relations that minimize if not wholly eliminate domination.

But, we must say more here about Burke's stress on cooperation, especially in acknowledgment of those who would call him "soft on aggression" (an allusion to post–World War II political discourse that we find apt here). Any complete theory of power must take into account the realities of deception, coercion, and mindlessness (what Aristotle would place under "inartistic proof"). So, even if Burke places his prescriptive emphasis on cooperation, as we believe that he does, he cannot overlook the *non*cooperative features of human relations (such as uses of force, both symbolic and material, and blind ideological obedience). Threats are real; so are bombs; so is imprisonment; so is the silencing of one person or group by another. And, what in Burke's nonjudgmental cooperative stance (his pluralism of perspectives, as Robert Heath and others have characterized it) gives us the "ammo" to identify and fight domination? Burke, unfortunately, is not explicit on this moral and practical question. He warns us against premature moral outrage; he cautions us against too easily seeing others as "vicious" rather than "mistaken"; and he reminds us that there is always the possibility of shifting one's point of view. At the same time, however, Burke shows us the shallowness of ideological adherence, the dangers of carrying our terms too far, and the kind of violence that is done with words (as in the prescient essay, "The Rhetoric of Hitler's 'Battle'"; see *Philosophy*).

Perhaps Burke would have addressed this important question thoroughly in the volume of ethics that he had hoped to write. But we will not see that volume, so we are left to speculate. Suffice it to say here that Burke gives us the tools for recognizing and countering verbal violence. Barbs usually precede bombs, just as *Mein Kampf* foreshadowed the Holocaust.

The question of cooperation, especially in terms of group action, slides us into a consideration of yet another theme with respect to Burke's implicit theory of power.

The Power of Collective Actors
and Power as Diffused throughout Society

This is an important matter in contemporary social and rhetorical theory. Traditional conceptions of power tend to focus on the resources of individual persons: power is typically conceived of as "the ability to get one's way." Such a conception, while wholly realistic in describing many situations, focuses the attention of the analyst on the question of "Who?" rather than on the question of "How?" with respect to power-in-action. We want to know more about the Wizard of Oz's capabilities because we infer from his trappings that he is a tremendous source of power ("He's clearly got it!").

Now, we know that power is exercised by groups, organizations, and societies. Burke knows this, too, and his emphasis on the social resource of language allows for a crucial shift from "I" to "we" and away from the simple question of "Who's got the power?" (as captured in the useful but limited "reputational" method of assessing power in a social system). Burke treats issues such as "socialization," worldview, and hegemony. In *A Rhetoric of Motives*, for example, Burke alerts us "to the ingredient of rhetoric in all *socialization*, considered as a *moralizing* process" (39). The ways in which we are acted upon by the larger social order and the fact of what we "appropriate" from that order provide a basis for a consideration of power that is (to take a term from the language of postmodernism) in many cases "de-centered." Put another way, power is "invested" in social systems, such as bureaucracies, and that power is often not easily identified with individual actors (e.g., "To which office do I complain?"; see the review by Mumby). This makes the question of "agency"—in either the terms of traditional social theory or the terms of Burke's pentad—extremely complicated (see

Cheney). The question of agency with respect to power is in fact crucial in terms of whether we see power principally as originating with persons or forces or as a basic dimension of social relations (see Clegg on this distinction).

In his 1985 essay that reviewed both the 1984 Burke conference and the ways in which Burke's writings presaged the contemporary concerns of poststructuralist and postmodernist criticism, Phillip K. Tompkins explains that Burke used the concept of "hegemony" in several different ways, although it was not a featured term in his theorizing. In *Permanence and Change*, Burke does use the word to point to "the hegemony of business" and other dominant institutions over the ages—the kind of dominance that infuses culture in such a way as to give a taken-for-granted quality to the relations of power. Burke writes:

> In "magical" stages (during the hegemony of customer) the productive order is mainly regulated by unquestioned tests of property. If there is a slave function in such a culture, the class that so functions does not know itself as such. A true slave morality is implicitly obeyed—and while such morality is intact, the slave does not consider his obedience as slavery, any more than a child normally considers obedience to its parent slavery. Before such obedience can be explicitly considered a state of slavery, a perspective by incongruity must arise. (*Language*, 186).

Thus we see, as Tompkins notes, the clear connection between Burke's conception of power relations on a broad societal level and the concept of hegemony, one central in the literature of power since Antonio Gramsci's early formulation of it inspired others such as Lukes to explore it further. (See also the partial reformulation of Lukes's theory in rhetorical and communicative terms in Tompkins and Cheney, "Communication.")

The trick here, though, is not to lose sight of human action; not to neglect the individual persons who inhabit society in an effort to capture larger social forces. Burke's rhetoric is the arbiter of the relationship between the "I" and the "we": it leaves room for individual choice and freedom, arguing simply that the resources that we use are mostly social. No *one* re-creates society or language, though we may do creative things with the resources at our disposal.

Burke's passage on the idea of a "constitution" in *A Grammar of Motives* helps somewhat to resolve the problem, allowing students of power to keep in mind simultaneously the power of individual action (or agency) and the power exercised through collective forces. Burke playfully considers the idea of a "constitution" in terms of its various definitions: the act or process of constituting, the state of being, the aggregate of one's powers as an individual, the aggregate of mental qualities, the fundamental laws of government as embodied in written documents, and an authoritative ordinance. In the rich ambiguity of the term *constitution* we find Burke's consideration of the individual and social resources of power. Constitutions for groups represent (in one way or another) the groups as well as their individual members. In the process of "constituting" a social body, individual contributions (in one way or another) are joined in the creation of something new, a social message or framework or force. A constitution comes to stand for or represent a collectivity. Once created, a social force—or, in more specific terms, a rule, law, norm, or governing document—in turn affects the individuals who would be governed by it. And the ongoing process of adherence (and, sometimes, revision or revolution) determines the shape of the social constitution for the future. (The parallel between this interpretation of Burke's notion of constitution and Anthony Giddens' theory of structuration, as explained in his *Constitution of Society*, should be evident.)

Pertinent here is Burke's discussion of "symbols of *author*-ity" (key symbolic loci in society; see especially his discussion of authority in *Attitudes*, 329–36). These are the sacred representations of the body politic and the body social that come to have our allegiance. In this regard, Burke captures the emotional aspects of power and shows affinity with the perspective of Richard Sennett. Sennett emphasizes the variety of types of emotional bonds, negative as well as positive, which power relations entail. As Burke maintains, "Obedience to the reigning symbols of authority is in itself natural and wholesome. The need to reject them is painful and bewildering" (*Attitudes*, 226). Outright rejection of key sources of authority—family, nation, religion, "boss," and so on—is usually acted out only at the cost of considerable pain for the person who then must seek alternative sources of authority or perpetually define himself or herself in opposition to the original, familiar ones.

The term *authority*, of course, is suggestive of its terminological cousin, *author*. And, authorship is suggestive of ownership, a key idea in Burke's formulation of authority. "One 'owns' his social structure insofar as one can subscribe to it by wholeheartedly feeling the reasonableness of its arrangements, and by being spared the need of segregational attitudes" (*Attitudes*, 330). As with Sennett's account of people who try to be independent of parental or other authorities and yet find themselves drawing on those authorities for self-definition, Burke recognizes the precarious position of the person who, although dissatisfied with important parts of her world, must still struggle to define herself with respect to those very parts of her world toward which she feels alienation. "Even the dispossessed tends to feel that he 'has a stake in' the authoritative structure that dispossesses him; for the influence exerted upon the policies of education by the authoritative structure encourages the dispossessed to feel that his only hope of repossession lies in his allegiance to the structure that has dispossessed him" (*Attitudes*, 329–30). This helps explain the tenacious adherence by some persons to the very system that disenfranchises or even abuses them.

Authority, for Burke, is not entirely alienating unless we declare it to be "unreason-able" (see E. Tompkins). Burke thus cleverly invokes a message- and reason-oriented conception of authority (and, by implication, certain types of power) where the "reasons" given for authority must be acceptable to the receiver—at least at the level of the logic of emotions—for the position of the authority to be maintained. Burke's ideas about authority thus show affinity with those of Lukes and Chester Barnard, who both shift the emphasis away from the person or group in authority to those who would find certain messages to be authoritative in governing action. Interestingly, this shift in emphasis is consistent with the trend in contemporary studies of leadership (see, e.g., Fairhurst and Sarr).

Intentionality

Intention is an important factor in any consideration of power. The question, "If a person does not intend to influence others but does so anyway—is he or she using power?" is enduring and troublesome. Burke incorporates Freudian insights about the unconscious (see especially *Rhetoric of Motives*); he also considers unintended consequences of actions (see especially *Permanence*). So, Burke is careful not to rest too heavily on either an Aristotelian consideration of "man" as the rational animal or on a Machiavellian emphasis on strategy. We could say instead that he chooses to establish a delicate balance between the two. This choice is evidenced by his notions of the implicit power of words, naming, and piety.

While Burke does consider the consequences of unintended actions and the unconscious, intentionality is difficult to address with regard to Burke, in large part because his stress on language tends to lead us away from a psychological consideration of motives (although he is ambivalent about the status of the latter; see Tompkins and Cheney, "Limits"). But it can be argued that words and form have implicit power because they encourage and satisfy the desires of an audience (see *Counter-*

Statement). The use of words and language, then, in the arousal and calming of an audience's desires, can be a subtle demonstration of power. It can be unintentional when speakers are merely "speaking," as in friends talking together. Conversation *qua* conversation, as a partnership of equals, does not necessarily include the intentional exercise of power. However, because of the use of words, power will be present in some incipient if not some overt form: each interlocutor can be limiting the other's horizon of vision with respect to values, beliefs, and potential actions. Can we say that this form of power is more cooperative than an explicit demonstration of domination? If an audience participates in the arousal and fulfillment of its collective or individual appetites, can that audience not be said to be cooperating in the facilitation of power? To what extent does the interlocutor "know" his or her best interests? The answers to such questions are themselves problematic but nevertheless central to making important distinctions between different critical perspectives on power in social behavior.

The power of words is further demonstrated in the magic of ostensibly descriptive naming. We noted before that the only way to escape mortification or victimization is to *rename* the situation. Burke notes the great potency of "accurate" naming: our drive to find the best label for something. How objects, feelings, and events are named affects orientation, interests, perspectives, and pieties. Whether we in the United States call a foreign movement "freedom fighters" or "rebels" has a profound implication for policy formation with respect to that other group in another country; each term, with its historical and ideological baggage, is highly suggestive of a policy. Naming can be an intentional or unintentional act. Naming something "our common mission," for example, suggests, whether intended or not, that those opposed to it in any way are peripheral or perhaps antagonistic. Declaring a meeting or a decision-making process to be highly political often heightens competition within a group. The final clause of Burke's "Definition of Man" brings the notion of perfection into the picture: "[a]nd rotten with perfection" is offered in an ironic tone but is ultimately related to language by Burke. The "entelechial motive" pervades language use, from the "mere desire to name something by its 'proper name'" (*Language*, 16) to finding the "perfect enemy" (18) in an entire population. Naming something or someone "properly" or perfectly" may allow for its eventual victimage and sacrifice by someone intent on protecting his or her property or status. These human motivations are significantly intertwined and interdependent, but they arise from the primary human characteristic, symbol usage. Yet, in such symbolic efforts, strategy and intention may be unapparent, concealed, or simply lacking.

Naming through symbols affects the pieties human beings adapt. Piety, according to Burke, is a method of orientation involving the intentional selection and putting together of experiences (*Permanence*). He also calls piety a "system builder," which has interesting connotations in our consideration of power. On a personal level, people will order their individual "selves" around "social recipes" (78) or organizing principles—often with little or no conscious knowledge. For example, the drug fiend, the criminal (Burke's examples), the politician, and the professor will purposefully formulate their behaviors and belief-systems by accepting the trappings, both personal and physical, of their life stations. Because piety is the "sense of what properly goes with what" or "the way we do things around here" (74), a person who wishes to perform a certain role must acquire the societally prescribed effects of that role. And much of this acquisition process may be unself-conscious. (We must observe the partial relationship between Burke's "piety" and Weber's "traditional authority," with both stressing adherence to the accustomed way of living. Perhaps traditional authority should be considered as a special case of piety in which social inertia dominates: "That's the way it's been done before, so that's the way we'll do it.")

New orientations or pieties can be acquired or instilled by receiving converting messages or "foretelling the future." It is conceivable that entities having power, whether they be religious leaders, government officials, or radical activists, can convince individuals and collectives to accept new ways of acting, if their visions of prophecies of the good life to be attained are believable enough. In Burke's words, "cogency . . . is the root of civilization" (81). The purpose behind movements of evangelism, education, and propaganda is the attainment or compelling of new beliefs and new organizations.

Burke notes the rationalization of Jewish and Christian movements, dietetics, and Marxism as examples of new ways of thinking that have been introduced and been persuasive enough to sway masses of people to a new piety. The good life is a powerful human incentive, and with its image we can be convinced of a new piety. New "orientative devices" (87) are regularly put into daily life: devices that hint at new ways of achieving the good life or attempt to convert us in various ways.

Therefore, piety can be manipulated and converted. As Burke says, "Where you discern the symptoms of great devotion to any kind of endeavor, you are in the realm of piety" (83). Burke's "orientative devices" can be introduced intentionally as a means of control or simply as good ideas that "catch on." Piety and its undoing through the introduction of new or counter pieties encapsulates Burke's perspective on possibilities for nonrevolutionary social change at a grand scale.

Conclusion

Here we address the question of Burke's implicit theory of power in relation to his explicit theory of rhetoric. With regard to domains, is power "bigger" than rhetoric? Is rhetoric "bigger" than power? How do they overlap? Why would one want to shift Burke's stress on rhetoric toward a consideration of power-in-use (cf. Mumby)?

If we were to depict this interconcept relationship using Venn diagrams, we would perhaps represent power as a domain somewhat larger than rhetoric but with there being significant (but never complete) overlap between the two. Just as Aristotle wanted to exclude certain aspects of human "influence" (e.g., contracts, torture, etc.) from his consideration of rhetorical exercise, so does Burke wish to focus his rhetorical theorizing and criticism on situations where human choice is present at least to some appreciable degree (although Burke would emphasize that often the decision maker does not see that she in fact has options): what we commonly might call a "rhetorical situation."

Certainly Burke sees the domain of power as being at least somewhat different than that of rhetoric in that power in part exists in Nature, prior to any use of language (or other symbol system, for that matter). Power is in this way primordial, as are *the conditions* for rhetoric. But rhetoric itself does not exist in Nature; it requires the establishment or the attempted establishment of symbolic linkages, connections that bridge distance and difference of various types (and often by implication establish new oppositions or divisions as well).

In a sense, by shifting the emphasis of Burke's theory of human relations from rhetoric (or persuasion plus identification) to power, we bring into clear view the picture of differences—both symbolic and non-symbolic—that exist in the world: differences in strength and ability, sexism, racism, homophobia, religious intolerance and prejudice, ethnocentrism, nationalism, elitism, differential access to the necessities of life, conquest, violence of various kinds, and so forth. But we still need to add richness of Burke's vocabulary to discuss those differences and what to do about them.

Burke's emphasis, in analyzing power or anything else, is obviously linguistic. But with respect to power in social relations, Burke offers much more than his many illustrations of the power of language itself. Burke indicates that much of the basis for hierarchy is in language use. He demystifies and undermines the usual reification of power while showing how both mystification and reification are possible and in fact inevitable in social practice. Burke explains how particular "symbols of authority" command the allegiances of groups of people in both emotional and rational ways. And Burke's implicit theory of power avoids the pitfalls of "locating" power with "sovereigns" or personal sources on the one hand and the problems with treating power as a quasi-mystical force that infuses society on the other (cf. Clegg). Burke's implicit theory of power is indeed language-centered, but it also allows for the realities of material constraint and physical force (though this is where Burke perhaps says too little). Burke's approach to power includes in its embrace both the direct instance of power-in-use, such as is often found in the moralizing force of the negative (e.g., "Thou shalt not . . ."), and the subtle manifestations of power in the ways people are socialized to hold a particular worldview or to suppress certain interests.

Of course, users of Burke should be cautious about adopting or applying an overly textual or logocentric perspective on power. Not only are there important material manifestations of power but also much of what is expressed as resistance (e.g., by slaves, secretaries, or mineworkers) does not appear in public discourse (see Scott). Too, many subordinate groups such as whole communities never think it in their interests to speak up (see Lukes), although the critic-observer in this case has the burden of trying to prove the counterfactual: that the interests of "the oppressed" would indeed have been expressed if the situation had been otherwise. Thus, the absence of the workings of power, references to it, and oppositional voices can be extremely important for the critic. Nothing in Burke's system precludes such an analysis, but Burke enthusiasts often overlook that which is unsaid.

Burke's implicit theory of power allows for the complexities that a good theory of power must have. As Stewart Clegg explains, there has been a tension, historically, between sovereign-centered theories of power that invest power in persons or groups (a view he traces back to Hobbes) and perspectives on power as a pervasive and often consciously strategic aspect of human relations (a view that for Clegg originates with Machiavelli). Burke's implicit theory of power includes both "sides" because it is at once social and individual, with language as the creative resource for formulating those two levels and their interrelationships.

References

Arendt, Hannah. "Communicative Power." In *Power*. Edited by Steven Lukes. New York: New York University Press, 1986 [1970].

Barnard, C. I. *The Functions of the Executive*. 30th anniv. ed. Cambridge, Mass.: Harvard University Press, 1968 [1938].

Burke, Kenneth. *Attitudes Toward History*. Berkeley: University of California Press, 1984 [1937].

———. *Counter-Statement*. Berkeley: University of California Press, 1968 [1931].

———. *Dramatism and Development*. Barre, Mass.: Clark University Press, 1972.

———. *A Grammar of Motives*. Berkeley: University of California Press, 1969 [1945].

———. *Language as Symbolic Action: Essays on Life, Literature, and Method*. Berkeley: University of California Press, 1966.

———. *Permanence and Change: An Anatomy of Purpose*. Berkeley: University of California Press, 1984 [1935].

———. Personal conversations with the first author and with Phillip K. Tompkins. February 1987; April 1984.

———. *The Philosophy of Literary Form: Studies in Symbolic Action*. Berkeley: University of California Press, 1973 [1941].

———. *A Rhetoric of Motives*. Berkeley: University of California Press, 1969 [1950].

———. *The Rhetoric of Religion: Studies in Logology*. Berkeley: University of California Press, 1961.

Cheney, George. *Rhetoric in an Organizational Society: Managing Multiple Identities*. Columbia: University of South Carolina Press. 1991.

Cheney, George, and Phillip K. Tompkins. "On the 'Facts' of the Text as the Basis of Human Communication Research." In *Communication Yearbook 11*. Edited by James A. Anderson. Beverly Hills: Sage, 1988.

Clegg, Stewart R. *Frameworks of Power*. London: Sage, 1988.

Condit, Celeste M. "Post-Burke: Transcending the Substance of Dramatism." *Quarterly Journal of Speech* 78 (1992): 349–55.

Douglas, Mary. *How Institutions Think*. Syracuse, N.Y.: Syracuse University Press, 1986.

Eisler, Riane Tennenhause. *The Chalice and the Blade: Our History, Our Future*. San Fransisco: Harper & Row, 1987.

Fairhurst, Gail and R. A. Sarr. *The Art of Framing: Managing the Language of Leadership*. San Fransisco: Jossey-Bass, 1996.

Foss, Sonja K., and Cindy Griffin. "A Feminist Perspective on Rhetorical Theory: Toward a Clarification of Boundaries." *Western Journal of Communication* 56 (1992): 330–49.

Foucault, Michel. *The Foucault Reader*. Edited by P. Rabinow. New York: Pantheon, 1984.

Gaonkar, D. P. "Rhetoric and Its Double: Reflections of the Rhetorical Turn in the Human Sciences." In *The Rhetorical Turn: Invention and Persuasion in the Conduct of Inquiry*. Edited by H. W. Simons. Chicago: University of Chicago Press, 1990.

Giddens, A. *The Constitution of Society*. Berkeley: University of California Press, 1984.

Gramsci, A. *A Reader*. Edited by M. Forgacs. New York: Schocken, 1988.

Habermas, Jürgen. *Communication and the Evolution of Society*. Translated by T. McCarthy. Boston, Mass.: Beacon, 1979.

Heath, R. L. *Realism and Relativism: A Perspective on Kenneth Burke*. Macon, Ga.: Mercer University Press, 1986.

Jameson, Fredric. "The Symbolic Inference; or, Kenneth Burke and Ideological Analysis." In *Representing Kenneth Burke*. Edited by H. White and Margaret Bros. Baltimore, Md.: The John Hopkins University Press, 1982.

Lannaman, J. W. "Interpersonal Communication Research as Ideological Practice." *Communication Theory* 1 (1991): 179–203.

Lukes, Steven. *Power: A Radical View*. London: Macmillan, 1974.

———. "Power and Authority." In *A History of Sociological Analysis*. Edited by Tom Bottomore and Richard Nisbet. New York: Basic, 1978.

Mumby, Dennis. "Power and Communication in Organizations." In *The New Handbook of Organizational Communication*. Edited by Fredric M. Jablin and Linda L. Putnam. Thousand Oaks, Calif.: Sage, in press.

Scott, J. C. *Domination and the Arts of Resistance: Hidden Transcripts*. New Haven, Conn.: Yale University Press, 1990.

Sennett, Richard. *Authority*. New York: Random House, 1980.

Tompkins, Elaine van den Bout. "On Alienation." Unpublished paper, Purdue University, 1986.

Tompkins, Phillip K. "On Hegemony—'He Gave It No Name'—and Critical Structuralism in the Work of Kenneth Burke." *Quarterly Journal of Speech* 71 (1985): 119–30.

Tompkins, Phillip K., and George Cheney. "On the Limits and Sub-stance of Kenneth Burke and His Critics." *Quarterly Journal of Speech* 79 (1993): 225–31.

———. "Communication and Unobtrusive Control in Contemporary Organizations." In *Organizational Communication: Traditional Themes and New Directions*. Edited by Robert D. McPhee and Phillip K. Tompkins. Beverly Hills: Sage, 1985.

Torrens, Kathleen. "An Indexical Exploration of the Concept of Hierarchy in the Corpus of Kenneth Burke." Unpublished master's thesis, University of Colorado–Boulder, 1993.

Weber, Max. *Economy and Society*. 2 vols. Translated by G. Roth and C. Wittich. Berkeley: University of California Press, 1978.

Whalen, Susan, and George Cheney. "Contemporary Social Theory and its Implications for Rhetorical and Communication Theory." *Quarterly Journal of Speech* 77 (1991): 467–79.

7

Dramatism and Deconstruction

Burke, de Man, and the Rhetorical Motive

Greig Henderson

Grammar versus Rhetoric

In his well-known essay, "Semiology and Rhetoric," Paul de Man distinguishes between the conception of language as rule-oriented grammar (the domain of literal meaning) and the conception of language as trope-oriented rhetoric (the domain of figural meaning). According to de Man, these domains inevitably clash, and the reader who tries to ascribe priority to one or the other always arrives at an impasse or aporia. He or she faces the simultaneous necessity and impossibility of choosing between incompatible options and is thereby left in the double bind of trying to master a self-subverting text. Because all texts undo or dismantle their putative referential content or semantic meaning by revealing the rhetorical nature of that content or meaning, all texts are riven by indeterminacies. This clash between the referential and rhetorical levels of discourse ineluctably produces undecidability. For de Man, the referential is a function of language, not something external to it and independently perceivable as a sense datum. His linguistic terminology "designates reference prior to designating the referent" and regards "language as a system of signs and of signification rather than as an established pattern of meanings" ("Resistance," 8, 9). Mimesis is but one trope among others.

At the beginning of "Semiology and Rhetoric," de Man concedes that the attempt "to reconcile the internal, formal private structures of literary language with their external, referential, and public effects" is a highly respectable moral enterprise (3). Nevertheless, he insists that it is an attempt foredoomed to failure. First, "literature cannot merely be recovered as a definite unit of referential meaning that can be decoded without leaving a residue" (4); form and content are not absolutely separable. Second, formalist critics who operate as if such a separation can be made never critically examine the assumptions and implications of the "inside/outside metaphor" (5) they routinely deploy. It is not simply their privileging of intrinsic over extrinsic modes of criticism that de Man questions; it is the viability of the distinction itself. How can we know the intrinsic from the extrinsic? How can we categorically distinguish between poetic and semantic meaning, between rhetoric and reference?

At first glance, semiology seems to avoid this problem, for "semiology, as opposed to semantics, is the science or study of signifiers; it does not ask what words mean but how they mean. . . . The entire question of meaning can be bracketed, thus freeing critical discourse from the debilitating burden of paraphrase" (5). Semiology, then, "explodes the myth of semantic correspondence between sign and referent" (5). But in spite of its salutary demythologizing power, semiology is committed to "the use of grammatical (especially syntactical) structures conjointly with rhetorical structures, without apparent awareness of a possible discrepancy between them" (5). Consequently, "the study of tropes and figures . . . becomes a mere extension of grammatical models, a particular subset of syntactical relations" (6). "This reduction of figure to grammar" (7) is anathema to de Man. For him, the formalist and semiological models, however different, are equally problematic. Both assume a continuity between grammar and rhetoric, and this assumed continuity is precisely what de Man's deconstructive analysis puts in jeopardy. Positing the essential figurality and rhetoricity of all signification, de Man insists that grammatical decoding can neither rationalize nor domesticate the figural and rhetorical dimensions of a text. For him, reading is "a negative process in which the grammatical cognition is undone, *at all times*, by its rhetorical displacement" ("Resistance," 17; emphasis added).

It is at this point in his argument that de Man enlists the support of Kenneth Burke's "well-known insistence on the distinction between grammar and rhetoric" ("Semiology," 8). "Burke," de Man writes, "mentions *deflection* (which he compares structurally to Freudian displacement), defined as 'any slight bias or unintended error,' as the rhetorical basis of language, and deflection is then conceived as a dialectical subversion of the consistent link between sign and meaning that operates within grammatical patterns" (8). While it is undeniably true that Burke insists on the distinction between grammar and rhetoric, not to mention the potential tension between them, it is not true, in my view, that Burke is committed to the claim that there is a necessary discontinuity between the grammatical and the rhetorical, any more than he is committed to the claim that there is a necessary continuity between them. In Burke's way of thinking, the various levels of discourse—grammatical, rhetorical, symbolical, and ethical—intersect ambiguously. Because rhetoric may either subvert or sustain grammar, every text is not condemned to tell the same predictable tale of its own uninterpretability; every text is not an allegory of rhetoric's subversion of grammar. Moreover, de Man tends to equate rhetoric more with tropes, schemes, and figures than with eloquence and persuasion. Using the parlance of classical rhetoric, one would say that he stresses style at the expense of invention and arrangement. Equating rhetoric with style, I shall later argue, is antithetical to the Burkean project. In my view, de Man is not dialectical enough. Despite his valorization of undecidability, he invokes a dualistic scheme that ultimately reduces aporia to a synchronic conceptualization within discourse. He thereby inadvertently embraces an intrinsic fallacy analogous to the semiotician's reduction of figure to grammar, namely, the reduction of rhetoric to figure. To say that grammatical cognition is undone, *at all times*, by its rhetorical displacement is to make the exposure of a text's unstable system of tropes purely an internal affair wherein grammatical cognition is foreordained to fail. Such a privileging of an epistemology of failure over the historical or diachronic aspects of the textual and intertextual system is anti-dramatistic in the extreme. According to this epistemology of failure, a discourse textualizes its own undecidability and thus fails to attain unity, self-coherence, or autonomy. This process is duplicated by the critic, who strives for totalization but fails to achieve it because of the aporia built into both the object-language of the text and the critical metalanguage that would seek to encompass it.

In de Man's account of how a text does things with words, much the same thing happens in each case. "We have, on the one hand, a literal meaning and on the other hand a figural meaning," and these two meanings "can be entirely incompatible," making it "impossible to decide by grammatical or other linguistic devices which of the two meanings . . . prevails. Rhetoric radically suspends logic and opens up vertiginous possibilities of referential aberration" ("Semiology," 10). Indeed, de Man goes so far as to "equate the rhetorical, figural potentiality of language with literature itself" (10). Every text, then, gives rise to two incompatible readings—one referential, one rhetorical—and we cannot "in any way make a valid decision as to which of the readings can be given priority over the other; none can exist in the other's absence" (10). "The deconstruction," he goes on to say, "is not something we have added to the text but it constituted the text in the first place. A literary text simultaneously asserts and denies the authority of its own rhetorical mode" (17). As J. Hillis Miller suggests, deconstruction is not a dismantling of the structure of a text but a demonstration that it has already dismantled itself.

Self-Dismantlement in a Poem by Yeats

As an example of how such textual self-dismantlement works, consider de Man's brilliant commentary on the ending of Yeats' poem, "Among School Children," the last four lines of which are:

> O chestnut-tree, great-rooted blossomer,
> Are you the leaf, the blossom or the bole?
> O body swayed to music, O brightening glance,
> How can we know the dancer from the dance?

In standard critical practice, the oft-quoted final line is seen as a dynamic image of order, an image of a living form that exemplifies the inextricability of individual figure and symbolic pattern. Such practice assumes a unity between space and time, form and experience, creator and creation, sign and referent. As de Man observes, traditional critics find in these lines "powerful and consecrated images of the continuity from part to whole that makes synecdoche into the most seductive of metaphors: the organic beauty of the tree, stated in the parallel syntax of a similar rhetorical question, or the convergence, in dance, of erotic desire with musical form" (11). De Man's strategic innovation is to ask what happens if the final line is construed as a real rather than a rhetorical question. Unlike the standard figural reading, this literal reading leads to greater complication of theme and statement; it may even lead to an epistemic desperation about the possibility of sign ever coinciding with referent or meaning. Rather than being a glorious affirmation of the unifying power of the romantic image, "How can we know the dancer from the dance?" becomes a real and urgent question that has the deconstructive power not only to unsettle symbolist assumptions about the coincidence of image and substance and the consubstantiality of parts and whole, but also to unravel the entire structure of the poem. "Two entirely coherent but entirely incompatible readings," de Man concludes, "can be made to hinge on one line, whose grammatical structure is devoid of ambiguity, but whose rhetorical mode turns the mood as well as the mode of the entire poem upside down" (12). Grammar and rhetoric, then, are warring forces of signification locked in a linguistic battle that ends perforce in undecidability.

Grammar, Rhetoric, and the Symbolic

Before contrasting de Man's understanding of the relationship between grammar and rhetoric with Burke's, I shall first consider Burke's conception of the grammatical, rhetorical, and symbolical levels of discourse. (For the purposes of economy, I am ignoring the ethical, the portrait of self and society that emerges from the symbolic action of language.)

Burke has a grammar in the Aristotelian sense of a set of verbal terms or categories by means of which a discourse can be analyzed. His dramatistic grammar centers on observations of this sort: for there to be an *act*, there must be an *agent*. Similarly, there must be a scene in which the agent acts. To act in a scene, the agent must employ some means or *agency*, and there cannot be an act, in the full sense of the term, unless there is a *purpose*. These five terms—*act, agent, scene, agency, purpose*—Burke labels the dramatistic pentad. (He later makes the pentad into a hexad by adding the term *attitude*, but that addition is inconsequential here.) His aim in *A Grammar of Motives* is to show how the designated functions of these terms operate in the imputing of motives.

The grammatical is a series of blanks to be filled out when one imputes motive to action, and any statement of motives involves the dramatistic pentad of act (what was done), agent (who did the act and under what subjective conditions), scene (the environment in which the act took place, the extrinsic factors that determined it), agency (how the act was done, what instruments were used), and purpose (why the act was done, its ultimate motive or final cause). The agent, however, need not be a human being. For Burke, even conceptual "terms are characters . . . an essay is an *attenuated* play. . . . Names are shorthand designations for certain fields and methods of action" (*Attitudes*, 311–12).

The grammatical blanks offer opportunities for "*dis*position and *trans*position" (*Grammar*, 402), and dialectic explores the combinatory, substitutive, and transformational possibilities. Different philosophical systems emphasize different parts of the pentad: realism emphasizes act, idealism emphasizes agent, materialism emphasizes scene, pragmatism emphasizes agency, and mysticism emphasizes purpose. The combinatory, substitutive, and transformational possibilities are endless, but Burke's point is that any statement of motives must deal with the five terms he has isolated even if it would foreground one and background the others. The grammatical resources are principles, and the various philosophies are casuistries in that they seek to apply these principles to the case of a particular cultural situation. Burke attempts an ingenious casuistry of his own, taking major philosophic systems as cases and developing their distinctive characters in terms of their variant stress on one or another of the terms of the dramatistic pentad.

What Burke was doing in 1945 has a decidedly contemporary ring, especially his view of the subject or agent as the function of a system. As a method of discourse analysis, *A Grammar of Motives* is protostructuralist to the extent that structure in all kinds of texts can be accounted for by the terms of the pentad, which in their combinations, substitutions, and transformations show forth the gamut of possibilities for verbal action. It is antistructuralist, however, to the extent that every grammar of motives implies a rhetoric of motives. Since every dialectic transposes and disposes the terms of the pentad in a uniquely constitutive fashion with a uniquely exhortative attitude, every dialectic implies a rhetoric of action. Though vulgar Marxists might see the historical and economic *scene* as determinative of the *acts* and attitudes that *agents* engage in, their "scenic" grammar implies a program of social change that urges the strategic deployment of linguistic and political *agency* for the *purpose* of revolution. "The dramatistic view of language, in terms of 'symbolic action,'" Burke writes, "is exercised about the necessarily *suasive* nature of even the most unemotional scientific nomenclatures" (*Language*, 45).

In contrast to grammar's attempt to furnish an exhaustive inventory of textual expression, rhetoric's function is to counteract the alienation that is endemic to every social order wherein differences of race, gender, sexual orientation, education, ethnicity, class, wealth, and so forth prevail. Through the operations of identification, rhetoric seeks to overcome these differences by inducing cooperation and community. Nevertheless, there is an obvious sense in which every identification rhetoric induces implies a concomitant dissociation, and vice versa. As Burke observes, rhetoric contains the ambiguities of substance. In identifying oneself with something or someone else, one is "at once a distinct substance and consubstantial with another" (*Rhetoric of Motives*, 21). "Put identification and division ambiguously together so that you cannot know for certain just where one ends and the other begins, and you have the characteristic invitation to rhetoric" (25). So although rhetoric involves the formation of identity and the establishment of community, it is predicated upon division and difference. If identification and consubstantiality were really possible, there would be no need to induce them. For Burke, then, grammar and rhetoric "are counterparts because to identify is to share substance with something or someone, the study of substance (or motivational essence) being the affair of dialectic [or grammar], the study of tactics for achieving identification (or consubstantiality) being the affair of rhetoric" (Crusius, 31).

The symbolic, which Burke associates with poetics per se, is grounded in the proposition that "a work is composed of implicit or explicit 'equations' (assumptions of 'what equals what'), in any work considered as one particular structure of terms, or symbol system" (*Philosophy*, 8). Along with identifications or equations (what equals what), there are also dissociations or agons (what versus what). And this apposition and opposition of terms unfolds in a certain way, making for dramatic resolution and dialectical transformation (what leads to what). The symbolic, then, should take at least three factors into account: associative clusters, dramatic alignments, and narrative progressions.

All told, then, there is symbolic action as designation (the grammatical), as communication (the rhetorical), and as expression (the symbolical). For Burke, however, the various levels of symbolic action are interdependent. "Since the work of art is a synthesis, summing up a myriad of social and personal factors at once, an analysis of it necessarily radiates in all directions at once" (*Attitudes*, 199). Burke's general approach, then, might be called pragmatic in the sense that he assumes that a work's structure is to be described most accurately by thinking always of the work's function. Form is function. What a text is, is what a text does.

In light of this synopsis of Burke's position, it would seem that de Man's endorsement of "Burke's well-known insistence on the distinction between grammar and rhetoric" is based on a misconception of what that distinction means. The grammatical for Burke is not simply the literal or the referential, though the realm of grammar does comprise logic, dialectic, information, and external reference. That is, the symbolic action of language has a reality-regarding element and has realistic content insofar as it encompasses the situation it represents, the encompassment, of course, being necessarily imperfect since we have no nonsymbolic or nonlinguistic access to the structure of the real. But in addition to this referential function, the grammatical is both a method and theory of discourse analysis, according to which one seeks to determine what components of the dramatistic pentad a given text emphasizes and downplays.

For de Man, the grammatical is equated with the literal and the referential and is part of a rigidly dualistic scheme: grammar versus rhetoric, symbolism (coincidence of image and substance) versus allegory (failure of coincidence of image and substance), metaphor versus metonymy, organic unity (interdependence of part and whole) versus undecidability (free play of signifiers), determinacy versus indeterminacy, semantic versus syntactic, constative versus performative, and so forth. In each case, the latter term is privileged. Yet however dialectical the relationship between these oppositions might appear to be on the surface, the relationship is in reality static and predictable, for the latter term at all times subverts the former.

Symbolism versus Allegory: The Rhetoric of Temporality

Take, for example, de Man's understanding of the opposition between symbolism and allegory. In "The Rhetoric of Temporality," he takes aim against the romantic privileging of symbol over allegory. Unlike allegory, which recognizes the difference between substance and image, symbolism posits the identity of substance and image and thus refuses to distinguish between experience and the representation of experience—refuses, in other words, to know the dancer from the dance. Symbol is synecdochic, a part of the whole it represents, whereas allegory is metonymic, a token for a meaning with which it is contiguous rather than continuous. "Whereas the symbol postulates the possibility of an identity or identification, allegory designates primarily a distance in relation to its own origin, and renouncing the nostalgia and the desire to coincide, it establishes its language in the void of this temporal difference. In so doing, it prevents the self from an illusory identification with the non-self, which is now fully, though painfully, recognized as non-self" (207). Properly deconstructed, the romantic image is revealed to be a compensatory gesture in the direction of an unrealizable wish-fulfillment, and the tenacity of the poet's belief in the unifying power of the image is unwitting testimony to the impossibility of establishing an organic relationship between mind and nature, subject and object, self and non-self. Enmeshed in illusion and mystification, the romantic poet is in reality an epistemologist of failure. "The dialectical relationship between subject and object is no longer the central statement of romantic thought, but this dialectic is now located entirely in the temporal relationships that exist within a system of allegorical signs. It becomes a conflict between a conception of the self seen in its authentically temporal predicament and a defensive strategy that tries to hide from this negative self-knowledge. On the level of language the asserted superiority of the symbol over allegory, so frequent during the nineteenth century, is one of the forms taken by this tenacious self-mystification" (208).

That the allegorically inclined demystifier avoids the pitfalls of tenacious self-mystification, however, does not mean that he or she attains full enlightenment. For de Man, irony is a master trope, for in both irony and allegory the relationship between sign and meaning is discontinuous: "the sign points to something that differs from its literal meaning and has for its function the thematization of this difference" (209). "The ironic language splits the subject into an empirical self that exists in a state of inauthenticity and a self that exists only in the form of a language that asserts the knowledge of this inauthenticity. This does not, however, make it into an authentic language, for to know inauthenticity is not the same as to be authentic" (214). For de Man, the subject of romantic irony is the isolated and alienated person who has become the object of his or her own reflection and whose consciousness has deprived him or her of the ability to act. His or her dialectic of self-destruction and self-invention is an endless process that leads to no synthesis. To know inauthenticity is not the same as to be authentic.

All of the oppositions that animate de Man's thought operate in a similar way. Anyone who favors the first term—grammar, symbolism, organic unity—over the second term—rhetoric, allegory, undecid-ability—is caught in the thralls of tenacious self-mystification and "text-istential" inauthenticity. Grammar, along with its cognates, therefore, is ultimately unproblematic and empty as far as de Man is concerned; its negative function is simply to offer a source of illusion for the tena-ciously self-mystified and tropologically impoverished literalist. As de Man suggests in "The Resistance to Theory," "tropes, unlike grammar, pertain primordially to language. They are text-producing functions that are not necessarily patterned on a non-verbal entity, whereas grammar is by definition capable of non-linguistic generalization" (15). Anyone who believes in grammatical cognition and the referential function of language is condemned to adopt a stance of naive verbal realism and to construe the relationship between signs and things in the most literalist, transparent, and unsophisticated way imaginable. He or she holds what Ian Hacking aptly calls nobody's theory of language.

Antinomies of Definition: The Paradox of Substance

For Burke, it is more complicated than that. Like rhetoric, grammar is a text-producing function which, though capable of nonlinguistic generalization, is still enmeshed in the labyrinths of language. In *A Grammar of Motives*, Burke's recurrent focus on the antinomies of definition and the paradox of substance infects his dialectical system with the virus of deconstruction from the outset. Moreover, the rela-tionship between the grammatical and the rhetorical is genuinely dialectical, not permanently agonistic.

Endorsing Spinoza's claim that all determination is negation, Burke concludes that the concept of substance is thereby endowed with an unresolvable ambiguity. As he reflects, "men are not only *in nature*. The cultural accretions made possible by language become a 'second nature' with them. Here again we confront the ambiguities of substance, since symbolic communication is not merely an external instrument, but also intrinsic to men as agents. Its motivational properties characterize both 'the human situation' and what men are 'in themselves.' Whereas there is an implicit irony in other notions of substance, with dialectic substance, the irony is explicit. For it derives its character from the systematic contemplation of the antinomies attendant upon the fact that we necessarily define a thing in terms of something else" (33). For Burke, this is "an *inevitable* paradox of definition." "To *define*, or *determine* a thing is to mark its boundaries, hence to use terms that possess, implicitly at least, contextual reference" (24). Substance, Burke notes, is etymologically a scenic word. "Literally, a person's or thing's sub-stance would be something that stands beneath or supports the person or thing" (22). The point is not to banish substance terms, but to be aware of their equivocal nature. Banishing the term *substance*, he maintains, does not banish its functions; it merely conceals them. Moreover, the unresolvable ambiguity built into the very concept of substance is precisely that which facilitates linguistic transformations and makes dialectic possible.

"Distinctions," Burke writes, "arise out of a great central moltenness, where all is merged. They have been thrown from a liquid center to the surface, where they have congealed. Let one of these crusted distinctions return to its source, and in this alchemic center it may be remade, again becoming molten liquid, and may enter into new combinations, whereat it may be again thrown forth as a new crust. So that A may become non-A" (xix). For Burke, as for Saussure, language is a system of differences without any positive terms, and from its "central moltenness, where all elements are fused into one togetherness, there are thrown forth, in separate crusts, such distinctions as those between freedom and necessity, activity and passivity, cooperation and competition, mechanism and teleology" (xix). Herein resides the tranformability that gives the terms of the dramatistic pentad their resourcefulness and flexibility.

Because of the antinomies of definition and the paradox of substance, one must invoke difference to constitute a meaning. In the Burkean system, as in the Derridean, meaning is disseminated. However substantial distinctions may appear, they become meaningful insofar as their terms are cast in opposition to each other, and they are forever capable of retreating into the moltenness of the alchemic center and reemerging as something else. Such an explicitly ironic conception of dialectic substance problematizes the grammatical project and makes any simple-minded equation of the grammatical with the referential or the literal impossible.

Unlike de Man's, then, Burke's conception of the grammatical is avowedly antifoundationalist. It would be difficult for any epistemology to anchor itself in the great central moltenness out of which such liquid distinctions emerge. To be fair, however, one must acknowledge that de Man's agenda is more to saddle his unnamed antagonists with a naively foundationalist epistemology and a naively mimetic view of language than to endorse such views himself. He thereby paves the way for his own deconstructive retextualization of the already textualized triumph of rhetoric over reference. By defining nobody's conception of grammar in such a reductively literalist fashion, de Man ensures that the triumph of rhetoric over grammar is a foregone conclusion, if being stoically mired in undecidability with one's ironic sensibility and failed epistemology intact can be thought of as a triumph at all.

Points of Affinity and Difference

This point notwithstanding, I am willing to concede that there is some affinity between the two theorists' critical practices. Burke's deconstructive analysis of *De Rerum Natura* in *The Philosophy of Literary Form* and *A Grammar of Motives*, an analysis in which he reveals the tension between Lucretius's literal and figural motives, between what Lucretius wants to *say* philosophically and what his language *does* poetically, makes the classic de Manian moves, well before de Man patented them. "In trying to make us feel the great relief that would come to us from the abolition of the gods," Burke writes, "Lucretius exposes himself to the full rigors of religious awe. He must make us realize *awe*, in the contemplation of heavenly distances and storms, in order to make us realize the full measure of the *relief* that would follow from the dissolution of this awe (by dissolving the gods which have become the symbols, the 'charismatic vessels,' of it). So he becomes somewhat an advocate against his own thesis. For in trying to build up a full realization of the awe, in order to build up a full realization of the freedom that would come of banishing this awe, he leaves us with an unforgettable image of the awe itself" (*Philosophy*, 152–53). The grammatical and the rhetorical are thus "working at cross purposes," for "something seems to have gone wrong with the *direction* of the poem, at least as regards to the philosophic ends of solace. The intention of showing that calamities are not acts of gods leads not to a *medical* treatment of symptoms, but to a *poetic* one, seeking to make the plague as vivid and picturesque as possible, and so building up in one way the disturbing thoughts it is designed to remove in another" (*Grammar*, 162).

Even though Burke's critical practice is at times as deconstructive as de Man's, the two theorists differ markedly in their conceptions of rhetoric. According to Burke, rhetoric regards the symbolic action of language as audience-directed discourse, focusing on its nature as communication, persuasion, exhortation, address, prayer, petition, and inducement to attitude and action. Through the use of identification, rhetoric seeks to overcome social estrangement, to foster cooperation, and to establish community. Of course, as I have noted, rhetoric, through the use of dissociation, may do exactly the opposite, and there is an obvious sense in which every identification implies a concomitant dissociation, and vice versa. Hierarchic psychosis is endemic to every society, and every work reflects the embarrassments, tensions, and alienations of a given sociopolitical hierarchy. This sociological aspect of rhetoric is largely missing in de Man, who, in stressing the necessarily mediated, hence duplicitous, nature of all discourse, holds that the inescapable tension between grammar and rhetoric accentuates rather than extirpates the inauthenticity of language and its users. In my view, such "textistentialism" runs counter to the spirit of dramatism.

For de Man, then, rhetoric is more an unstable system of tropes (intrinsic substance) than an art of persuasion (extrinsic effect). Grammar, in turn, is essentially an unstable system of concepts that bear within them figural traces that referential language vainly tries to efface. A concept is a trope whose tropological status has been forgotten, and deconstructive analysis inaugurates a return of the repressed that is already implicit in the symbolic action of the text. But cannot one concede that the contradictory strains of substance and effect inhabit all manifestations of rhetoric in discursive texts without seeing the resultant aporia in exclusively synchronic terms, that is, without seeing it as a built-in feature of all discourse? Is it not possible to construe trope not as semantic error, a swerve away from the literal, but as rhetorical will-to-power, a strategy for fighting on one's own terms? Surely both trope and concept, rhetoric and reference, do their work in the diachronic realm of intertextual and intersubjective meaning as well as in the synchronic realm of intratextual meaning. That is, they operate in the sociohistorical realm of practical effects; they do not have a merely textual existence wherein their inexorable fate is but to reveal the indeterminacies of their own intrinsic substance. To emphasize the latter is to reintroduce at a different level the discredited distinction between intrinsic and extrinsic as well as to ignore the whole hegemonic aspect of rhetoric.

For Burke, by contrast, the rhetorical is not synonymous with the figural. In fact, much of what de Man regards as part of rhetoric Burke regards as part of the symbolic, but this difference, of course, is only a matter of nomenclature and not important in and of itself. What is important is that Burke's notion of rhetoric pertains to discovery and arrangement as well as to style, to effect as well as to substance. Burke's conception of form is unabashedly rhetorical. "Form," he writes, is "the psychology of the audience . . . the creation of an appetite in the mind of the auditor, and the adequate satisfying of that appetite" (*Counter-Statement*, 31). Burke's conception of the fourfold nature of form—progressive, repetitive, conventional, and minor—shows how formal motives generate verbal substance, constrain discursive practice, and condition reader response. The rhetoric of form not only has a suasive impact on the audience; it also has a suasive impact, conscious or unconscious, on the author. While we are using formal structures and rhetorical strategies, they are using us. The rhetoric of form shapes both the discovery and arrangement of our concepts and tropes, constrains our discursive practice in ways that are often invisible to us, and arouses, shapes, and controls the responses of our audience. In this context, is not de Man's implicit reduction of rhetoric to figure as impoverishing as "the reduction of figure to grammar" that he imputes to formalism and semiology? Why are ideation and imagery, concept and trope, philosophy and literature, reference and rhetoric, necessarily at odds with one another?

Symbolic Action in *Mein Kampf*

Consider Burke's analysis of Hitler's *Mein Kampf* (*Philosophy*, 191–220), an essay in which he examines Hitler's use of sexual symbolism, of the imagery of blood, pollution, and disease, and of the rhetoric of identification and dissociation. Germany is a dehorned Siegfried; its masses are feminine and desire to be led by a dominating male; this male must overcome the rival Jewish male, a seducer who would poison Aryan blood by intermingling with the folk. An associative cluster emerges: blood poisoning, syphilis, prostitution, incest, and so on are equated materially with the infection of Jewish blood and spiritually with the infection of Jewish ideas. Burke's whole point in this essay is to show how imagery and ideation, rhetoric and grammar, sustain each other in Hitler's sinister and nightmarish text. Because of Hitler's resistance to a purely environmental account of social problems, his grammar of motives systematically elevates agent at the expense of scene. The superagent is none other than Hitler himself, the living incarnation of Aryan will-to-power. Although it takes a great deal of sophistical ingenuity to distinguish benign Aryan superindividualism from malign Jewish individualism, these are the only factors that really matter in Hitler's diagnosis of and remedy for Germany's woes. The extrinsic causal factors that have in large measure shaped and determined the economic scene are completely disregarded. This truncated grammar of motives implies a concomitant rhetoric of motives: a rhetoric of identification, which induces the people to see themselves as consubstantial with their leader, and a rhetoric of dissociation, which induces the people to alienate themselves from the Jews and makes possible the brutal victimization. Hitler's psychotic dream, rife with its obsessive images and fanatical hatreds, is thereby converted into a grammar of the agent and a rhetoric of persecution. He spontaneously evolves his cure-all on the grammatical and rhetorical levels in response to inner necessities and compulsions on the symbolical level. His grammar and rhetoric sustain rather than subvert each other.

It is difficult to imagine a deconstructive reading of *Mein Kampf* claiming the opposite: that the racist and totalitarian ideology prosecuted on the referential level of Hitler's text is undermined on the rhetorical level by an unstable system of figures and tropes. Yet if we accept the rigid dualism of de Man's thinking, are we not *at all times* committed to uncovering rhetoric's subversion of grammar? Whereas one would prefer, paraleptically, of course, not to advert to de Man's collaborationist wartime writings, it is difficult not to detect a guilty conscience underlying his "textistentialist" irony vis-à-vis the impossibility of authenticity and historical knowledge. Whether these wartime writings, as one of his apologists maintains, "serve as examples—in advance—of the (precritical, ideological) blindness that the later (critical, theoretical) insight will expose, unsparingly, as such," is open to debate" (Esch, 36). As Burke pointed out in 1937, well before de Man appropriated "blindness and insight" as a title for a collection of his essays, "*every* insight contains its own special kind of blindness" (*Attitudes*, 41). Is it the blindness of de Man's flirtation with fascism that makes possible the insight of his deconstructive analyses along with "the fatalistic theory of history," "the absolutization of language," "the epistemology of failure," and the attitude of ironic quietism that undergird these analyses (Lentricchia, 48, 43, 42)?

Whether one sees this as a real or a rhetorical question, it points to the virtues and limitations of de Man's deconstructive practice, both of which are rendered incisively by Frank Lentricchia: "Deconstruction's useful work is to undercut the epistemological claims of representation, but that work in no way touches the real work of representation—its work of power. To put it another way: deconstruction can show that representations are not and cannot be adequate to the task of representation, but it has nothing to say about the social work that representation can and does do. Deconstruction confuses the act of exposing epistemological fraud with the neutralization of political force" (200–201). That Hitler's representations were ontologically unanchored and obscenely false did not matter at all; their consequences were invidiously real. In mapping out "the grand coalitión of [Hitler's] ideational imagery, or imagistic ideation" (*Philosophy*, 207), Burke never loses of sight of the fact that systems of ideas and images, concepts and tropes, however unstable in their intrinsic substance, do their brutal work of power in the extrinsic realm of practical effects regardless of our epistemologies.

References

Burke, Kenneth. *Attitudes Toward History*. 3rd ed. Berkeley: University of California Press, 1984.

———. *Counter-Statement*. 2nd ed. Berkeley: University of California Press, 1968.

———. *A Grammar of Motives*. Berkeley: University of California Press, 1969.

———. *Language as Symbolic Action: Essays on Life, Literature, and Method*. Berkeley: University of California Press, 1966.

———. *The Philosophy of Literary Form: Studies in Symbolic Action*. 3rd ed. Berkeley: University of California Press, 1973.

———. *A Rhetoric of Motives*. Berkeley: University of California Press, 1969.

Crusius, Timothy. "A Case for Kenneth Burke's Dialectic and Rhetoric." *Philosophy and Rhetoric* 19, no. 1 (1986): 23–37.

de Man, Paul. "The Resistance to Theory." In *The Resistance to Theory*. Minneapolis: University of Minnesota Press, 1986.

———. "The Rhetoric of Temporality." In *Blindness and Insight: Essays in the Rhetoric of Contemporary Criticism*. 2nd ed. Minneapolis: University of Minnesota Press, 1983.

———. "Semiology and Rhetoric." In *Allegories of Reading: Figural Language in Rousseau, Nietzsche, Rilke, and Proust*. New Haven, Conn.: Yale University Press, 1979.

Esch, Deborah. "The Work to Come." *Diacritics*, Fall 1990, 28–49.

Lentricchia, Frank. *Criticism and Social Change*. Chicago: University of Chicago Press, 1983.

8

Multiculturalism and the Burkean System

Limitations and Extensions

James W. Chesebro

Kenneth Burke's system for analyzing human communication was introduced in the journals of the discipline of speech communication in the early 1950s (Nicholas; Holland, "Rhetorical Criticism," "Dramatistic Approach"). During the past forty years, Burke's approach has been extensively employed in virtually every area of communication:

> Burke's dramatistic approach has been widely accepted as a critical method; speech communication journals reflect Burkeian conceptions in numerous ways. His theories of identification, substance, form, transcendence, representative anecdote, and pentad have been explained and interpreted. Burke's ideas have been applied in a number of specialties within speech communication . . . in theatre, . . . organizational communication, . . . political communication, . . . small group communication, . . . [and] interpersonal communication, . . . [as well as to provide analyses of] multiple murder and suicide, . . . generic criticism, . . . selected presidential war messages, . . . social movements, . . . feminist rhetoric, . . . [and] prime time television series. These articles, and others, certainly demonstrate that Burke's dramatism can be applied to rhetorical acts in a variety of fashions. (Brock, Scott, and Chesebro 174–76)[1]

While recognizing the pervasiveness and insightfulness of Burke's critical approach, this essay focuses, in general, on the degree to which any critic's ideology affects what is viewed as an object of criticism and how the object of criticism is interpreted and evaluated. This exploration is challenging, for rhetorical criticism itself has traditionally been conceived as more than epideictic discourse. Given special attributions as a class of discourse, rhetorical criticism has been understood as a "criticism of scholarship" (Rosenfield, 119), and in some cases even as discourse whose purpose is to "discover the truth, the whole truth, and nothing but the truth" (Hill, 122). In contrast, Wander maintained that rhetorical criticism necessarily will and should reflect the ideological posture of the critic:

> Criticism takes an ideological turn when it recognizes the existence of powerful vested interests benefitting from and consistently urging policies and technology that threaten life on this planet, when it realizes that we search for alternatives. The situation is being constructed; it will not be averted either by ignoring it or placing it beyond our provence. An ideological turn in modern criticism reflects the existence of crisis, acknowledges the influence of established interests and the reality of alternative world-views, and commends rhetorical analyses not only of the actions implied but also the interests represented. More than "informed talk about matters of importance," criticism carries us to the point of recognizing good reasons and engaging in right action. What an ideological view does is to situate "good" and "right" in an historical context, the efforts of real people to create a better world. ("Ideological Turn," 18)

The responses of other rhetorical critics have been protracted and detailed, with several qualifying, if not denying, Wander's thesis (Megill; Rosenfield; Hill; Campbell; McGee; Francesconi; Corcoran).

In this context, one of the issues generated by Burke's critical analyses turns on the question of the cultural orientation of a critic and how a critic's cultural orientation affects the decisions made by a critic to describe, interpret, and evaluate communicative acts.[2] Specifically, regarding Burke's system, it seems appropriate and useful to ask if Burke's system necessarily possesses an "ethnocentric bias" that affects how the critical perspective is shaped and how the critic describes, interprets, and evaluates.

Yet the discipline of communication has exempted Burke from a detailed consideration of his ethnocentric biases and how these biases might have shaped his critical system. Wander has initially observed that Burke was decisively ideological and political in all of his early criticism when he was "less interested in the academic implications of his work than in its contribution to the political, cultural, and intellectual struggles of the period" ("Ideological Turn," 5). Indeed, Wander has aptly maintained that, especially in the 1930s and 1940s, "Burke considered himself a Marxist and was strongly sympathetic to the Communist party," "thought that 'fostering intellectual distrust' in established parties would hasten the victory of socialism," and "pursued a Marxist, even at times Marxist-Leninist, critique, though his commitment to the independence of the intellectual cut him off from vanguardism and the imperatives of party discipline" (5).

Despite these tendencies, in the discipline of communication, Burke has been amazingly perceived in nonideological and apolitical terms. As Wander has explained: "In the academic world, however, the fact that Burke oriented his project around 'rhetoric' and traced its origins back to Aristotle, and had, by the 1950s, begun to detach himself from radical politics to meditate on literary texts, made him an acceptable candidate for canonization in the field—even by those for whom efforts to deal with sociopolitical issues reached beyond the pale of legitimate scholarship" (5–6). Additionally, Wander has reported that

> In the field of speech, however, Burkeanism rarely carried with it the emancipatory sociopolitical critique that made it an intellectual force in the social sciences. Among speech and rhetorical critics, Burkeanism, refracted through a pentagonal prism, became an alternative to the prevailing but intellectually embarrassing schematic known as "neo-Aristotelianism" which, as [Edwin] Black made clear in the early 1960s, was little more than a set of categories lifted, with slight emanation, out of Wichelns' early essay. (6)

In another context, I have already raised the issue that Burke's ideological orientation is profoundly grounded in his special and specific cultural conditioning:

> Thus, the issue is not whether Burke and his system of analysis are a product and reflection of his culture. They are. Being human, Burke cannot escape his cultural conditioning. There is no reason to apologize for one's cultural orientation, but it is necessary to recognize the selective and limiting conditioning generated by one's cultural orientation when creating a critical system. Burke's quest for a universal system is limited by his own cultural conditioning. (86–87)

This issue has been the subject of a scholarly debate that began in August 1992 (Condit, "Post-Burke"; Chesebro, "Extensions"; Tompkins and Cheney; Chesebro, "Extending"; Condit, "Framing"; Tompkins).

These critical and philosophical debates, exchanges, and speculations are important, and they are likely to continue. Nonetheless, it may also be appropriate to consider an alternative to the kind of philosophical exchanges occurring in the pages of academic journals. Rather than respond only to what Burke has written, a different approach to these issues may be equally appropriate, if not more useful.

If we assume that specific issues have been articulated in these published debates, it may now be appropriate to formulate researchable and testable hypotheses and procedures to resolve these issues. To achieve this end, I want to test a specific set of Burkean concepts in an applied field and context. This test is guided by one general question, "Is there an ethnic bias in Burke's system?" More specifically, the test is designed to answer the question, "Does Burke presume an Anglo perspective in the way in which he has constructed and applied his system?"

Two major steps are necessary if these questions are to be addressed adequately. First, specific Burkean concepts must be selected for analysis. In this case, because the notion is central to his entire discussion of the rhetorical nature of symbol-using, Burke's concept of *form* in general and his particular typography of forms in particular have been chosen for analysis. Second, having selected specific Burkean concepts to be tested, an object of study is intentionally selected because it constitutes a rigorous test[3] of Burke's implicit claim of universality, specifically, that his four major forms account for how all meanings are socially constructed and developed. In this specific case, Pedro Albizu Campos's[4] two-and-one-half-hour, October 12, 1933 address,[5] entitled "Day of the Race" (i.e., "El Dia de la Raza"[6]), given in Ponce, Puerto Rico, is used as a "test case" to determine if Burke's scheme of forms can adequately account for the development of ideas contained within this speech.

Burke's Conception of Form

Burke's concept of form has been selected as the point of departure, because the concept is central to Burke's concept of symbol-using as a rhetorical process. As Burke has maintained, "*Form* in literature is an arousing and fulfillment of desires. A work has form in so far as one part of it leads a reader to anticipate another part, to be gratified by the sequence" (*Counter-Statement*, 124).

Burke has further posited that there are four major forms and several "minor or incidental forms" (*Counter-Statement*, 127). One of these major forms is the "syllogistic progression," which Burke defined as "a perfectly conducted argument, advancing step by step" (127). A second of the major forms is the "qualitative progression," in which "one quality prepares us for the introduction of another" (125). The third major form is the "repetitive form," in which one "principle" is consistently maintained "under new guises" (125). The fourth major form is the "conventional form," which "involves to some degree the appeal of form as form" (126). Finally, rather than defining the "minor or incidental forms," Burke listed some of them and included "metaphor, paradox, disclosure, reversal, contradiction, expansion, bathos, apostrophe, series, [and] chiasmas." Of these "minor forms," Burke held that they may "manifest sufficient evidences of episodic distinctness to bear consideration apart from their context," but he has also maintained that "Their effect partially depends upon their function in the whole" (127).

Given Burke's analysis, the four major forms become central. In the context established here, the question becomes: "Do the four major forms account for communicative and rhetorical activities in non-Anglo cultures?"

The Rhetoric of Pedro Albizu Campos

In giving his address, Albizu Campos served as the spokesperson and "designated leader of the Nationalist Party [in Puerto Rico]," a position he held "for over three decades, [from] 1930– [to] 1960" (Ferri, 6). Accordingly, his addresses constituted a mandate for Puerto Rican independence, and was perhaps the most significant of all of the early calls for Puerto Rican independence.

"Day of the Race" itself falls roughly into two major parts. In the first part, Albizu Campos seeks to define the essential nature of the "character" of Puerto Rico. Believing that social divisions based on race in Puerto Rico were counterproductive, because "skin color is an accident" (134), Albizu Campos sought to develop a sense of unity in Puerto Ricans based on what he perceived to be their shared culture. Part of this cultural unity was to be based on the fact that Puerto Ricans are part of a larger "Latin American race" (134), for "the Latin American nations" form "the core of civilization" itself (145). Part of this cultural unity was to be based on the fact that Spain—the "mother country" (136)—secured its historical independence from Rome, much as Puerto Rico must secure its independence from the "Yankees" (138). Part of this cultural unity was to be based on the civilizing influence of Christopher Columbus (142). In terms of Columbus's role as a unifying force for Puerto Rican culture, Albizu Campos was passionate: "We, the

Nationalists of Puerto Rico, venerate with pride, goodwill, fervor, and with reverence imposed by the greatness of his name, the great image and sublime figure of the Navigator par excellence in the history of the world" (143).

In the second part of the speech, Albizu Campos maintained that Puerto Rico's unifying culture could and should provide a foundation for the political independence of Puerto Rico. As Albizu Campos succinctly stated his case: "Puerto Rico will be free. Puerto Rico will be sovereign" (139). In support of this basic thesis, four lines of thought are developed by Albizu Campos.

First, for Albizu Campos, political independence is the only course of action available to Puerto Rico, for the "Yankees" are exploiting Puerto Rican wealth. As Albizu Campos stated the case:

> Imagine how much we are worth in dollars. The commercial balance of our nation—that is, the excess of the value of what Puerto Rico exports over that which it imports, the value of what we sell compared to the value of what we buy, the commercial balance which Puerto Rico has had during thirty-five years—amounts to twelve hundred and fifty million in gold.
>
> To those who say that Puerto Rico cannot be independent because it is very poor, I say don't be ignorant. You should read your own history, know about these things and who your fathers and mothers were, so you can talk about the independence of your homeland. (145–46)

Second, Albizu Campos maintained that a continued relationship with the United States could only spell disaster for Puerto Rico. He used Ponce as his example:

> Ponce has fallen; it has cruelly fallen. Today, Ponce is a shapeless mass in Puerto Rico. Ponce responds to nothing. There is no unity. A small group over here, another small group over there, insulting and abusing each other: that is Ponce. It is a very painful and shameful spectacle. All intelligence has sunk. Everything is sad, shameful. All intelligence has sunk. All is sad, shameful. All intelligence sinks. Everyone in Ponce is digging his/her neighbor's grave and is burying the honor of the homeland. (147)

Third, Albizu Campos argued that "the Yankee" will only "talk" about "equality, fraternity, and liberty," for the "Yankees," as revealed in a congressional investigation, "have only twenty-four men who control seventy-six percent of all the riches of a nation of a hundred and twenty-five million people. The Yankee people are an enslaved people" (151).

Fourth, Albizu Campos maintained that the United States is godless: "There is no Christianity in the United States. That is why when a Negro sits where he is not allowed on a bus, they [the Yankees] simply tie him to the rear of the bus and drag him through the streets, so other Negroes can see what will happen to them!" (151).

Accordingly, the call for revolution was therefore an appropriate and necessary solution for Albizu Campos. For Albizu Campos, the electoral process would not work: "I was here for the elections. It was immoral! Everyone here was selling votes for a dollar on election day; in the afternoon, they sold them for five dollars. A shameful struggle among the sugar manufacturers of Ponce." Thus, in Albizu Campos's view, rather than "stand in lines" waiting "for a young girl to hand you a small loaf of bread," Puerto Ricans should take a "dagger, a stick of dynamite, a bomb or a cannon to blow up the sugar centrals of Puerto Rico" (151). Albizu Campos's final appeal is vivid:

> Puerto Rico has to play its part in history and has to be free in order to look posterity straight in the eye. Here is history, here is our flag, the flag of our parents, the flag of our brothers, the flag of our sisters. Here is our flag as well as the flag for Puerto Rico's posterity. Brandish it and die for her! Ladies and gentlemen, I have spoken. (156)

Albizu Campos's speech is rich in its rhetorical appeals, devices, and strategies. Indeed, Ferri has already argued for the significance of this address as a subject of rhetorical analysis, and he has provided a comprehensive description, interpretation, and evaluation of the rhetorical strategies contained in it.[7] Given the objective in this analysis, no purpose is served by duplicating Ferri's effort. Accordingly, the question I would raise about Albizu Campos's address can appropriately deal with whether Burke's four major forms account for the progression in his speech. If Burke's system is universal or cross-cultural, one of his four major forms should adequately account for the development of ideas contained in Albizu Campos's address.

The Rhetoric of Pedro Albizu Campos:
A Test of the Adequacy and Comprehensiveness
of Burke's Theory of Forms

Because of the detailed analyses already provided by others, such as Ferri, regarding the specific objectives, context, and strategies employed by Albizu Campos, attention can be directed to the question raised at the outset of this analysis: Do Burke's four major forms account for communicative and rhetorical activities in non-Anglo cultures and specifically for the progression of ideas contained in Albizu Campos's October 12, 1933 address? In response to this question, the answer is apparently "no," for none of Burke's forms accounts for the progression developed in Albizu Campos's speech.

Characterizing the Form of the Albizu Campos Speech

The overall progression and major features of the Albizu Campos speech are not accounted for in terms of Burke's four forms.

The Syllogistic Progression

Without intending any negative assessment, the speech does not adhere to the syllogistic form, for it is not a "perfectly conducted argument, advancing step by step" (Burke, *Counter-Statement*, 124). If nothing else, the speech commits a logical error by excluding a major premise required to draw a conclusion (i.e., it commits the logical fallacy of the "excluded middle"). Albizu Campos fails to establish that political independence is a necessary consequence of enhancing Puerto Rican cultural unity—a host of different political systems (such as commonwealth status) can also be derived from cultural unity.

The Qualitative Progression

The qualitative progression, in which "the presence of one quality prepares us for the introduction of another" (Burke, Counter-Statement, 124–25), does not adequately account for the development of ideas in Albizu Campos's speech either. The description of Puerto Ricans as "docile" and sentencing "their children to a life in 'shameless slavery'" (cited in Ferri, 77) at the outset of speech does not prepare the audience for his concluding call for revolution: "Citizens! Citizens of Hell! Slavery does not have a citizenship; it has death for every person who embraces the Goddess of Infamy" (154).

This qualitative disjuncture may ultimately stem from a more profound paradox facing all radicals. The political radical traditionally characterizes an audience as powerless, which underscores the need for action. But, given the radical's commitment to self-determination, the radical must then call on the powerless to exert sufficient power to create a revolution and overthrow a system already described as possessing excessive and mindless power. In equally useful terms, Brock has also identified and characterized a qualitative disjuncture in radical discourse. He has maintained that the political radical creates "a negative mood" when calling for "the rejection of the hierarchy" (343), and then must attempt to construct a frame of "acceptance" when arguing for an agency that "is not completely accepted within the present system" (350).

The Repetitive Form

As conceived by Burke (*Counter-Statement*, 125), the repetitive form consistently features the same principle under "new guises." An aesthetic issue, Burke has aptly noted that the repetitive form "is basic to any work of art," particularly when attempting to "sustain" a certain attitude and establish a "lyric mood" (125). Yet Albizu Campos's discourse is not directed toward a literary or aesthetic end. While epideictic moments characterize the outset and conclusion of the speech, he seeks a change in attitudes, a change in existing actions, and a radical dismantling of the existing order. While it is conceivable that a "call to revolution" might be refeatured as a governing principle in multiple guises throughout a speech, Albizu Campos seeks to establish two—not one—governing principles: disapproval of an existing political system and a commitment to an alternative political system. Thus, Albizu Campos pointedly rejects the repetitive form. While the October 12 date, as "El Dia de la Raza," possesses potential celebratory or epideictic overtones in Puerto Rico, Albizu Campos's effort is to transform this epideictic event into a series of discrete deliberative or political stages. Such an objective is not readily achievable with a repetitive form, given its tendency to feature a single principle.

The Conventional Form

Possessing many of the epideictic characteristics of the repetitive form, the conventional form "involves to some degree the appeal to form *as form*" (Burke, *Counter-Statement*, 126). However, while "anticipations and gratifications . . . arise *during the process* of reading" in other forms, the conventional form possesses expectations "*anterior to* the reading" (126–27). In other words, with the conventional form, the audience celebrates in the unfolding of a process that it already knows will occur.

As has already been suggested, Albizu Campos's effort was to use and to transform a conventional holiday into a decisively deliberative or political event. In this sense, while a conventional form is the rationale for the decision to speak, the speaker dramatically transformed the conventional moment, proposing a change from existing conventions to an unknown vision and system.

In all, the overall progression and major features of the Albizu Campos speech are not accounted for in terms of Burke's four forms. Thus, if the Burkean system of forms is employed, there is no readily available method for characterizing the development of Albizu Campos's address.

Explaining the Selective Nature of the Burkean System

This raises an equally important key question: "Why doesn't Burke's conception of form account for the progression in Albizu Campos' speech?" While several reasons might be posited as responses to this question, two possibilities are explored here.

Linear and Spiral Patterns[8]

First, the nature and power of two radically different culture-bound consciousnesses may be one of the reasons why Burke's forms do not account for the development of Albizu Campos's speech.

In Burke's culture, forms are linear, for understanding itself can be equated with knowing an idea has undergone a progression from one manifestation to another. In this sense, understanding itself is equated with recognizing the specific and discrete stages an idea passed through from its origin to a subsequent and altered state or stage.

In Albizu Campos's culture, another kind of form is possible, the spiral form, for understanding itself can be equated with knowing the complex and multiple factors that are simultaneously affecting an idea. In this sense, understanding itself is equated with recognizing how an idea is a reflection of and product of diverse associations and contextual possibilities. When the spiral form dominates, the quest is intentionally to emphasize an appreciation for and understanding of the essence, integrity, completeness, nuances, and comprehensiveness of an idea.

If a scheme is too narrow in scope, or simply inappropriate, for a critic's task, it may be useful to ask how the scheme can be extended to function more effectively. In terms of Burke's discussion of form, two extensions may be appropriate.

It is initially useful to ask what principle unifies Burke's conception of the various forms he discussed. Burke informed us that audience expectations determine the nature of form. However, the forms themselves also seem to possess at least one common content feature. All of the forms presume a linear progression. This linear feature may be a function of the printed page, and its sequential formula in moving from left to right, from one discrete word to the next discrete word, and then from top to bottom, as one moves from one line to the next, and finally from one page to the next. At the same time, Burke also characterized each of the forms as a "progression." The word *progression* is noteworthy in this context, for it implies the kind of analytical, dichotomous, and linear orientation reflected in its equivalent terms *sequence, movement forward,* and *connected series* (*Webster's*).

Second, an alternative conception—although it may ultimately complement and function as a useful addition to Burke's linear conception—of a form must be invoked to account for what occurs in Albizu Campos's address. The form of Albizu Campos's prepared remarks follows a spiral, cyclical, or circular pattern. The spiral pattern is not a common argumentative form in Anglo culture, and it can mistakenly be equated with the kind of "circular reasoning" that is discouraged in argumentation and debate textbooks. Moreover, the spiral form is not equivalent to Burke's notion of the repetitive form, which holds that a single principle is refeatured in several guises for instrumental objectives. Rather, a central focus of spiral reasoning is its emphasis on a synthesis directed toward expressive ends (Ting-Toomey, 78). While functioning as an argumentation form, spiral forms also create a mood (i.e., the emotional relationship between speaker and audience) and tone (i.e., the emotional relationship between speaker and the topic of a speech).[9] Accordingly, within a spiral form, words such as *soul* and *spirit* can easily be invoked as unifying rhetorical concepts.

The spiral form departs significantly from the progressions outlined by Burke. The spiral form does not gain its significance as a form of reasoning from the kind of spatial metaphor that casts ideas as a sequential movement from one location to another. Indeed, the notion of a spiral implies an evolution of circular changes within a relatively contained space and time. Indeed, a spiral is "the path of a point in a plane moving around a centered point while continuously receding from or approaching it" (*Webster's*).

Rhetorically, the spiral form is not merely a series of progressive qualities (i.e., Burke's qualitative form), nor it is merely a repetition of the same principle under new guises (i.e., Burke's repetitive form), and it is not merely a convention in which an appeal is made to form as form (i.e., Burke's conventional form). As Albizu Campos's discourse has suggested, the metaphor of the spiral form is *not* the sequential steps of the syllogism but rather a circular pattern that invokes a series of approach–avoidance interactions. Similarly, while the spiral form is designed to invoke a series of qualities and please the audience with its form, the spiral form is substantive—the spiral form is a "working rhetoric" that explicitly seeks to refashion and change attitudes, beliefs, and actions. And, finally, while the spiral form can define a single principle by revealing it in multiple guises, it is more likely to deal with a series of basic principles, redefine these principles, and ultimately offer a reconception of the configuration of these basic principles.

Perhaps equally important, the spiral form is not a solely ideational construct. It admits—it celebrates—the recognition that emotions are facts, and that emotions are as central to the human condition as facts and concepts. Indeed, in a thoughtful definition of the spiral form, it can be understood as a form that intentionally transcends and merges the expressive and instrumental functions of communication, implicitly holding that humans are persuaded simultaneously by both facts and emotions.[10]

The spiral form is vividly reflected in Albizu Campos's speech. The synthesizing nature of the spiral form is reflected, not only in the mood and tone Albizu Campos sought to establish with his audience, but also in the ideas he expressed. Albizu Campos argued for the existence and recognition of a Puerto Rican "character" (cited in Ferri, 132). This "character" transcended racial differences, and indeed, Albizu Campos argued that the various races of Puerto Rico were already mixed and that these diverse racial combinations constituted a critical feature that created the sentiments or mood and tones of the Puerto Rican character. For Albizu Campos, the October 12 date itself was one of the most powerful reflections of the synthesizing nature of the Puerto Rican character. As Albizu Campos discussed "El Dia de la Raza," he also moved from its consideration as an international and national holiday, to its role in domestic decision making, to its meaning in his personal life. This spiral progression, then, is reflected in the mood and tone of the speech as well as in the ideational development of the speech. In the initial stages of his argument, he maintained:

> The other significant occasion which defines our culture is October 12, the Discovery of the New World. Regarding this, ladies and gentlemen, so that you may understand something about history and be aware of what the celebration of this date has meant for all the nations of the New World, I'm going to point out only a few facts.
>
> President Irigoyen was governing the great nation of Argentina, and he came up with the idea that October 12 should be celebrated in all of Latin America as the Day of the

Race. Many laughed and asked: "Day of which race? Of the Negroes? Of the Indians? Of the Italians in America? Of the Portuguese in America? Of the French in America? Of the Spanish in America? Of the Yankees in America? Of the Germans in America? Of the British in America? Of the Chinese in America? Of the Japanese in America? To which race is he referring?

And that brings us to the problem of resolving what is understood by the term. (132–33)

As Albizu Campos turned to the issue of domestic decision making, "El Dia de la Raza" took on additional meanings:

the national structure is not the structure of the epidermis. . . . Only ignorant minds separate men because of their epidermis. This would only cross the mind of the stupid North Americans. Only a savage nation would consider this. But civilized countries, mother countries, those countries always live with the unity that emanates from within every person, with the indestructible unity of people. They see that skin is an accident and the blondest man with the bluest eyes and the handsomest face, and the most attractive Negro with the most vibrant eyes and the most powerful physique could be either a saint or a sinner. This depends on what they carry in their spirit and on what they carry in their soul. This quality is what distinguishes man from beast. (134)

Finally, moving the conception to a more personal level, Albizu Campos asked a series of powerful questions that reflect both the emotional and ideational synthesizing nature of the spiral form:

Does African blood exist? It flows through my veins, and I carry it with the supreme pride of human dignity.

Here we have Indian blood. Here we have pure archetypes of Indian blood. I also have Indian blood which is why I feel perfectly American, an autochthonal American in the true sense of the word.

Do we have white blood? I also carry it in my veins. My father was Biscayan, and he came from the purest race in all of Europe.

And the type of person who is creating unity of feeling and day-to-day homogeneity of action in our country is also

forming racial unity in the biological sense and is restoring man
to his pristine origin since man did not begin yellow, or white,
or black, but only man, like the Divine Creator. (135)

This pattern of development led Albizu Campos to conclude his line of
thought in this fashion: "We are a country predestined in history because
Puerto Rico is the first nation in the world where a union of the spirit
and of the body has been formed. That is why, ladies and gentlemen, we
celebrate the Day of the Race" (135).

Thus, at least two classes of basic argumentation forms exist, the
linear and the *spiral*. Each class reflects and constitutes a different way of
understanding and, ultimately, a distinct cognitive system. All of Burke's
forms presume a linear movement. The spiral form of reasoning, more
expressive in its focus, describes various pathways surrounding a central
core, and seeks to provide readjustments and realignments of the attitudes, beliefs, and actions people hold in relationship to this central core.
It may be tempting to presume that the spiral form of reasoning is
unique, or at least a dominant, form in the Latino/Latina culture. However, the explorations conducted here do not provide a warrant for such
an exclusionary statement. Indeed, the spiral form may also account for
the development of ideas employed by some significant, albeit anti-
establishment, Anglo speakers.[11]

Modality—Orality and Literacy as Defining Variables
A critic's modality can affect how form is described, interpreted,
and assessed. In this sense, the critic's "natural" modality can affect what
the critic perceives and understands to exist.

Burke's conception of a form presumes a written or literate framework, and his conception of a form therefore emphasizes different
variations of a self-contained, text-centered model. As I have argued
elsewhere:

Burke's writings and critical perspective provide insight when
we are examining the discourse mediated by the written mode
of communication. Whether intended or not, virtually all of
Burke's examples of how communication functions are drawn
from literature or the printed page. Burke's viewpoint and his
theory of criticism is persistently shaped by and illustrated by
the written mode of communication. For example, while other
communication critics have focused upon the dynamics of
Hitler's oral mode, Burke focused upon the strategies contained
in Hitler's published volume *Mein Kampf* [Burke, *Philosophy*,

191–220]. Burke's choice, in this case, is not exceptional. In almost every case, Burke's examples—or the evidence for his claims—come from the written or printed domain.

In this regard, Burke's conception of "the nature of form" clearly focuses upon how audiences' "desires" are aroused and fulfilled. But, the key question is what type of audience does Burke have in mind. As I see Burke's discussion of the types of forms that exist, Burke's audiences are groups of readers of printed pages. For example, Burke's discussion of the syllogistic progression as a "form of a perfectly conducted argument" turns on our *reading* of Brutus' speech in the printed play *Julius Caesar* (Burke, *Counter-Statement*, 124). In this context, Burke provides insight when we deal with the printed page. (Chesebro, "Toward What?")

Yet Albizu Campos functioned within an alternative context, an oral context.[12] In the oral context, a dynamic, live, face-to-face, and complex interplay occurs between the speaker and audience. The progression of ideas contained within a verbal message constitutes only one of several variables that affect how the relationship between the speaker and audience members develops. Indeed, the relationship between speaker and audience changes and evolves as the speaker receives feedback from the audience, as the audience perceives and attributes various levels of credibility to the speaker, and as the speaker and audience establish and react to the extremely powerful nonverbal relationships that emerge between them.

In the case of Albizu Campos, the role of the audience is decisive in shaping the content and development of his October 12, 1933 speech. During his speech, Albizu Campos explicitly recognized the reactions and feedback of the audience, and these reactions altered how the speech was developed. At one point, for example, in the middle of a discussion of the role of women in the Puerto Rico, Albizu Campos abruptly stated:

> I'm going to ask those two gentlemen to please be silent. Those two gentlemen who are arguing over there. Let's wait until they are finished. Please, gentlemen, I would appreciate it, for it is very difficult to speak in a public square when everyone wants to speak. Those who want to speak to their fellowmen about the transcendental problems that they are occupied with, let them go to the plaza—well, ladies and gentlemen, it is with Queen Isabella that the principles of Spain's unity crystallized.

The moral catalyst of that unity was a woman, just as the catalyst of Puerto Rico's unity has to be the Puerto Rican woman.

Puerto Rico will be free, Puerto Rico will be sovereign, Puerto Rico will be independent when the Puerto Rican woman feels free, feels sovereign, feels independent. In order for the Puerto Rican woman to attain unity, she has to feel within her being—ladies and gentlemen, we are still in a state of barbarity (He refers to the music of a parade that interrupts his speech). (cited in Ferri 139–40)

A host of such "adjustments" to the audience are to be found throughout Albizu Campos's address.

Burke's perspective of form is not directly designed to deal with discourse mediated by the dynamic speaker-audience oral interaction. As I have previously argued:

If we return to Burke's discussion of form, we may find it particularly difficult to discover Burke's conception of the syllogistic progression in either oral or electronic systems. In the oral communication context, for example, the [speaker–audience] interaction is simply too complicated to be adequately accounted for in terms of the syllogistic progression as "a perfectly conducted argument." Among other variables, an audience's perception of an "argument" will depend on how they perceive the credibility of the speaker. Additionally, the nonverbal relationship between audience and speaker will define what social meanings are conveyed. Finally, the nature of the feedback the speaker receives from the audience will affect how the speaker develops an argument.

The complex interactions of the oral situation do not seem reducible to a form such as the syllogistic progression. At best, it would appear that forms of this order—be they syllogistic, qualitative, repetitive, conventional, and minor incidental forms—would appear to give us insight into only a small portion of the dynamic relationships which exist when humans engage in oral communication. (Chesebro, "Toward What?")

In all, this perspective suggests that how one describes, characterizes, and distinguishes forms will depend on the nature of the medium. In the printed medium Burke has traditionally employed, form is a function of how *ideas* are systematically or progressively developed. Indeed, whenever each of us writes or reads, with full concentration, we essentially and ultimately engage in a series of private, isolated, and individual acts. External circumstances have a way of fading from consciousness, the text itself has a way of functioning as the only variable affecting the social meanings understood, and even the author or source of the message—who may be completely unknown to the reader—seems to dissolve as the ideas conveyed in print begin to dominate. In this context, the nature of a form will have certain characteristics.

In sharp contrast, forms are described, characterized, and distinguished in dramatically different ways if the effort is to account for the dynamic interplay of variables that occur as speakers and audiences interact during public, live, face-to-face encounters. At best, a syllogistic-qualitative-repetitive-conventional scheme of forms will account for only a small portion of what occurs within an oral communication field. At worse, such a scheme will appear woefully inadequate, given the full range of functional variables affecting the interaction, and given the descriptive, interpretative, and evaluative tasks a critic must undertake.

Conclusion

Every critical system reflects the cultural orientation of its creator. Critics cannot and do not escape the conditioning of their cultures. As Gregg has maintained, "Human perceptions of the physical and social environment—our system of belief about the world we live in—and our responses to the environment are all patterned by culture. . . . Culture not only controls the way we perceive reality, but also the way in which we 'prove' these perceptions are valid or 'real'" (92–93). The scheme proposed by Kenneth Burke is no exception. The issue is not whether Burke and his system of analysis were a product and reflection of his culture. They are. Being human, Burke could not escape his cultural conditioning. There is no reason to apologize for one's cultural orientation, but it is necessary to recognize the selective and limiting conditioning generated by one's cultural orientation when creating a critical system.[13] Burke's quest for a universal system was limited by his own cultural conditioning. Accordingly, the basic premises of Burke's system must be continually reexamined and extended if the system is to remain a viable mode of analysis in social environments dominated by multicultural communication.

Notes

1. Kenneth Burke died on November 19, 1993, in Andover, New Jersey (see Lyons). This essay was originally written before Burke's death, and it was presented for the first time two weeks after his death. In this context, a statement of my motives is appropriate. I have not written this essay as a postmortem. Rather, I perceive this essay as a celebration of the kind of issues and arguments which Burke would have enjoyed if he were alive today. Indeed, I believe Burke found the type of arguments included in this essay to be one of the factors that contributed to the popularity of his writings.

In terms of my basic stance in relationship to Burke, I have maintained that Burke is "one of the leading U.S. critics in the second half of the 20th century," and I have concluded that "few critics have revealed the scope, imagination, insight, and dazzling concern for symbol-using which Kenneth Burke possesses" (Chesebro, 350, 365). I continue to hold this position.

As I now reflect on Burke's death, I believe that his passing has subjected the discipline of communication and the literary world to a profound loss (see, e.g., Lyons). Yet, I also believe that Burke's published works will live after him, and they will continue to function as a significant corpus for communication theorists and critics.

As might be expected, whenever a system is as widely employed and applied as Burke's system is, issues regarding the system are likely to emerge. To ignore these issues now, because of Burke's death, would be viewed by Burke as an inappropriate reaction, for Burke sought and enjoyed the responses he generated among his colleagues (see, e.g., Brock, Burke, Burgess, and Simons). Because of the critical body of issues raised by Burke, the lines of thought he developed should continue to be examined.

2. This issue has also been explored in the discipline of communication in terms of the ideological nature of rhetorical criticism. Beyond Wander's earlier essay, more recent extensions of these issues are available in special publications such as the spring 1993 issue of the *Western Journal of Communication*, which is devoted to "Ideology and Communication." Additionally, as this discussion implies, I presume that an intimate relationship exists between ideology and cultural conditioning. Specifically, I view ideology as a sociopolitical program— manifest in a set of integrated assertions, theories, and aims—which is characteristic of the thinking of an individual, group, or class, with culture functioning as one of the socialization processes shaping an individual's, group's, or class's ideology.

3. This "test" is profound in several respects, particularly from a rhetorical perspective. Prior to his October 12, 1933 address, Albizu Campos had employed traditional persuasion and accommodation strategies rather than the confrontation strategies his Party was subsequently and formally associated with in 1935 and thereafter. Ferri has argued that the strategies used by Albizu Campos prior to that address were predominantly traditional: "At this point in his political life, Albizu Campos still believed in democratic persuasion and in the modification of

the colonial system by working from within" (71). Ferri has maintained, however, that: " by the 1933 speech, Albizu Campos had moved from the position of urging a political challenge made from within the system to a militant position, challenging the system itself and urging its overthrow" (75).

4. Pedro Albizu Campos was born in Puerto Rico in 1893, graduated from high school in 1912, received a scholarship to study at the University of Vermont in 1912, transferred to Harvard University in 1913, and entered the Harvard School of Law in 1917. After serving in the U.S. Army, he resumed his law studies in 1920 and following administrative delays, he officially received his law degree from the Harvard School of Law in 1923. He returned to Puerto Rico in 1922 and joined the Nationalist Party in 1924. From 1926 through 1930, he traveled in the Caribbean area and South America as a representative of the Nationalist Party. He ran for and lost the office of senator-at-large for the Nationalist Party in 1932. In 1935, the Nationalist Party adopted a resolution to boycott the 1936 elections and to organize and recruit an army of national liberation, and declared the Party to be at war with the United States. In 1936, Albizu Campos was arrested and convicted of conspiracy to overthrow the government, recruit soldiers, and incite rebellion against the United States. In 1943, he was paroled and given permission to live in New York. In 1948, his parole ended, and he returned to Puerto Rico, where he resumed leadership of the Nationalist Party. In 1950, after armed rebellion in Puerto Rico and the Nationalists' attempt to kill President Truman, Albizu Campos was sentenced to life imprisonment. In 1953, he was pardoned, but the pardon was revoked after the attack by the Nationalists on the U.S. House of Representatives in 1954. In 1956, he suffered a stroke in prison, and he was transferred to Presbyterian Hospital in Santurce, Puerto Rico. In 1964, he was pardoned again, and he was removed from the hospital to a private home. In 1965, Pedro Albizu Campos died from pneumonia complicated by a kidney ailment. (These biographical details are provided by Ferri [8–9]).

5. All quotations from Albizu Campos's October 12, 1933 speech used in this analysis are taken from the translation provided by Ferri (131–56).

6. For a discussion of the issues involved in the translation of la raza, see Ferri (68–69); Simounet-Geigel and Geigel.

7. Ferri has identified eight major rhetorical strategies in this speech, including the use of familial substance, allusion, definition, repetition, the rhetorical question, labeling, depiction, and polarization (88–97).

8. The linear-cyclical framework employed here is derived primarily from Ting-Toomey (78), and secondarily from Hall.

9. Mood and tone have been examined as critical concepts by Brower (19–30).

10. It may also be useful to explore how musical variables, such as rhythm and rhymes, constitute significant, if not essential, examples of the spiral form.

11. The author is currently exploring the possibility that Mary Baker Eddy may constitute an example of an Anglo who employed the spiral form as a basic cognitive and organizing pattern. When used by Anglos, or understood within an

186   James W. Chesebro

Anglo context, the meaning and use of the spiral form may change profoundly, and it may be more appropriately understood as a mode of development that some radical and reactionary rhetors employ to establish the power of an alternative lifestyle for an individual, group, or culture. Additionally, as maintained in note 10 immediately above, variables such as rhythm and rhymes may be essentially constituted from and a reflection or manifestation of the spiral form when employed by Latins or within a Latin context. However, it remains unclear if variables such as rhythm and rhyme are retained when used by Anglos or understood within an Anglo context. All of these claims require additional analyses, and they ultimately constitute claims for further research.

     12. A more extended treatment of the concept of an "oral culture" has been provided by others; see, e.g., Ong.

     13. These claims have been illustrated by comparing the linear assumptions governing Burke's concept of a *form* with the spiral assumptions of *form* that can be detected in certain Latin discourse. Implications of this comparison are richly and dramatically illustrated in essays by Shah and Thornton (157) and Martin, Hammer, and Bradford (esp. 172–74).

References

Brock, Bernard L. "A Definition of Four Political Positions and a Description of Their Rhetorical Characteristics." Diss., Northwestern University, 1965.

Brock, Bernard L., Kenneth Burke, Parke G. Burgess, and Herbert W. Simons. "Dramatism as Ontology or Epistemology: A Symposium." *Communication Quarterly* 33 (1985): 17–33.

Brock, Bernard L., Robert L. Scott, and James W. Chesebro. Introduction. In *Methods of Rhetorical Criticism: A Twentieth-Century Perspective*. Edited by B. L. Brock, R. L. Scott, and J. W. Chesebro. Detroit, Mich.: Wayne State University Press, 1990.

Brower, Reuben Arthur. *The Fields of Light: An Experiment in Critical Reading.* New York: Oxford University Press, 1951.

Burke, Kenneth. *Counter-Statement*. Berkeley: University of California Press, 1968 [1931].

——. *The Philosophy of Literary Form: Studies in Symbolic Action.* 3rd ed. Berkeley: University of California Press, 1973 [1941].

Campbell, Karlyn Kohrs. "Response to Forbes Hill." *Central States Speech Journal* 34 (1983): 126–27.

Chesebro, James W. "Extensions of the Burkeian System." *Quarterly Journal of Speech* 78 (1992): 356–68.

——. "Toward What? Insight and Blindness on the Way to 'Consciousness.'" Speech Communication Association Convention. Miami Beach, FL. 1993.

——. "Extending the Burkeian System: A Response to Tompkins and Cheney." Quarterly Journal of Speech 80 (1994): 83–90.

Chesebro, James W., ed. *Extensions of the Burkeian System.* Tuscaloosa: University of Alabama Press, 1993.

Condit, Celeste M. "Post-Burke: Transcending the Sub-stance of Dramatism." *Quarterly Journal of Speech* 78 (1992): 349–55.

———. "Framing Kenneth Burke: Sad Tragedy or Comic Dance?" *Quarterly Journal of Speech* 80 (1994): 77–82.

Corcoran, F. "The Widening Gyre: Another Look at Ideology in Wander and His Critics." *Central States Speech Journal* 35 (1984): 50–53.

Eddy, Mary Baker. *Science and Health with Key to the Scriptures.* Boston, Mass.: The First Church of Christ, Scientist, 1934 [1875].

Ferri, Joseph Michael. "Pedro Albizu Campos, 'El Maestro': Translation and Rhetorical Analysis of Selected Speeches." Diss., Temple University, 1987.

Francesconi, R. "Heidegger and Ideology: Reflections of an Innocent Bystander." *Central States Speech Journal* 35 (1984): 50–53.

Gregg, J. Y. *Communication and Culture: A Reading-Writing Text.* 2nd ed. Belmont, Calif.: Wadsworth, 1985.

Hall, Edward T. *Beyond Culture.* New York: Anchor, 1976.

Hill, Forbes. "A Turn Against Ideology: Reply to Professor Wander." *Central States Speech Journal* 34 (1983): 121–26.

Holland, Virginia. "Rhetorical Criticism: A Burkeian Method." *Quarterly Journal of Speech* 39 (1953): 444–50.

———. "Kenneth Burke's Dramatistic Approach in Speech Criticism." *Quarterly Journal of Speech* 41 (1955): 352–58.

Lyons, R. D. "Kenneth Burke, Philosopher, 96, and New Criticism Founder, Dies." *New York Times*, November 21, 1993, 21.

Martin, J. N., M. R. Hammer, and L. Bradford. "The Influence of Cultural and Situational Contexts on Hispanic and Non-Hispanic Communication Competence Behavior." *Communication Quarterly* 42 (1994): 160–79.

McGee, Michael C. "Another Philippic: Notes on the Ideological Turn in Criticism." *Central States Speech Journal* 35 (1984): 43–50.

Megill, A. "Heidegger, Wander, and Ideology." *Central States Speech Journal* 34 (1983): 114–19.

Nicholas, Marie Hochmuth. (1952). "Kenneth Burke and the 'New Rhetoric.'" *Quarterly Journal of Speech* 38 (1952): 133–44.

Ong, Walter J. *Orality and Literacy: The Technologizing of the Word.* New York: Methuen, 1982.

Rosenfield, Lawrence. R. "Ideological Miasma." *Central States Speech Journal* 34 (1983): 119–21.

Shah, H., and M. C. Thornton. "Racial Ideology in U.S. Mainstream News Magazine Coverage of Black–Latino Interaction, 1980–1992." *Critical Studies in Mass Communication* 11 (1994): 141–61.

Simounet-Geigel, Alma, and Wilfredo A. Geigel. "'La Raza': The Search for Identity." Paper presented at the Speech Communication Association convention, Atlanta, Ga., 1991.

Ting-Toomey, Stella. "Toward a Theory of Conflict and Culture." In *Communication, Culture, and Organizational Processes*. Edited by William L. Gudykunst, L. Stewart, and Stella Ting-Toomey. Beverly Hills, Calif.: Sage, 1985.

Tompkins, Phillip K. "A Note on Burke, Goethe and the Jews." *Quarterly Journal of Speech* 81 (1995): 507–10.

Tompkins, Phillip K., and George Cheney. "On the Limits and Sub-stance of Kenneth Burke and His Critics." *Quarterly Journal of Speech* 79 (1993): 225–31.

Wander, Phillip. "The Ideological Turn in Modern Criticism." *Central States Speech Journal* 34 (1983): 1–18.

Wander, Phillip, ed. Special Issue on "Ideology and Communication." *Western Journal of Communication* 57, no. 2 (1993).

Part IV

The Burkean System

9

Lacan, Burke, and Human Motive

Dina Stevenson

Language is a human universal—our most significant distinguishing characteristic—both intimately personal and public property. The consequences deriving from its use are immediate as well as long-term; it affects our lives in ways simple and complex, profound and commonplace. Naturally we are acutely curious about this thing, this tool, this way of being in the world, and in our curiosity we have problematized issues regarding both its nature and its uses in communication and persuasion.

The problems we have legitimized as subjects of study allow us to consider mysteries apparently inherent in both the structures and the ways we manipulate language to achieve our various ends. The particular ways we have problematized language and its uses have led us to select and have informed our inquiry into, among other things, the processes of text production, metaphor, speech acts, sentence parsing, the role of situation and audience, and the nature of claims and evidence. However, perhaps because it lies hidden beneath language itself, we tend to take for granted the issue of linguistic motive, which remains largely invisible and unconsidered. Burkean theory is therefore unusual in that it problematizes the linguistic motive itself, making it a subject worthy of investigation. Burke's search for a clear understanding of motive not only encompasses insights into the underlying human reasons for discourse production, but is also intended to improve our assessment of the techniques we employ in persuasion.

However, although an investigation into the nature of linguistic motive from its inception to its results in discourse is an outstanding element of Kenneth Burke's rhetorical opus, his theory suffers by not taking into account two significant related disciplines. The first of these is central to the notion of motive itself. If we examine the key terms—pollution, purification, and redemption—whereby Burke explores and explains the linguistic motive and the actions that result from it, we will find that they require an understanding of the psychological responses to our separation from others and of the relationship between aspects of language and psychological development.

Pollution, which each of us experiences at an unaware level from the time we first enter the symbolic order, is a categorical guilt, a feeling of worthlessness that we are driven to overcome. Symbolic acts of purification, through which we attempt to remove the negative experience of pollution, inevitably follow. To engage in purification we must first perceive that certain actions, tied to the values and emotionally weighted facets of particular symbols, will eliminate the guilt of pollution and provide the emotional relief of consubstantiality—a symbolic rejoining with others from whom we have felt separate since the moment of entry into the symbolic.

Symbolic consubstantiality provides a feeling of redemption, an experience of increased self-worth. However, emotional disappointment is also inherent in redemption; it necessarily follows relief because symbolic consubstantiality is not actual rejoining, and pollution, the self-blame for separation, remains and must inevitably reassert itself.

Clearly, then, the concept of motive in general and pollution, purification, and redemption in particular deal with issues profoundly psychological in nature. Thus one noteworthy limitation of Burke's analysis, representing a substantial weakness in his theory of motive, is the lack of specific theoretical grounding in psychological or psychoanalytic theory.

Surprisingly, the second significant inadequacy in his search for motive has to do with language. As Gusfield points out, it is "at the point where the context in which symbols emerge or exist is approached" (41) that a crucial deficiency in Burke's rhetorical theory becomes apparent. Although language is central to his theory of motive and its consequences for rhetorical action, his understanding of language is inadequate to the task he has undertaken.

Therefore, although Burke has had both the insight to problematize linguistic motive and the intuition that an understanding of this motive will lead us to better comprehend both how and why we engage in persuasive discourse, he has fallen short in his investigation of two essential perspectives on which his theory of motive implicitly rests. If we are to accept that the Burkean theory of motive has something significant to offer the field of rhetoric and to move toward applying that theory, we must first overcome its deficiency in the areas of psychology and linguistics.

I propose that we look to Lacanian theory, with its psychoanalytic explanation of human motive and its firm grounding in Saussurian linguistic theory, to overcome these considerable lacks in Burke's theory. It offers a detailed and well-developed account of the complex relationships among language, human psychological development, and motive, which both parallels and complements the Burkean inquiry into rhetorical motive and action.

Language and Division

In his *Rhetoric of Religion*, Burke describes the prelinguistic, premotive infant as inhabiting a realm of "formlessness" (214). Lacan also presents us with a "formless" infant, significantly premature at birth, which he calls a *hommelette*—a play on the words *homme* (man) and omelette, a being without structure or well-defined boundaries. The prelinguistic *hommelette* has developed neither psychostructures nor the fundamentally linguistic ability to differentiate, categorize, evaluate, and understand the chaos of sensory information with which it is bombarded.

Lacan's well-developed theory of the language-using subject is, in both function and formation, congruent with the language-motivated, language-created human being of Burkean theory. Like Burke, Lacan identifies the universal human situation as the emergence from formlessness into the symbolic order that brings recognition of our separateness from others and creates the endless desire to experience oneness with others, or what Burke calls consubstantiality. For Lacan, "there is no escape from the process of symbolization, which is essentially the process of alienation, in the relationship of self to other, and self to self" (MacCannell, 135). Burke also sees symbolicity as that which forms man-as-human, and as that which alienates him from the natural, animal condition of pure motion (Rueckert, 136). For both theorists, alienation results directly from an unbridgeable rift between the symbolic and the real or natural world. But Burke is weak in his explication of this aspect of language and of the psychological factors affecting and affected by language. Lacanian theory, however, has integrated Saussurian linguistics into a clear and well-developed psychoanalytic theory, and this linguistic perspective adds a great deal to his interpretation of the human subject's emergence and motives. A brief examination of Saussurian linguistics is therefore important to our understanding of the ways in which Lacan's work can enhance Burkean theory.

Saussure divides words, or signs, into signifiers and signifieds, often represented as "S/s." Roughly, the signifier is the word itself—marks on a page or vocalized sounds—and the signified is a "meaning" that exists outside the symbolic order but to which we have imperfect, indirect access through more words. Although we experience the S/s pair as "united in one, like two sides of a sheet of paper"(Benvenuto and Kennedy, 114), "the relationship between the sound and the word concept is discontinuous" (Wilden, 212) and therefore arbitrary. That is, although we *experience* signifier and signified as a natural and indivisible unit, this experience merely "creates the illusion of the transparency of language" (Belsey, 38). We are led to assume that meaning and word are one because we have no access to meanings (signifieds) except by naming them in other words (signifiers), which, of course, have signifieds of their own, only accessible through still more words. But in spite of the perceived natural connection between signifier and signified there can be no one-to-one correspondence between a word and the real world that we take it to signify, since "arbitrariness lies between the signifier and 'reality'—whatever that is—between signifier and either 'real objects' or whatever is represented as reality by the social consensus of mutually shared presentations or referents" (Wilden, 216).

These "mutually shared . . . referents" provide, through conventional acceptance, the experience of loosely agreed-upon meanings in language. Such agreement is implicit and normally invisible: "the linguistic community 'agrees' to attach a specific signified to a specific signifier, though in reality, of course, its agreement is not explicitly sought but merely manifested in the fact that certain linguistic units are used and understood" (Belsey, 41). Because each of us is born into a preexisting community, we learn the complex system of conventional consensus by which that community displays its own particular arbitrary relationships between signifiers and signifieds.

According to Saussure, meaning in language is not only disconnected from the real; it also exists in purely relational form. There are no positive terms, and the meaning or signified of a given sign exists exclusively through negative contrasts with all other signifieds in the system. Although Burke is also interested in studying language as a system with internal relational meanings, he approaches it not through linguistics, but rather through logology which looks, for example, at the language of Christianity as a well-developed subsystem. His assumption is that such a quasi-closed subsystem, one that has evolved over a long period of time, will have developed its own distinctive network of relational meanings. His work, however, does not take us much beyond specific examples and results in no clear theoretical insight.

For Burke, the verbal separates us from the nonverbal world, necessarily reducing and distorting it. Paradoxically, it is only through the verbal that we can conceive of the nonverbal, however inaccurately, and we "have no objects without language" (Burke, *Language*, 61). Although this leaves him in agreement with Saussure, who tells us that "there are no pre-existing ideas, and nothing is distinct before the appearance of language" (Saussure, 112), Burke's weakness in the area of linguistic theory leaves him unable to account for the nonrepresentational nature of language, which is central to his conclusions regarding motive, symbolicity, and, in a larger sense, rhetoric itself. Lacan, however, does account for this significant aspect of language; for him, "reality" is a linguistic construct, located in the absolute split between signifier and signified, which results in the arbitrary and conventional nature of language. Inevitably, then, language—while creating ideas and objects— distorts, transcends, and separates us from the real.

It is here that we find theoretical support for Burke's assertion that division from the real and from other people is caused by entry into the symbolic. Since objects exist for us only when they can be named, and since naming in itself separates us from the real, to which it cannot actually refer, we must conclude that entry into the symbolic, our very ability to name, must lead to the experience of separation not only from things, but from other humans who become for us elements of the named, external real.

The Mirror Phase

Before entry into the symbolic with its absolute split from the unmediated experience of the nonverbal real, the infant must, according to Lacanian theory, move through the mirror and Oedipal phases. As we have already seen, the Lacanian *hommelette*, like the Burkean formless infant, experiences oneness with others and with its sur- roundings. Burkean theory does not explicate the stages or lay the groundwork for the infant's emergence from formlessness into language and subjectivity, although this emergence is critical to his analysis of motive. The mirror and Oedipal phases not only provide further infor- mation regarding the prelinguistic experience, they also demonstrate the necessary steps that lead the infant through a transformation from formlessness to subjectivity.

The first of these to occur is the mirror phase, between six and twenty-one months of age, during which the proto-subject first recog- nizes its reflection as its own, or, metaphorically realizes its own physical coherence through visual correlation with the image of another, perhaps its mother or another child. For Lacan, the idealized metaphor for this phase is the proto-subject's sighting of its own image in a mirror, at which point he

seems to go through an initial stage of confusing the image
with reality, and may try to grasp hold of the image behind the
mirror. . . . Then comes the discovery of the existence of an
image with its own properties. Finally, there is the realization
that the image is his own. (Benvenuto and Kennedy, 53)

However, the infant does not see himself in the mirror image as he truly
is, that is, "sunk in motor incapacity, turbulent movement, and fragmentation" (Muller and Richardson, 29), but rather in an apparently integrated, coherent, and purposeful form. Moving from the *hommelette*'s
complete lack of self-concept through its identification with the mirror
image, the proto-subject undergoes a profound transformation. Lacan
describes the infant's experience as one of "orthopaedic" totality
(Sheridan, 4), that is, a prelinguistic concept of physical unity and
control. Through identification with the mirror image a specular "I," a
visual discernment of its body as distinct from surrounding space, comes
into being.

Two noteworthy attributes of the specular "I" are that it is fictional
and that it prefigures the subject's alienation from itself and others in the
symbolic (Sheridan, 2). The first sense in which the specular "I" is fictional is that it gives the infant, whose actual body experience has been
one of incoherence, the false impression of a coherent "self" whose
apparent unity and control can never actually be achieved. This fictional
unity and physical control thrill the infant, representing an ideal
(Sheridan, 2) as it "constitute[s] a registration of the totality of a body
previously lived as fragmented" (Lemaire, 78).

It is also fictional in the sense that it presents the infant with a
reversed form of its image, distorting the experience of the external real.
The distortion and apparent but unattainable coherence constitute the
initial instance of *meconnaissance* or misrecognition. Misrecognition,
which results in misrepresentation, is an inherent quality of language—
which can after all only perceive and talk about what is "out there" in
arbitrary terms that have no direct correspondence to the real they seem
to name. Thus the concept of misrecognition/misrepresentation in the
mirror phase provides a precedent in the infant's psychological development, a virtual space, if you will, for Burke's notion that language distorts but never truly names the real.

The infant's mistaken interpretation of its own mirror image begins
the process of alienation from its original being, from its formless "self"
that has until now experienced the world in a completely unmediated
way. The specular "I" provides the prototype for a concept of "self" that
will later, with the advent of language, be more formally misrecognized/

misrepresented by the linguistic "I" of the developed subject. It presages the subject's final alienation from the real, from itself, and from other subjects who will, inevitably, later be misrecognized and misnamed in language and thereby foreshadows the division caused by entry into the symbolic which, according to Burke, is at the very root of human motive.

The Hortatory Negative and the Lacanian Negative

Burke tells us that the negative is "the very essence of language" (*Language*, 457) because without the negative there can be no drawing of distinctions, no sense of "this, not that" which we must have if we are to distinguish among the myriad of items and actions named in the symbolic. The specular "I" of the mirror phase furnishes the first instance of "self" in context and institutes the proto-symbolic distinction of "self" and "not-self." The concept of the negative is born here in a primordial form and illustrates the sense of the negative required if the infant is to finally emerge as a human subject in the realm of the symbolic. It is the negative that allows for the naming of a thing by a symbol that is not the thing itself but that is instead always a misrecognition/misrepresentation.

Burke tells us that the hortatory is necessarily the significant initial negative that moves the proto-subject into the symbolic, making him fully human. Although Burke offers such metaphors of the original hortatory negative as the "thou-shalt-nots" of the ten commandments (*Rhetoric of Religion*, 20), he does not go beyond these examples to make explicit the particular, universal hortatory negative whereby each infant moves into its truly human state. Lacan, however, does present us with an account of the distinctive initial hortatory negative in his explication of the Oedipal phase.

The *hommelette* experienced himself as one with the mother in the total identification of the original dyadic relationship. He was unable to differentiate himself from her; she seemed an extension of himself, providing food, comfort, warmth, physical contact, attention, and stimulation. Registering the first inkling of his own physical separateness through orthopedic totality and the specular "I," he has become fearful that she may, as a separate being herself, not require him absolutely; he has become driven to make his attachment to her even stronger, trying to coerce her into choosing him above everything else in her world. His need for the mother is so great that he wants to be her desire, that is, to be all that she desires, obviating the possibility of her needing or giving her attention to anyone or anything else.

The mirror phase sets the stage for the linguistic negative, whereby the infant will learn to distinguish himself from others and from all that constitutes the real. As he develops beyond the mirror phase, he inevitably becomes aware that his mother has other relations, symbolized in the Oedipal myth by the father, and that he can be neither wholly one with the mother nor her exclusive desire. This happens as the father, who represents the law of culture and language, intervenes with what Lacan calls *le nom du pere*. Because name (*nom*) and no (*non*) are pronounced identically in French, this phrase has a double meaning: the name of the father and/or the no of the father. The name of the father is significant because it is the child's ability to name concepts and objects, which first occurs in the Oedipal phase, that signals his new capability of distinguishing person from person and thing from thing. When he can name the father, he is also potentially able to name himself, to distinguish himself as an entity separate from his surroundings and from other people.

For Lacan, however, the "no" of the father is of more profound significance because it "is perceived as an implicit 'no' (*non*) to total identification with the mother" (Ragland-Sullivan, 55). The father "renders the mother-child fusion impossible by his interdiction and marks the child with a fundamental lack of being" (Lemaire, 87). The child experiences this lack because his sense of "self" until now has existed through an identification so complete that he has felt himself to be both part of the mother and the incarnation of her desire. In his lack he feels worthless for the first time, and this feeling of worthlessness, along with his recognition of separateness, creates the guilt to which Burke attributes the motive for discourse. The child feels responsible for the loss of unity with the (m)other; had he been in some way "better," she would not have rejected him in favor of the symbolic father. He therefore sets out, in the symbolic, to prove to her, or to her symbolic substitutes, that he is in fact worthy of her desire.

It is important to observe that the characters of the Oedipal drama are metaphoric and may be interpreted rather loosely. The caregiver on whom the infant relies may not be the actual mother; she (or he) may therefore be referred to as the "(m)other," a person who is not merely "other" but who is in fact the *primary* other in the infant's life, the prototype for all of the "others" through whom the subject will eventually attempt to fulfill desire in the symbolic. Lacan refers to the father as the *symbolic* father since this may be any significant third person who, by coming between (m)other and child via the negative, can "teach the infant that the mother and itself are not one but two beings" (Ragland-Sullivan, 55). The paternal "no" provides us with what Burke lacks: a specific, universal hortatory negative whereby each subject enters the world of symbolic action.

In addition to irrevocably dividing the infant from the external real, the initial hortatory negative creates internal divisions: the psychostructures. Up to this point, the infant has been without the psychological divisions of the truly human subject. The paternal hortatory negative renders the child's perception that he is the desire of the (m)other patently untrue. In addition, the authority of the symbolic father makes desire a threat to the child's safety and must be repressed. The unconscious comes into being as a prison for desire, and with it the conscious and the preconscious.

The conscious is the aware, "thinking" mind. The preconscious is "the repository of cultural norms and prohibitions . . . which are capable of becoming conscious" (Silverman, 56). Language, with all of its cultural ideologies, taboos, rules, and values, exists in the preconscious and mediates between the subject and both the internal (unconscious) and external real. The multiple taboos and perceptual limitations of the preconscious law of language repress all prohibited impulses into the unconscious; they will not be available to consciousness "except in disguised form" (Silverman, 55). The subject's "truth," the remnants of the unmediated real that can never be articulated or directly accessed, is submerged in the unconscious as well. Although the contents of the unconscious disappear from awareness, although they can't be named or recognized in language, they attempt throughout life to make themselves known and to find fulfillment.

There is an ongoing tension, perhaps even a war, between the unconscious and the preconscious as the processes of the latter limit and distort expression of unconscious materials. The preconscious, through its cultural-linguistic negatives, acts as a censor, "a repressive authority, determining not only which unconscious materials may gain access to consciousness, but the shape which those materials must take" (Silverman, 60). The "shape" is that of Lacanian demand.

Desire, the most significant element in the unconscious, is not a generalized concept: there is, in fact, only one desire, and that is always the desire to be the desire of the (m)other. Lacan tells us that desire is necessarily distorted, is misrepresented in the symbolic, where it cannot be named but can only be misnamed; the repressions of the preconscious are bypassed through condensation and displacement, which disguise unnameable desire by putting it in terms acceptable to the internalized law of language. The disguised product Lacan calls "demand," which is always a symbolic substitute for desire, or rather a virtually endless chain of necessarily inadequate symbolic substitutes. Through demand, the inaccessibly buried desire to be the desire of the (m)other is misrepresented as the desire to be the desire of the *other*, or others who substitute for the (m)other in the symbolic.

Each demand, while reflecting active unconscious desire, must nevertheless misrepresent it, as language always misrecognizes and misrepresents the real. Demand inevitably leads to disappointment; even if a demand is met, as a product of misrecognition and misrepresentation it cannot lead to fulfillment of desire. Although it is repeatedly denied satisfaction, unconscious desire is not thwarted but continues to appear in new symbolic demands, and these inevitably lead to new disappointments.

Pollution

The hortatory negative of the Oedipal phase creates in us a permanent sense of guilt or pollution, not because we break the law it represents, but "from the mere formulation of the law" (Burke, *Rhetoric of Religion*, 228). Because the "no" and its implicit threat to the child repress into the unconscious the desire to be the desire of the (m)other, the child feels inadequate, divided both externally from the "other" who once made it feel whole, and internally by the newly formed psychostructures.

Burke claims that entry into the symbolic is "analogous to a kind of 'fall' into a technical state of 'grace' that 'perfects' nature" ("Action vs. Motion," 822). It is true that, by imposing an apparent order, the symbolic "perfects," or gives us the reassuring illusion of a nature both ideal and accessible. For Lacan, just as the image of the "self" in the mirror offers the proto-subject "freedom" from its nature as fragmented and incoherent, language-caused separation from the internal and external real offers "the freedom from nature that only culture could provide" (MacCannell, 69). Our tendency to subscribe to the commonsense acceptance of linguistic convention as true reference reenforces the belief that language actually names things in the material world. Thus language, although it is actually always a *meconnaissance*, provides the experience of freedom from the chaos of nonordered nature, and we call this freedom "reality." However, language offers an uncomfortable freedom at best; its price is the lifelong search in the symbolic for a unity and coherence that can never be, and which were only misrecognitions in the first place.

Because "order is impossible without hierarchy" (Burke, *Attitudes*, 374), hierarchic arrangement of symbolic values and substances is inevitable in the language that "orders" our world. MacCannell tells us that

for Lacan as well the symbolic "does not arrange without also eval-
uating" (60), and that only the sign "can create value hierarchies" (110).
Hierarchies derive "directly from the nature of language and [Burke]
discusses [them] as linguistic traits or as evidence of man's 'language-
ridden view' of the world and human relations" (Rueckert, 135).

Burke tells us that "the child's early experiences within the family
reveal the operations of the hierarchic motive" (*Rhetoric of Motives*,
284). Lacanian theory enriches and clarifies this notion with a specific
theoretical description of the original and originating symbolic hierarchy
for all subjects. Through the *nom/non du pere* delivered by the symbolic
father in the Oedipal phase, we learn that it is "good" to renounce the
desire of the (m)other, and that it is "bad," even punishable, to retain
that desire. This sets the prototypical pattern of a "good" (obedience to
the law of language) above a "bad" (desire for unity with the [m]other).

There is also a second hierarchy implicit in the Oedipal phase, one
in which the father, (m)other, and child are represented in descending
order of power and importance. The father has the power; it is he who is
able to break into the primary dyadic relationship. He does so with the
(m)other's implicit or explicit consent, through her recognition of his
right to say "no" to the child. The child experiences himself as outside
the newly perceived parental relationship, as the lowest or least valuable
element in the familial hierarchy, and the feelings of low self-worth that
come with this hierarchic position create and perpetuate guilt.

The first hierarchy participates in the creation and repression of
desire; the second makes it inevitable that the newly created subject will
identify with the father, the power figure, and with the symbolic law he
represents in hopes of becoming once again the focus of the (m)other's
attention and of replacing the father as her desire. Desire and the identification with the law of the father thus lead to what Burke calls the
incurable "hierarchic psychosis" (Rueckert, 132), an irrepressible drive
to assert self-worth through the demand of discourse, misrepresenting
true desire in attempts to symbolically reestablish the original dyadic
relationship.

The categorical guilt that Burke tells us we experience due to our
separation from others, and which is a major factor in his theory of
motive, is a consequence of both hierarchies. The child feels insufficient,
unable to compete with the father for the attention of the (m)other. He is
left with the sense that, if only he could be good enough, he would
regain the lost unity that provided the feeling of safety and love during
infancy.

Burke's definition of man tells us that we are "rotten with perfection,"
(*Language*, 5) and by this he means that "there is a principle of perfection

implicit in the nature of symbol systems; and in keeping with his nature as symbol-using animal, man is moved by this principle" as he strives endlessly to identify himself with "higher" levels of symbolic hierarchies.

Hierarchy requires not only concepts of "higher" and "lower," but a "highest" element, a "godhead." This godhead is "that which is most valuable in a given value system, whether it happens to be moral excellence, material wealth, physical beauty, athletic prowess, or scholarly excellence" (Rueckert, 148). The godhead is always an ideal, a principle of perfection in a given realm, and as an ideal it is always in fact unattainable. The unattainable nature of godheads inevitably leads to guilt, or pollution, and if we take the desire to be the desire of the (m)other as the original, repressed godhead, we are "rotten" because we feel responsible for having lost the original unity of the mother–infant relationship, and we are driven by the desire for, and inability to regain, that perfect union, that quintessential godhead.

The original hierarchies of the Oedipal phase are not the only ones operative in human motive. A language/culture embodies the possibility, indeed the inevitability, of multiple, conflicting hierarchies, which themselves shift internally depending on the situation in which they are called into play. Each hierarchy has a godhead or point of highest perfection. However, were we to symbolically achieve, in our own eyes, the highest level of a given hierarchy—to reach that which has symbolized perfection—the hierarchy would inevitably shift and grow such that there would be a new godhead, misrepresenting in new ways desire, which remains out of reach. Because the perfection we see in a godhead exists only in the symbolic, it is a misrepresentation, a false cognate for desire; therefore, reaching hierarchic perfection cannot provide fulfillment of desire. To come to terms with the feeling of unworthiness that persists in spite of our achievements, we adjust hierarchies, we set new terms for perfection, new symbolic goals to re-represent the possibility that desire is attainable.

The hierarchies by which we judge ourselves to be inadequate exist in the preconscious. Desire remains active, though repressed in the unconscious. It tries repeatedly to make itself known and to achieve perfection in the form of reunification, as well as perpetuating guilt because reunification is unattainable. The unattainable nature of true perfection ensures the perpetuation of guilt.

Purification

Through purification techniques, we attempt to experience ourselves as symbolically higher on one or more of the many shifting and reforming hierarchies that represent the internalized law of language. By doing so we hope to become desirable to the (m)other, to regain the oneness of infancy—to become consubstantial with the other and to thereby undo division.

After the Oedipal phase, one thing the newly emerged subject does in the symbolic to live with the pain of separation and his own lack is to "seek . . . what Lacan calls symbolic identification with the father—that is to say, he must take over the *function* of the father" (Wilden, 165). The child prepares to do this as he internalizes the laws, values, taboos, and imperatives inherent in the language/culture into which he is born and which the symbolic father represents. According to Burke, we enter a covenant with language, what Lacan might see as a compulsion to obey and enforce the law of language in order to be as powerful as the father, to best him at his own game, and to thereby replace him as the mother's desire. Burke tells us that the laws of language are arranged hierarchically and embody the motives peculiar to the symbolic ("Action/ Motion," 813). However, a given language/culture can only provide secondary motives. They are misrepresentations of the real, the motives of demand rather than of desire, and they exist because we assume that language names the real, that its taboos and beliefs are objectively valid and that therefore its hierarchies have real value. Because we take over the function of the father through the Oedipal phase, we are motivated to act in accordance with the law of language, to obey the hierarchic dictates of preconscious symbolic contents.

In symbolic action we attempt to persuade substitute "others" of our value and to experience their approval as evidence that we are worthy of being the desire of the (m)other. In this way, although "[t]he signifier . . . separates us from each other [and] disrupts any 'communication' we might have with each other," it also, according to Lacan, "puts us on a route, a path, that goes towards the other" (MacCannell, 9). Demand, then, is the essence of rhetoric; it is expression, however misrepresentative, of the fundamental human motive. Because desire, the primary, immutable motivating force, is inaccessible, it is through demand, desire's symbolic distortion, that we try repeatedly through discourse to overcome the inevitable separation of subject from subject instituted with the advent of language, to reunite and fulfill desire.

Burke gives the name *purification* to the rhetorical means by which we attempt to rid ourselves of pollution, and with this term he lays out the function of Lacanian demand in rhetoric. The misrepresentations of demand make use of the secondary motives of language itself, controlled by our belief in the particular, hierarchically arranged, value-laden laws of culture. Because symbolic hierarchies are culture-specific, the culture's values will be reflected in any instance of demand. Culture-specific symbolic hierarchies tell us what is "good" and therefore to be identified with and attained as evidence of our successful takeover of the function of the symbolic father, of our integration into the law of language. Identification with higher levels of linguistic/cultural hierarchies will, we hope, allow us to succeed, however metaphorically, in the ongoing competition with the father for the attention of the (m)other whose desire we desire to be.

Burke defines two kinds of demand in purification: scapegoating and self-mortification. Scapegoating is a symbolic projection of pollution onto some external object or person; it is a defensive denial of guilt by which we attempt to feel pure, hierarchically elevated above others, desirable to the (m)other substitutes in the symbolic, and therefore, by extension, desirable to the (m)other.

Self-mortification, on the other hand, involves implicitly taking responsibility for guilt. To eliminate guilt by self-mortification we symbolically punish and purify ourselves, we deny ourselves pleasures in order to hierarchically elevate and make ourselves desirable. We may inflict the symbolic punishments of self-mortification through language, as with self-denigration, or by engaging in symbolic physical acts. From cosmetic surgery to dieting to voluntarily giving up things we really want, we find ways to "apologize" through self-mortification for the worthlessness we feel in response to the Oedipal event. Each of these is an instance of demand, a plea for forgiveness by which we hope to become again one with—and the desire of—the (m)other through her symbolic substitutes.

Redemption

Redemption, or the elimination of categorical guilt and the fulfillment of desire, is the goal of each act of purification. However, although we may experience enhanced desirability through symbolic improvement of our hierarchic status, the resulting redemption is always short-lived. From Lacan we learn that this must be so because each demand is a *meconnaissance* of desire: even if the demand is met, as a product of misrecognition its fulfillment cannot be the fulfillment of desire. Each time, therefore, purification must lead to disappointment. What we gain is only a temporary feeling of desirability, verified by the experience of consubstantiality with a substitute other or others. Although we will try, through successive misrepresentations in the demand of discourse, we can never again achieve the original, prelinguistic experience of total, coherent identity with the other, and we remain permanently burdened with unfulfillable desire and feelings of worthlessness.

Burke provides the example of courtly love, with its unattainable goal of unity. Just as all human subjects have the impossible desire to be the desire of the (m)other as a main motivating force, a knight ideally wooed a married or otherwise unattainable woman, courting her

> in terms of eternity, that is, in perpetual repetition. . . . On firm moral and legalistic grounds, their union was . . . impossible. Hence he could safely become her knight . . . he could . . . court her in terms of the infinite, the incommensurable, the absurd, the faith that will somehow bring about the impossible. (*Rhetoric of Motives*, 250)

Since success is impossible from the outset, courtly love is a form of self-mortification in which the knight asks for what must be denied him, has his worthlessness confirmed by his inability to attain his goal, and is purified by his suffering. The unattainable woman functions as a metaphor for the (m)other, who is also impossibly wooed in the symbolic. It is significant that Burke refers to the wooing as "infinite . . . incommensurable . . . [and] absurd." It must be infinite and absurd in its repetitions, since no attempt can possibly succeed; it is incommensurable because it cannot be measured against the true unquantifiable desire that it misrepresents. The knight also courts his lady in faith, and this is the implicit, mistaken faith that demand actually does represent desire and can therefore lead to fulfillment.

Conclusion

Human motive, then, is both created by and acted on in the symbolic. Pollution is the result of division from others in the Oedipal phase; purification is the action of demand in repeated and hopeless attempts to regain lost unity; redemption is the temporary and counterfeit feeling of goodness, of shedding guilt through acts of purification. When Burkean pollution, purification, and redemption are viewed through Lacanian psychoanalytic theory, they become more than behaviors in which we engage in order to persuade. They are the inevitable results of our particular construction through language, of desire, of the psychostructures, and of the failure and repetition of demand.

Rhetoric, then, is the manipulation of situation-appropriate, symbolic purification devices whereby we follow the route of demand as we attempt to achieve consubstantiality, to overcome the gap in our humanness—the gap, which we may never truly cross—to unity.

References

Belsey, Catherine. *Critical Practice*. New York: Methuen, 1980.

Benvenuto, Bice, and Roger Kennedy. *The Works of Jacques Lacan: An Introduction*. New York: St. Martin's, 1986.

Burke, Kenneth. *Attitudes Toward History*. 3rd ed. Berkeley: University of California Press, 1984.

————. *A Grammar of Motives*. Berkeley: University of California Press, 1969 [1945].

————. *Language as Symbolic Action: Essays on Life, Literature, and Method*. Berkeley: University of California Press, 1966.

————. "(Nonsymbolic) Motion/(Symbolic) Action." *Critical Inquiry* 4 (1978): 809–38.

————. *A Rhetoric of Motives*. Berkeley: University of California Press, 1969 [1950].

————. *The Rhetoric of Religion: Studies in Logology*. Berkeley: University of California Press, 1970.

Gusfield, Joseph R., ed. *Kenneth Burke: On Symbols and Society*. Chicago: University of Chicago Press, 1989.

Lemaire, Anika. *Jacques Lacan*. Translated by David Macey. Boston, Mass.: Routledge & Kegan Paul, 1977.

MacCannell, Juliet Flower. *Figuring Lacan: Criticism and the Cultural Unconscious*. Lincoln: University of Nebraska Press, 1986.

Muller, John P., and William J. Richardson. *Lacan and Language*. New York: International Universities Press, 1982.

Ragland-Sullivan, Ellie. *Jacques Lacan and the Philosophy of Psychoanalysis*. Urbana: University of Illinois Press, 1987.

Rueckert, William H. *Kenneth Burke and the Drama of Human Relations*. Minneapolis: University of Minnesota Press, 1963.

Saussure, Ferdinand de. *Course in General Linguistics*. Translated by Wade Baskin. New York: McGraw-Hill, 1966.

Sheridan, Alan, trans. *Ecrits by Jacques Lacan*. New York: Norton, 1977.

Silverman, Kaja. *The Subject of Semiotics*. New York: Oxford University Press, 1983.

Simons, Herbert W. and Trevor Melia, eds. *The Legacy of Kenneth Burke*. Madison: University of Wisconsin Press, 1988.

Wilden, Anthony (ed.). *Jacques Lacan: Speech and Language in Psychoanalysis*. Baltimore, Md.: The Johns Hopkins University Press, 1968.

10

Burkean Social Hierarchy and the Ironic Investment of Martin Luther King

James F. Klumpp

In the opening decades of the twenty-first century, social demographics will pose their greatest challenge yet to the American culture: the point will be passed when Americans whose ancestors arrived on these shores from Europe will slip from a majority to a plurality. In the time of this great change, Americans will face the need to reinvent power relationships to construct a less graded society, drawing life from its rich ethnic and racial mix. To make this future, Americans must begin from a past and present rife with differentiated power. They must confront a long history of racism—from 250 years of slavery to the internment of Japanese Americans—from which they must fashion a multiracial culture. And they must confront the resistance of male and white power in their own time—documented in the glass ceiling and anti-immigrant agitation—that must be overcome if a productive and just society is to be accomplished. Will the American strength—the diversity of heritage and experience—be its advantage or its downfall?

All of the resources of the society will need to contribute to assure creation of a better society, including the devoted energies of the custodians of discourse. Discourse can be a resource through which we achieve the just and productive society that manifests a community for all, or it can be the poison that precludes the "better life." The challenge to those of us who study discourse is all the greater because discourse is a domain that reveals a particular obstacle to such cultural transformations: oftentimes sorting friend from foe and advance from retreat is surprisingly difficult. Rhetoric is the art in which discourse is turned toward inventing the future from the material of the past and present. The process through which adaptation emerges from the midst of reaffirmation is a delicate process that defines the tentativeness inherent in peaceful change. Understanding the transformation and meeting the challenge of facilitating its success will require all the resources our understanding of discourse can muster.

In the face of this complicated challenge, the need for the resources of Kenneth Burke's writings on rhetoric seems compelling. A plethora of Burkean concepts present themselves to students of discourse as powerful perspectives on the challenge: language as equipment for living, permanence and change, perspective by incongruity, the power of symbolic motivation, symbols of authority, symbolic transformation, attitudes toward history, and, of course, hierarchy. Perhaps no concept rushes as quickly to the heart of the challenge society faces as hierarchy. The central questions of the time seem posed by the fact of social hierarchy: Can a society be constructed that is consistent with the equitable values of democracy when the differences of a diverse population offer so many opportunities for social gradation? Or, perhaps even closer to the point, can the tension between equality and merit yield to social forms that maximize productivity *and* social justice? Burke theorizes the difficulties and opportunities inherent in the intertwining of hierarchy and discourse. This interpenetration of discourse and social form—so prevalent in Burke's many concepts—defines precisely the challenge to, and thus the opportunity for, students of discourse.

The potential contribution of the Burkean perspective, particularly his concept of hierarchy, is threatened, however, by the rush to simplify the Burkean notion to help locate him as either friend or foe. I believe that two tasks are critical to reinstall the power of the concept to play its potential role in meeting the coming challenge: to expand the texture of the concept by reacquiring its place in Burke's system and to explore the potential power of the concept to help us negotiate the complicated hierarchical impact of discourse. A revitalized Burkean concept provides another tool with which critics can approach the challenging problems of the next century.

Thus, I will argue for the vitality of criticism grounded in the Burkean notion of hierarchy. I will argue that the Burkean notion is a complex set of arguments, rife with ambiguity that permit friendly and unfriendly constructions as the notion is taken beyond the Burkean corpus. I should preface such a project by shunning a commitment to "purify" misinterpretation of Burke's words or thoughts. Although much of the dispute over the implications and usefulness of hierarchy in the Burkean system results from extrapolations that depart from Burke in important ways, I recognize that the dispute begins in the ambiguities in Burke's work. I will deal with Burke's words, to be sure, but by using them to explore the issues with dramatistic or logological criticism as the context. I will begin by identifying the notion of hierarchy in the Burkean viewpoint, then will explore its possibilities for criticism, and finally will illustrate with an examination of a foundational plea for equality.

A Burkean Viewpoint on Hierarchy

Over my years of teaching Burkean criticism, no element of Burke's theory has been as controversial with my students as the assertion that "hierarchy is inevitable." Of course, the assertion read as a statement about social hierarchy goes against a basic faith of the American left. Among the most virulent reactions to this statement are colleagues and students identifying themselves as feminists who view hierarchy as a characteristic of patriarchy and whose personal commitments to constructing social equality seem challenged. This history justifies a focus on Burke's position on the inevitability of hierarchy. If Burkean criticism is, in fact, rooted in the assumption that gradations of social station are intractable and beyond the influence of discourse, the current project is a nonstarter. So close attention is mandated to axioms and assumptions about hierarchy in working the relationship between hierarchy and discourse.

Such attention reveals that Burke's argument for hierarchy is neither as straightforward nor as simple as its centrality to his system would indicate. The claim of intractability is often stated in terms of social hierarchy: "social hierarchy is an inevitable part of the human condition."[1] Furthermore, the claim is taken to be a characteristic of what political scientists used to call the "distribution of power in society," a rather static characterization of pecking order; in pentadic terms, hierarchy is an empirically documented fact about the social scene. By rooting hierarchy in a scenic-dominated account of human relations, this account makes hierarchy's place in symbolic action derivative.

This image fits the metaphysics of a social scientist that Burke explicitly rejects (*Permanence*, li) more than that of a humanist whose system evolves from literary interests. I will attempt to locate the latter interest as a more fruitful stance for rhetorical criticism, thus rooting social hierarchy in interpretive processes. Explicating this position will require exploring (1) the claim of inevitability and (2) the arguments that establish the claim.

Locating the Claim

There are, in fact, at least three possible constructions of the claim that "social hierarchy is inevitable." The first is to take the claim as an *empirical claim* about status relations in human society. "Inevitable" in this construction implies the universality of the generalization. The second would take hierarchy to be a *dimension of status relations,* useful to grade societies from authoritarian to egalitarian. With this interpretation "inevitability" would be not so much an empirical claim as an operational entailment definitionally ancillary to a particular system for understanding culture. The third possibility would take hierarchy to be what social scientists would call a "variable," one of the *alterable dimensions of ongoing social life* through which social relations are accomplished. This third possibility is a more fluid construction, in which "inevitable" has some of the flavor of operational fact that characterizes the second possibility, but is grounded in social praxis rather than a "scientific model."

These three possibilities are neither a continuum nor are they mutually exclusive but, as primary stances, they enact dramatically different moralities. Lurking behind the first is a hint of authoritarian societies with rigid caste gradients. A claim of "inevitability" in this context entails a resignation from the possibility of alternative social relations. This attitude of resignation precludes meaningful moral judgment. The second stance, by contrast, opens the possibility of categorizing and then passing moral judgment on societies. Because this possibility is based in categorical method, it also introduces the possibility of setting off particular societies in which Burke's method might be appropriate from others in which it would fail. The third stance opens the possibility of the richest morality of choice by individuals and societies but based on what is *done* with hierarchy rather than the *fact* of hierarchy. I will argue that this final stance opens a place for symbolic action and therefore offers the most promise for insightful criticism.

Arguments to Support the Claim

The question that sorts various arguments for the inevitability of hierarchy are summarized by this question: In Burke's account of hierarchy, is hierarchical social status posited as the source of hierarchy in social systems, or is hierarchical social status viewed as derived from some more basic hierarchical action? The empirical claim among the three possible stances would entail the former position; the other stances are consistent with either of these positions. By tracing Burke's arguments for hierarchy, I will indicate my claim that the third stance with a focus on hierarchy in language offers the most fruitful approach to criticism. To do so, I examine three potential lines of argument.

Hierarchy Is Empirically Characteristic of All Human Societies. The empirical claim about social status implies a test by an immediate search for disproving examples. I have never found a place in the Burkean corpus where I believe that empirical generalization is the main force of his claim nor where Burke offers a proof based solely on generalization across societies. Although Burke has penned many claims, and "never" is a bold assertion, argument by empirical generalization would seem unlikely given the typical contextualist moves of his systematic inquiry.[2] Typically, only two universals—the common experience as biological animals and symbol using—mark Burke's discussion of humans (see, for example, *Permanence*, 275). Furthermore, Burke is far more likely to generate proof from the rich variety of human societies than to generalize across them.[3]

Hierarchic Structure Is Inherent in Systematization. The second line of argument is proffered in *Rhetoric of Motives*:

> The hierarchic principle itself is inevitable in systematic thought. It is embodied in the mere process of growth, which is synonymous with the class divisions of youth and age, stronger and weaker, male and female, or the stages of learning, from apprentice to journeyman to master. (141)

Burke's argument here is that the act of systematization—roughly arrangement—trades on the ordering of elements. Such orderings establish hierarchies. This becomes especially true when the ordering has an aura of development. So-called natural hierarchies thus emerge, such as age being superior to youth and master being superior to apprentice.

Three things are important to observe from this line of argument. First, Burke explicitly refers to the hierarchial *principle* as the inevitable element. The assertion is that systematization elevates the principle of the system over the *specific content* of the system. In developmental series, this is the entelechial principle evident in the "end" of the series. Thus, the principle of age takes precedent over the ages of a group of people. Age is a natural entelechial principle, so the older among the group of people are elevated over the younger. In this way, the hierarchic elevation of the principle reaches down into social order and imposes status hierarchy. Thus, the force of the argument for the claim about the social system is not empirical but derivative from the claim about systematization.

Second, the argument reverses the relative power of social status and interpretive construal, linking the two by elevating the latter to

primary. Burke continues in the paragraph to explain how he moves from
the claim about the definition of systematization to social hierarchy:

> But this last hierarchy [apprentice to journeyman to master] is
> as good an indication as any of the way in which the "natural-
> ness" of grades rhetorically reënforces the protection of priv-
> ilege. Though in its essence purely developmental, the series is
> readily transformed into rigid social classifications, and these
> interfere with the very process of development that was its
> reason for being. (*Rhetoric of Motives*, 141)

System requires a rhetoric—perhaps it is better at this point to say
motive or orientation—which pronounces the differentiations and
grading that define it. When the abstract orientation of the system is
turned toward humans, social hierarchy results. Furthermore, the social
hierarchy performed in the motive then shapes social action. Now
hierarchy has become a living social system in which masters assert their
superiority, consumers seek the work of masters rather than apprentices,
and apprentices strive to learn so that they may pass through the
structure of social rituals that will see them arriving at the level of the
masters. In short, if systems are to be lived within, then the notion of
hierarchy that is inherent in the notion of system—the *supremacy* of the
systemic principle—infuses the lived-within system with social hierarchy.

Third, the ironic voice enters this relationship between systemness
and social hierarchy to introduce variation within the hierarchy. The
final clause of the last quotation indicates that hierarchies contain
internal irony. The tendency to create social structure with rigid class
gradients mutes the developmental energy: masters attempt to protect
their privilege. Of course, equally plausibly, the developmental principle
provides power that can be employed to weaken the rigidity of social
hierarchy: a master without an apprentice is less a master. This irony
infuses the rhetoric of ritual. If rituals are too open, their social significance is lost; if too closed, pressure builds to dethrone masters. Thus, a
rhetoric develops in which the master richly praises the achievement of
the apprentice and the apprentice proudly celebrates the master. The
resources of this rhetoric permit variation in the relative power of each
within the hierarchy. In sum, the relationship between the principle of
systemness and the social hierarchy is rhetorical, therefore rests on a
paradox, and is capable of generating reconfigured power relationships.

The analysis performed on master and apprentice can equally be
performed on other principles based on time, or value, or natural
sequences. There are, no doubt, other systemic principles as well, and

each has potential as rhetorical force to create social hierarchy. But is a principle of hierarchy evident in all ordering? Or, does Burke's argument merely apply to those orderings which do obviously build on such a principle? Two examples from Burke's series in *Rhetoric of Motives*— "stronger and weaker" and "male and female"—may help explore these question. These two pairs are not naturally developmental, and Burke never provides a similar account of hierarchical entailment in ordering them. The viability of this second argument depends on doing so.

The first is fairly straightforward from the act of valuing. "To value" is to elevate (and thus a particular type of systematization). In language, valuing is performed through differentiation and grading. "Stronger" is a value based in a particular hierarchical principle (although not a natural one like aging, but grounded in the language act of valuing). One can certainly imagine other hierarchical principles, including, I believe, a hierarchical principle that values weakness over strength (one can imagine two psychologists discussing their patients in a way that makes the "best" one the one with the "best" weaknesses). The act of elevation that inheres in valuing, however, does imply a graded differentiation which, through the same logic as in the developmental series, becomes a principle of social structure.

Burke's inclusion of "male and female" is even more interesting and goes to the heart of the dispute about the inevitability of hierarchy. (Certainly, it is as much a manifestation of sexism as "White" and "Black" would be a manifestation of racism, although in Burke's defense, it is not clear whether he is asserting or reporting here.) A differentiation of male and female is an ordering of a kind. It also contains a principle— either biological or gendered differentiation—but neither term naturally defines itself as the entelechial principle that transforms differentiation into hierarchy. This seems to represent a principle that requires something more to transform into social hierarchy. We would have to look beyond the natural resources of developmental principles to find another resource that can create a hierarchical principle to order male and female—the story of Adam and Eve, for example—and thus serve as a basis for transforming the distinction into social hierarchy. These two examples, "stronger/weaker" and "male/female," thus entail the resources of language beyond mere organizing, and thus bring us to the third potential line of argument.

Hierarchy Is Entailed in the Character of Language. There are several ways of constructing such an argument. Allow me to develop one.[4] It begins with the character of naming. A name marks off particular parts of undifferentiated experience as important (*Grammar*, 24;

Permanence, 92). In doing so, a name must inherently elevate its principle over other possible principles, thus a hierarchic principle lies at the center of definition. To define is to "mark off" and to stress that which is marked off (*Grammar*, 24).

As an inherent resource of naming, one of language's native powers is to systemize experience into hierarchy. A name creates a hierarchy of the elements of lived experience—those to which we attend elevated above those we ignore. To name me a "professor" invokes several hierarchic principles simultaneously: for example, one's work (or one's employment) as one's identity, or bureaucratic title over activity (cf. teacher as an alternative). In fact, more than elements of experience are elevated in the simple act of naming—the name invokes a cluster of vocabulary that may be called on as a way of understanding. Names are not isolated in a sort of dictionary singleness in language-in-use, but are tied to complexes of vocabulary that accompany invocation. When a single word is considered within these complexes taken as a whole, invoking "professor" as my moniker places me in the context of an activity in which the name signifies my success. An act of language carries attitudes that further elevate particular elements of experience and disparage others: in our example, the name "*professor*" uttered with contempt—"He is one of those tax-sucking purveyors of venom to our young"—or with awe—"You must meet Professor Klumpp. He is on the faculty at the University of Maryland."

These resources of language may be overt or implicit in language. So-called scientific vocabularies—what Burke calls semantic meaning (*Philosophy*, 140–43)—work to avoid elevating, yet they implicitly contain hierarchic principles that value objectivity and precision over motive and ambiguity (*Permanence*, 95–96).

The central argument here is that hierarchy, its creation or invocation, is intrinsic in language. This does not yet, of course, indicate that social order inherently invokes hierarchical principle. To the central argument must be added the power of language to structure social order. There are three alternative relationships that may form this bridge. First is the link between language and action. Burke punctuates characterizations of action not in the single space-time metaphysics of a moment but in the complex patterns of behavior that he calls "motives." "Motives are distinctly linguistic products," Burke writes in *Permanence and Change*.

> We discern situational patterns by means of the particular vocabulary of the cultural group into which we are born. Our minds, as linguistic products, are composed of concepts (ver-

bally molded) which select certain relationships as meaningful. Other groups may select other relationships as meaningful. (35)

Motives thus structure our action. In *Attitudes Toward History* Burke writes:

> "Action" by all means. But in a complex world, there are many kinds of action. Action requires programs—programs require vocabulary. To act wisely, in concert, we must use many words.
> . . .
> Names shape our relations with our fellows. They prepare us *for* some functions and *against* others, *for* or *against* the persons representing these functions. (4).

The complexes of action that we recognize as social hierarchies are played out in the distribution of value with particular vocabularies of motive.

This is the principle evoked in the second bridge and Burke's most obnoxious statement to those who are concerned about social hierarchy: the clause in his "Definition of Man," where he characterizes humans as "goaded by the spirit of hierarchy" (*Language*, 15).[5] Upon introducing this phrase, Burke immediately offers an alternative phrasing, "moved by a sense of order," thus tying the point with his argument from systemization. He then discusses the phrase in terms of his discussion of hierarchy in *Rhetoric of Motives*. But the phrase may be fleshed out equally well by reference to the principle of piety and system-building discussed in *Permanence and Change*. Once humans have named something, they work to *perfect* the name; that is, they respond to the thing in terms of the name they have applied and the names that cluster with it in a motive (*Permanence*, 74+). This is the same impulse that gives rise to the "well-rounded statement about motives" in *Grammar of Motives* (xv; thus, the pentad), and the fifth clause of his definition "rotten with perfection" (*Language*, 16). "The principle of perfection," he writes, "is central to the nature of language as motive. The mere desire to name something by its 'proper name,' or to speak a language in its distinctive ways is intrinsically 'perfectionist'" (16). The language-user carries the hierarchical impulse that singles out "the significant" from linguistic naming into social acting. Actions then order the social order.

The third basis for the merger of language and social structure Burke explains in a scheme of "hierarchies of terminology" explicated in *Language as Symbolic Action* (373–76). Burke differentiates vocabularies in four domains: the physical, the grammatical, the sociopolitical, and the supernatural. Burke argues that we draw names from one of these domains to allow us to pronounce relationships in the other. For example, we employ the invocation "Father" toward God (supernatural) in a gesture that recognizes His elevation over us with a terminology and hierarchical principle drawn from the domain of the family (socio-political). In addition, of course, the invocation's use in religious authority (creator) also reinforces the terminology's power within the family (my father created this family in his image). "Father" and "child" also invoke the physical in asserted biological link. In fact, in a culture whose metaphysics is dominated by physical scientism, the sociopolitical is often experienced as less real than the physical, so the metaphorical move from the physical to the sociopolitical is more powerful than the move from the supernatural to the sociopolitical.

Our example has by now illustrated the resources of language that can harden into hierarchies of social order—for example, sexism and patriarchy. Language provides the mode by which these hierarchies are performed in social action. But does their emergence represent an inherent characteristic of language, or merely an avoidable perversion of language's power? Burke answers:

> To say that hierarchy is inevitable is not to say that any particular hierarchy is inevitable; the crumbling of hierarchies is as true a fact about them as their formation. But to say that the hierarchic principle is indigenous to all well-rounded human thinking, is to state a very important fact about the rhetorical appeal of dialectical symmetry. And it reminds us, on hearing talk of equality, to ask ourselves, without so much as questioning the possibility that things might be otherwise: "Just how does the hierarchic principle work in this particular scheme of equality?"
>
> Though *hierarchy* is exclusive, the *principle* of hierarchy is not; all ranks can "share in it alike." (*Rhetoric of Motives*, 141)[6]

Equality of human relationship is possible in social status. It is one of the possible distributions of power. But two things must always be said about such equality. First, to seek it invokes the hierarchic principle in which equality is elevated over inequality.[7] Second, equality is established rhetorically (the metaphor of equality seems to evoke the physical metaphor of a scale with each tray equally distant from the horizontal plane) based on some hierarchical principle: thus, (hierarchic principle 1) gender is not a *proper* principle of social inequality, (hierarchic principle 2) those who *discriminate* on that basis are to be *condemned*.

Thus, the essential position of this line of argument is that hierarchy is born in the inherent hierarchical principle in the nature of language and derivatively experienced in social order. Language neither dictates a particular hierarchy nor precludes relationships of equality. Language merely dictates that ordering will follow from the inevitability of a hierarchical principle.

My preference is for this last line of argument. Burke never explicitly and completely develops the line of argument in his work, but at many places he indicates this justification. In *Rhetoric of Motives* he writes: "In any order, there will be the mysteries of hierarchy, since such a principle is grounded in the very nature of language" (279). In many places in his work, Burke stresses that (1) no single hierarchical principle is inevitable, and (2) human action is shaped by the hierarchical principle, *not* by the hierarchy per se. Burke's assertion, therefore, is not fundamentally an empirical assertion, but the following of an inherent characteristic of language into its implications in human action.

Of course, one final argument needs to be examined: merely saying Burke does not base his claim in empirical generalization does not release us from the empirical obligation. If nonhierarchical societies can be found, isn't the line of reasoning defeated? It is at this point that Burke's commitment to the hierarchical principle rather than to hierarchy becomes crucial. Even a society that values equality, or a society that lives out equality, operates on the hierarchical principle that elevates equality over inequality and invokes some hierarchical principle to declare the basis of equality in social status. In one sense, we could therefore challenge anyone to point empirically to a social order they believe escapes hierarchical principle and we would point out the hierarchic principle.

But is the game rigged? Is this not a manifestation of what Stephen Pepper has called contextualism's "catch me if you can" theory of truth? The charges assume that Burke's "game" is empirically sorting social orders into hierarchical and nonhierarchical and asserting that the latter set is empty. On the contrary, his assertion is more dramatic, a part of his major methodological move: removing language from the traditional viewpoint that contextualizes it within a radical institutional functionalism,[8] to conversely view the power of discourse forms as a context for society.[9] In an addendum to *Counter-Statement* (218) Burke explains this difference: that his primary empirical facts are language practices and sociality and, contrary to traditional social science, his task is to view the latter from the perspective of the former rather than the other way around.

Does such a focus make Burke only relevant to societies founded on inequality? Although the question would seem natural, it merely reiterates the emphasis on social function over language and the sorting task that preoccupies traditional social science. Burke would displace the question itself, stating the basic task of social science differently: the *pragmatic* task is to work with the powers of language in society toward a more humane social order. Indeed, *Permanence and Change* is a plea for such a "program."

The notion of hierarchy in Burke's work is part and parcel of his primary task: to explore the implications of a viewpoint that features language as the primary human act infusing social order. Burke's work is, therefore, contextualist in viewpoint, and the empirical question of social hierarchy becomes a methodological correlate of the method's power to explain variety of social form, rather than a threshold test of the method's assumptions.

An Attitude Toward Hierarchy

Before exploring the implication for criticism, a visit to Burke's attitude toward hierarchy will illuminate the critical stance implied in his viewpoint. In fact, "attitude"—complete with the ambiguity it has for Burke—is just the right word. Burke sees attitude as a pre-action closely tied to the body. When he proposes to add it to the pentad to create a hexad, the move is designed to add the body to the mix (*Grammar*, 237–38). The representative anecdote is "we are ready to grasp the hammer before we reach it, and the attitude of manipulatory response directs the approach" (George Herbert Mead, cited on 238). So we are interested in Burke's predisposition toward the struggles entailed in hierarchy.

The most unfortunate result of locating Burke's notion of hierarchy in social status is to therefore identify him with a rhetoric of domination (see, for example, Foss and Griffin, 340). This characterization ignores the major leveling social project in Burke's work, and leaves us with a portrayal at great variance with his activism. Burks is certainly correct biographically when he characterizes Burke's attitude as "an endless questioning of bureaucratic hierarchy" (229). Burke mixes a linguistic realism with a social activism.[10] Hierarchy is an inevitable part of the former, and a central dimension of the latter upon which rhetoric plays out. In fact, Burke's tracing of the power of hierarchy as a linguistic resource into social hierarchy is to focus on the rich possibilities for linguistic strategies that create a wide variety of forms in social hierarchy. Those resources have been exploited in power relationships of domination, and Burke is concerned with unmasking this domination (for example, in his greatest criticism, "The Rhetoric of Hitler's 'Battle,'"

Philosophy). But these are the same resources with which democratic institutions, or other projects toward greater social equality, must construct the rhetorical motives for greater equality. Burke's interest as a social critic—from his program in *Counter-Statement*, to his communistic call for social leveling in *Permanence and Change*, to his call for the comic corrective in *Attitudes Toward History*—is far more egalitarian than the identification of Burke's project with a rhetoric of domination implies.

This does not, in the end, merge Burke's objectives with the feminist project, nor indicate that other feminist arguments that identify sexist elements in Burke's work are unjust.[11] Certainly Burke more easily locates our current hierarchical pain in capitalism and productionism than he does in a patriarchy, and there is still plenty of room for considering the Burkean dialectic route to equality versus the formal idealism that derives rhetorical theory from social circumstance. But locating the Burkean position on hierarchy as a characteristic of social form rather than rhetorical form distracts attention from more crucial issues. Burke's mix of social activism with linguistic realism posits *social* hierarchy as an act and a scene rather than an agency and charges those who would change social hierarchy with recognizing the promise and traps inherent in language as an agency for doing so.

Hierarchy in Rhetorical Criticism

The pragmatic contribution of Burkeans to the twenty-first century will not, however, be in theory. Although we read Burke's collected works as a theory of language, their power is ultimately in the interpretation empowered by the perspective. So my focus on the placement of hierarchy within Burke's theoretical system is instrumental to the payoff in criticism. To introduce criticism into the complex, the characteristic Burkean move is to make a space for the critic. I now turn, therefore, to the task of opening the relationship between linguistic hierarchy and social form and placing the critic into the space thus created.

Burke develops the critical resources of hierarchy most fully in *Rhetoric of Motives*. The central importance of hierarchy in that discussion has probably been underemphasized by rhetorical critics. Burke had introduced the concept of rhetorical motive in Counter-Statement under the rubric of "patterns of experience" (150–61), defined it in *Permanence and Change* (19–21), considered its possibilities as a method for understanding the power of language in *Philosophy of Literary Form* (106n), and finally explicated it in *Grammar of Motives*. In *Rhetoric of Motives*, Burke opens the concept of motive to see the possibilities for criticism within it.

Of course, rhetoric fills the inside of such motives. Motives move people in particular directions, largely by socially appropriating value among the elements of the context created through the strategies of the motive. In *Permanence and Change*, Burke explains the relationships among language, sociality, and motive: "The question of motive brings us to the subject of communication, since motives are distinctly linguistic products. We discern situational patterns by means of the particular vocabulary of the cultural group into which we are born" (35). Burke stresses the social invention of rhetorical strategy: "Our very concepts of character depend upon the verbalizations of our group. In its origins, language is an implement of action, a device which takes its shape by the coöperative patterns of the group that uses it" (*Permanence*, 173). Thus, the intricate dance of interlocking social action is founded in the possibilities of rhetorical strategy.

I have slipped into a metaphor of internality now, and that choice is important for the critic. Social hierarchy becomes scenic in the critic's account of the rhetorical act. This, in turn, leads the critic to consider questions of power and domination that mediate between the rhetorical act and social hierarchy with scenic ratios. My argument is that this metaphor best emphasizes Burke's merger of the linguistic power of hierarchy and the social power of hierarchy. The metaphor of an interior space, therefore, allows us to consider the implications for the critic.

If critics are to enter these hierarchies, they must punctuate accounts of the rhetorical act more socially. Burke recommends decoding social hierarchy by reconstructing the motive's cycle of terms (*Rhetoric of Religion*, 174–207) or by considering the culture's response to its historical situation (*Attitudes*). The latter is particularly striking because it provides a diachronic account of the shifting authority in human history. If history is viewed as the empowering and disempowering of symbols of authority, and their corresponding social hierarchy (*Permanence*, 282), the critic of discourse enters as an actor in the social drama. This is the Burke of *Permanence and Change*, who argues for the superiority of a poetic motive for human discourse.

Traditionally, rhetorical criticism has favored accounts of narrower circumference constituted around the choices of individual rhetors. Hierarchy facilitates criticism of individual works in at least two ways. First, critics constituting the rhetorical act as a response to the rhetor's situation (Bitzer; *Permanence*, 220; *Attitudes*, 3–4) can work social hierarchy as the scene of the rhetorical act. This encourages a construction of the rhetor as a user and reviser of rhetorical hierarchy. The merger of rhetorical and social hierarchy is thus accomplished to provide the critic a vocabulary that entails social commentary in rhetorical commentary.

A second approach to individual rhetorical moments connects the rhetorical act to hierarchy through a familiar rhetorical concept—appeal. Individuals interpret moments through rhetorical choice constrained by the rhetorical hierarchies of their social group. The rhetor's facility with the interpretive resources of familiar motives identifies him with the group's hierarchical frame. Rhetorical messages acquire appeal as they mold their interpretation with the language of appropriate motives— Burke calls it "'cashing in on' a given historical situation" (*Attitudes*, 93). Strategies for selecting motives, contextualizing interpretation within the motives, and developing identity within the possibilities of the motive become inquiries for the critic.

Burke's treatment of hierarchy in *Rhetoric of Motives* suggests an intermediate approach to criticism between the story of the culture organizing human action hierarchically and the individual nestled within hierarchy. This construction views the rhetorical act as fundamentally about hierarchy. The interior of social hierarchy becomes the stage for the rhetorical drama. The hierarchy presents its players with possibilities that the players track down. There emerges for the critic a kind of dialectic of freedom and domination played out with rhetorical motive.

Burke urges the critic to understand the power of social hierarchy to limit human possibility. Hierarchies empower authorities to wield language to dominate others. A critic's account of such social domination can strengthen or weaken the social hierarchy. But the interior of a social hierarchy is more complicated than simple domination. Burke observes that humans caught on the bottom end of hierarchy do not always act as we would expect them to act—to resist their low station. Burke develops the concept of "weigh[ing] objective resources . . . to decide how to oppose them" that he introduces in *Attitudes Toward History* (3–4), into what he calls "the mystification" of the hierarchy of the motive. In perhaps his closest brush with orthodox Marxism's condemnation of the power of rhetoric for disempowerment, Burke argues that those at the lower range of the social hierarchy develop valuings that lead to acceptance of their condition.

In Burke's hands this "opiate" becomes grist for criticism, however. He writes:

> Though *hierarchy* is exclusive, the *principle* of hierarchy is not; all ranks can "share in it alike." But: It includes also the entelechial tendency, the treatment of the "top" or "culminating" stage as the "image" that best represents the entire "idea." This leads to "mystifications" that cloak the state of division, since the "universal" principle of the hierarchy also

happens to be the principle by which the most distinguished rank in the hierarchy enjoys, in the realm of worldly property, its special privileges. Hence, the turn from courtship to ill will, with ironic intermediate grades. (*Rhetoric of Motives*, 141)

In *Attitudes Toward History* and *Rhetoric of Motives*, Burke elaborates the dialectic stresses in any motive that make it at once the home of contentment and discontent. Indeed, frames of acceptance give way to rejection in what Burke labels the "Malthusian limits" of a motive (*Attitudes*, 27–28): though humans are "rotten with perfection," moving toward perfecting a motive will stimulate counterforces diverting stresses toward opposition. The irony thus produced infuses rhetoric within motives.

Together, these concepts create a rich rhetorical environment within motives ripe for the insights of interpretive critics. Burke closes *Rhetoric of Motives* with a challenge to critics:

Since, for better or worse, the mystery of the hierarchic is forever with us, let us, as students of rhetoric, scrutinize its range of entrancements, both with dismay and in delight. And finally let us observe, all about us, forever goading us, though it be in fragments, the motive that attains its ultimate identification in the thought, not of the universal holocaust, but of the universal order. (333)

Motives are rich complexes of rhetorical resources that support ironic hierarchies and exploit their valuings to change acceptance to rejection in another moment.[12] Critics may study the ways in which the rhetoric of the motive conserves the motive and strengthens it, opens up the possibility of change by reversing hierarchies or altering focus, the ways in which single hierarchies contain both the seeds of their power and the seeds of their destruction. Burke provides the tools to operate within the motive toward these ends.

"I Have a Dream": The Irony in Hierarchical Investment

The metaphor of space and the power of transformation present the Burkean critic with perspective that authorizes involvement in the tracking of hierarchic possibilities. Because the metaphor of space also locates the critic and the power of transformation also empowers the critic, they charge the critic to work within the changing hierarchical dynamics of our time. A rich texture of criticism results. Critics will be optimistic and pessimistic. They will egg on, and chide. Always conscious of Burkean irony, critics will track down the possibilities of discourse. To illustrate resources hierarchy brings to criticism, perhaps no American text could be more exemplary than the one that comes closest to being a culminating plea for equality—Martin Luther King's speech to the National March on Washington for Civil Rights of August 28, 1963, commonly known as the "I Have a Dream" speech.

At the heart of the "I Have a Dream" speech is a fundamental irony: the speech is the centerpiece of the most successful assault on American social privilege since the Civil War, yet it is fundamentally what Burke would call a speech of acceptance—embracing central symbols of the American social order.[13] We might in that sense call it "conservative," although the term will be more useful in setting up our irony than in locating the speech in American politics. The speech's appeal to dominant American social hierarchies to interpret African American aspirations predestines the Pandora's box of King's movement: the speech aspires to racial equality by exploiting all the progressive resources of American hierarchy, and demarcates its aspirations in the limits of that hierarchy.

Burke's entailment of rhetorical and social hierarchy creates a theory of rhetoric that features irony. The irony at the heart of "I Have a Dream" is, from that perspective, a prototype of the essential rhetorical problem. Throughout his work, when characterizing how humans respond to symbols, Burke stresses the interrelationship between the rhetorical and social power of symbols. The most powerful symbols for rhetorical appeal are the most familiar, and they are most familiar because they are performed incessantly to order our mundane daily lived experience. The most powerful social forms are those that are performed with such a familiar rhetoric that those living within the form have ceased to sense the language of its performance as rhetorical. When the distinctions and gradients performed in the everyday language of rhetorical forms (Burke calls them "motives" of course) are sublimated into rituals of social status, rhetorical hierarchies and social hierarchies have merged. In particular, social movements that seek to alter everyday social status confront the irony most starkly: the most rhetorically potent motives they may invoke trade in the very power they would destroy.

Within the general intertwining of the rhetorical and the social, hierarchy is a dimension of both linguistic and social ordering. Rhetoric works through hierarchy—this is more important than *that*; *this* is good, *that* is bad; do *this* instead of *that*. Rhetoric works by bringing schemes of ordering from, and back into, experience. When the "this" and "that" are people, social hierarchy is recognizable in the ongoing, day-to-day elevating of some over others and the struggle to maintain, diminish, or rearrange social status. Burke's insight is to mutually implicate rhetorical and social hierarchy and then to trace the implications thus created. Rhetorical messages must create a space within the allure of the familiar for the novel, and doing so is the message's working of the dialectics of permanence and change, identity and identification.

My reading of Martin Luther King's "I Have a Dream" argues that the speech taps powerful rhetorical hierarchies to motivate change, but ironically these motives trap King in languages and social structures that reinforce the hierarchy he seeks to supplant. To proceed, I will examine the use of rhetorical hierarchy that structures the King speech from simple contrast to more complex developmental metaphors, and finally into the fully implicated socio-rhetorical motives. The rhetorical appeals at each level present opportunities and dangers, but the most complex and powerful rhetorical forms—the hierarchical motivational structures—ironically trade most heavily in the social hierarchies King must change.

Antithesis and Metaphors of Difference

Speeches that we identify as exemplars for social change trade on the rhetorical creation of dramatic contrast. The contrast may be between despair and hope, or problem and solution, or simply today and tomorrow, but the rhetorical form that places moments of choice as the pivot for change depend on contrast opening the room for choice. Martin Luther King selects powerful experiential metaphors to establish the overwhelming sense of contrast between today and tomorrow in the speech. In their experiential power, these metaphors call on both the liberating and oppressive in American social hierarchy. Their nearness to basic themes fills King's speech with moving dynamism; their implication in latent yet basic rhetoric of domination defines limits on their power to liberate.

Many stylistic metaphors contribute to the basic contrast of bad and good, old and new that values in this speech. These antitheses include several that are used sparingly, such as the contrast of quicksand with solid rock, or jangled discord with beautiful symphony. Two figures of contrast dominate the speech, however. The first is the light/dark metaphor. "Now is the time to rise from the dark and desolate valley of segregation to the sunlit path of racial justice." This triple metaphor—rise, dark to sunlit, and wandering desolation to guiding path—combines the major rhetorical resources that establish the movement in the speech.

The light/dark metaphor is common in American discourse. Its dual source in our experience of day and night and in our Judeo-Christian myth of Genesis spreads its motivational quality through other metaphors, such as heat and cold and the seasonal cycle. Michael Osborn identified the power of the light/dark family to "express intense value judgments and . . . elicit significant value responses from an audience" (117). He also noted the connection of the light/dark cycle with inevitability—"day will follow night with the certainty of the laws of the universe"—provides a kind of inevitability as a rhetorical entailment of the contrast. In short, the metaphor of contrast becomes a metaphor of development (117–18). The metaphor presages the inevitable victory of the social movement and faith in triumph releases a power toward change in the permanence/change dialectic.

Martin Luther King's problem in exploiting the fiery potential of the light/dark metaphor is that a metaphor used powerfully is empowered for uses King does not control: there is light and heat to be found from a fire intensified, but the fire brought to a blaze is the fire that can also consume all that you cherish. The light/dark metaphor has such a power to endanger the things that King cherishes because in our civilization it embodies a sinister power—its place as rhetorical support in the historical development and perpetuation of Western racism. In this power we encounter the ironic danger of King's strategy even at the simplest rhetorical level. In a detailed history of language and oppression, Joel Kovel traces the linguistic resources of the light/dark contrast to maintain White racist power over Blacks. Kovel argues that the rhetorical forms that first developed the racist hierarchy of African slavery exploited the grading power of the light/dark metaphor in myth and social rela- tionship—the preference of light over dark in biology; God's creating lightness out of darkness and declaring it good; Africa as the dark continent; and many more (62). This myth was wedded with practical necessity when the difference of skin color conquered a major problem of the American institution of slavery, providing a badge that would mark the social distinction and make slave laws more easily enforceable. A Black was assumed to be a slave unless he could prove otherwise in the American South, and a White was assumed to be a freeman. Today, slavery is gone, but in our cities the light/dark metaphor constructs a matrix of rhetorical practice in which crime and security implicate racial hierarchy: Black youth are often assumed to wear the badge of physical threat—the darker the more sinister; the darkness of the night is assumed to be the time of danger; and the electric companies champion the protection that comes from making our dark neighborhoods light. In short, within King's most potent antithesis—the light/dark metaphor— lurks a rhetorical resource (Kovel calls it "aversive racism") in which American social hierarchy practices racist oppression. The light/dark metaphor merges immediate oratorical power with more subtle oppressive power to complicate the path from dominance to freedom.

The second major antithesis is King's use of the up/down metaphor. Up is good and down is bad in the metaphoric scheme of this speech. This is the most common metaphor used to value in the speech. Those things that King values are cloaked in the metaphor—the "high plane of dignity" or "the majestic heights of meeting physical force with soul force." The upward movement is central—"Now is the time to lift our nation" or "we must rise to the majestic heights." The topographic variation is the basis of the famous peroration where freedom is to ring from hills and mountaintops all through the nation.

The up/down metaphor is identified by Lakoff and Johnson as a fundamental metaphor employed across cultures, but with particular implications in each culture (14). Like the light/dark metaphor, the up/down metaphor soon entails other contrasts such as high/low, climb/fall, or top/bottom. We have to go no further than the expressions "on the bottom of the social hierarchy" and "to climb to a higher station" to find the central link between the metaphors and the everyday living of social status. The metaphor functions for King to locate his movement as a movement of social hierarchy—he would move his people from a lower to a higher station. Thus, the antithetical contrast is converted into a developmental direction achieved by commitment and effort—"pull oneself up" as a common expression of social improvement. The up/down metaphor also contains ironic resistance—a fear of "uppity Blacks," for example.

But the fundamental irony of the metaphor is that its power of appeal is focused into its limited vision. The up/down orientation performed in the language of the American hierarchy trades on the society's powerful motives for "improving one's self." Within this motive, this strategy provides socially authorized resources for a rhetoric of change. But the up/down metaphor can become a prison of limited vision— perhaps "vision up the well shaft" communicates the irony. "Up" frames movement within an orientation from current position to the end that defines the hierarchy. It thus displaces strategies to transform the hierarchy (alter the scene to relocate the agent) in favor of strategies to modify place within the hierarchy (relocate the agent within a stable scene). A vision articulated in the strong motivational terminology of the American hierarchy, in fact, forfeits the power to define vision beyond the hierarchy.

These two metaphors—light/dark and up/down—take standard American rhetorical devices and create the values that guide the speech. They are powerful devices that achieve their purpose of creating an exalted emotion to energize the civil rights movement. Yet the metaphors that accomplish this end are implicated in the origins of the racism King fights and the limitation of the vision he urges. Thus, the power of King's message turns on the ironic tension between the opening of the possibility of change and invoking the rhetoric of oppression in a hierarchy.

Developmental Metaphors

The term *social movement* is itself a metaphor that encompasses the dynamism that is a prerequisite for the rhetoric of social movements. Well-selected developmental metaphors are an asset within social movements because they provide the dynamism by taking the contrast of antithesis (as we have seen, the light/dark and up/down metaphors have particular strengths in this task) and arraying the contrast into human time and space to create progress. They entail rhetorical hierarchy because their dynamism comes from casting the envisioned future as a completion of past and present. These more complex metaphors move the simpler orientational metaphors toward fully developed motives. The greater power of developmental metaphors presents the possibility of containing the ironic dangers through the greater strictures of form, or spreading them into social action through more complex metaphoric strategies. King's speech taps powerful developmental metaphors, but they are metaphors that divide his movement for change.

Two developmental metaphors contain the ironic tension within King's speech: the journey and the dream/fulfillment forms. The speech divides into two parts, each featuring one of these forms. The early portion of the speech is a history of the movement and a history of the unfulfilled commitment of America to integrate her African American citizens. This portion is structured in the form of the journey.

The journey is a well-rounded figure of the speech with deep roots in the American experience. The first notable public address in American experience—John Winthrop's speech aboard the *Arabella* in Salem harbor in 1630—began the portrayal of American life as a journey with purpose. Historians from Bancroft to Turner to Boorstin have described the power of the journey west to motivate Americans. With King's choices, his movement joins the American journey. Burke observes that a key moment in the rhetorical construction of journey is the fixing of the destination. King uses the ideograph of <freedom> as the destination in the journey. That potent ideograph is overtly located in American sacred documents that identify King's movement within the flow of American political history.

When the architects of *our* Republic wrote the magnificent words of the *Constitution* and the *Declaration of Independence*, they were signing a promissory note to which *every American* was to fall heir. This note was a promise that *all men—yes, black men as well as white men*—would be guaranteed the *unalienable rights of life, liberty, and the pursuit of happiness.* (emphasis added)

This grounding early in the speech—elaborating freedom's definition in sacred American documents—establishes King's journey within the history of the American experience. Later, King overtly discusses the union of his movement with progressive America. He warns his Black followers against distrusting Whites and points explicitly to Whites attending the rally: "They have come to realize that their freedom is inextricably bound to our freedom. We cannot walk alone."

The later portion of the speech moves from locating the movement in history to inspiring the movement to action. It draws on a different rhetorical form—the dream and its fulfillment. King declares his dream in a series of moments that combine parallelism, antithesis, rhythm, and pace to build to crescendo. So powerful is this building rhetorical structure that it covers completely a mixing of metaphor (the up/down metaphor of the mountaintop in nexus with a figure of mountains being lowered and valleys raised to express equality) that would jar in ordinary speeches.[14] Furthermore, the movement from dream to fulfillment is not, on its face, a natural movement, yet it is powerful. This power resides in three sources: King's delivery, the strong vignettes of equality that portray the dream fulfilled, and the link of dream to fulfillment in secular American mythology. Little needs to be said about King's delivery. Each sentence or two, each two to four clauses, are delivered with crescendo in volume and pace, providing the sense of movement. The stating of the dreams in the form of vignettes—descriptions of common equality seen in a future time—suggests that the dream is of their fulfillment.

But the strongest power in establishing the developmental form in dream and fulfillment is their linkage in the American dream. King is overt: "[Mine] is a dream deeply rooted in the American dream." From the story of the building of the frontier to the gold fever of the 49ers to the motivation in the immigrant experience to Walt Disney's "When you wish upon a star," the theme of America as the place where achievement begins in a dream is a powerful cultural form. Its most obvious recent incantation is Ronald Reagan's use of it to build a political coalition: "Why shouldn't we dream? After all, we are Americans."[15] Identifying his dream, and the dreams of his African American followers with the

American dream, King is calling on the American pattern of progressivism to provide the motivational frame for his movement.

King's choice of these two American symbols—the developmental metaphors of the journey and fulfillment of the dream—stresses the continuity of his movement with the American experience. Burke stresses that identification always brings a compensatory division, and King's identification with the dominant American symbols splits the movement for Black liberation.[16] The leaders of the Black Power movement sought Black identity and the right of African Americans to define their own vision, and rejected integration into the White-controlled social structure. King's embracing of White brothers in their progressive journey toward the American dream of equality sets King against other Black leaders of the time. Black Power's more violent metaphors of war and nationalism and distinctiveness and pride are forsaken in this speech for the metaphor of the American journey.

The hierarchic implications of King's speech carry beyond the dispute with the goals of the Black Power movement; the developmental metaphors of this speech elevate King to a position of leadership in the movement for African American aspirations. Journeys are led. Their linearity creates leaders and followers. With the journey as a context for the speech, the rhetorical act itself—the natural social differentiation of public speaking in which speaker is elevated above listener—is converted into the act of leading the journey. King's persona in the speech assumes that position. This is didactic style. The preacher's "Thou shalt not . . . " is the implicit rhetorical form, tempered only by the prophet's dreams of freedom as the journey's destination (cf. Patton). The persona turns the split in the African American community into the elevation of King's personal power. There is, of course, irony here as well. King—the representative of the Black race, who consciously identifies with the poor classes, who builds a movement outside mainstream American political parties—celebrates the songs of the American nation in the shadow of one of its central political memorials and climbs the hierarchy and transcends the Black movement to become a hero of American progressivism worthy of a *national* holiday.

King's embrace of American progressivism opened up many new opportunities for his movement as well as a rich storehouse of rhetorical strategies for altering the status of his people in the dominant American hierarchy. But his choice to work with the rhetorical resources provided by the hierarchy also closed other African American leaders out. King became an accomplice in the strategy called "co-optation." His segment of the movement was differentiated as the "good Blacks" who accept the American hierarchy, and were admitted on the terms of that hierarchy.

Those the hierarchy ostracized as the "bad Blacks" were denied admission to the hierarchy, now strengthened by its even wider appeal. Thus, the advances in civil rights are bought at the expense of new hierarchical divisions within Black America. The assertion of the power of the developmental metaphors performs rhetorical action that divides King's movement and brings him and his followers into hierarchy on circumscribed terms.

The Hierarchical Motives of Lived Experience

The developmental frames of this speech are not yet, however, a full motivational hierarchy. That full power is provided by the three motive structures of the speech—the economy, religion, and the American political motive. Each of these are structures where action and rhetoric intertwine in ongoing social action performed within defined social status. Each is a hierarchy of power relationships interconnected in a wide range of actions performed with characteristic rhetorical forms. Each has a vocabulary and characteristic patterns of description, justification, and sanction that acquire power and grant legitimacy to acceptable action within a social structure. Ultimately, these motivational structures with powers to direct daily life far beyond the speech contextualize the speech. King's choices of hierarchies and his choices of where to open the hierarchies for greater access play against the background of the ongoing rhetorical-social motive.

The implications of choices of motivational hierarchy are evident in the weakest of these motivational structures in the speech, the economic motive. King invokes it but once in the early part of the speech:

In a sense we've come to our nation's capital to cash a check. When the architects of our Republic wrote the Constitution and the Declaration of Independence, they were signing a promissory note to which every American was to fall heir. . . . It is obvious today that America has defaulted on this promissory note insofar as her citizens of color are concerned. Instead of honoring this sacred obligation, America has given the Negro people a bad check, a check which has come back marked "insufficient funds." But we refuse to believe that the bank of justice is bankrupt.

The economic motive is a full motive of behavior. Within its vocabulary, metaphors, and rhetorical forms are performed the billions of transactions that each day shape the American economy. The motive constructs a full social hierarchy with levels of social status (graded by dollar signs and stars in the symbols of the famous board game, "The Game of Life"). The most important sign of its fullness is that it provides a rich rhetoric that allows those of lower status to rationalize their position, including the role of education, risk, hard work, and luck in authorizing wealth and economic control. In conjunction with this rhetoric is a full vocabulary and style of discourse that differentiates the status levels.

King carves out but a simple part of that motive—the cashing of a check. This is not an act that requires high status in this hierarchy. On the contrary, the cashing of a check is but part of the role known as "consumer." In fact, of course, King's movement was focused on opening up places for consumption to Black Americans. In the language of a later decade he opened up a vast market, previously closed, to the goods and services of capitalism. This limited vision underscores that *none* of King's dreams envision African Americans controlling the economy, operating in the upper reaches of the hierarchy with control of vast corporations or the junk bonds of Wall Street.[17] Toward the end of his life King began to turn his attention to questions of economic power. Perhaps symbolically, he was killed as he turned to aid a union in its fight for economic power. But King could not command the rhetorical resources of the economic motive as he could other motives. "I Have a Dream" is not a speech that opens the business hierarchy to make rhetorical space for freedom.

Perhaps the space for freedom is in the second motivational hierarchy that shapes "I Have a Dream," the religious motive. The metaphors, allusions, and figures of Protestant Christianity are the most pervasive in the speech. In many ways the hierarchy of Protestant Christianity is the least differentiated of the hierarchies invoked by the speech. The discourse reaches into the supernatural to array social relations within the power of *Logos*, of God's word—the Old Testament power to create and sanction, the New Testament power of grace and redemption. Humankind is theologically leveled under the "fatherhood of God and the brotherhood of man," but that phrase does not define the total hierarchy of Christianity. In an Old Testament tradition, ministers of God are called and raised above the people to present God's word; in a New Testament tradition, the redeemed are generally given higher status than the unredeemed.

The myth that supports the hierarchy is the righteousness of God embodied in a doctrine of sanction (Old Testament) or of love (New Testament). But the sense of justice in the hierarchy rests in God's goodness and power. The spiritual hierarchy fosters an accompanying political hierarchy that organizes the institutional church and elevates bishops or synods, or some such officers, over parishioners. In these more practical hierarchies, the church more rigidly restricts elevation through its hierarchy. The doctrines of redemption and glorification, and in some denominations, the calling of the preacher, provide some sense of movement within the hierarchy, but the power of this hierarchy lies in its righteous justice rather than in its openness.[18]

Martin Luther King calls on the religious motive metaphorically at various moments when key relationships are in need of expression. "I have a dream that one day on the red hills of Georgia the sons of former slaves and the sons of former slaveowners will be able to sit down together at the table of brotherhood." "You have been the veterans of creative suffering. Continue to work with the faith that unearned suffering is redemptive." The religious motive is deeply meaningful to his people and its shadow casts throughout the address. The journey on which he and his people are engaged is at least minimally the coming up of the Children of Israel from their bondage in Egypt. King is to some extent the Black Moses so long sought. The use of the metaphor of fire to describe the oppression of African Americans and the promise of deliverance from these fires is allusion to the deliverance from the fires of hell. And all this is sealed in the climax of the speech: "join hands and sing in the words of the old Negro spiritual, 'Free at last! Free at last! Thank God Almighty, we are free at last!'"

The elegance of this strategy is built on an ambiguous mixing of religion and politics in which the spiritual becomes political anthem and "free" transforms from its spiritual to political meaning. The Negro spiritual had more of a religious than a political meaning for its slave chorus. Death and resurrection were the final release from the bondage of the devil below and the slavemaster on earth (see Cox, 202). When preaching by African Americans was outlawed in the 1830s, the message of "Free at last!" was delivered by the White clergy to slaves who were being told that their bondage on earth was insignificant in light of their rapture hereafter. The irony of the ambiguity in the phrase then has a paradoxical power. Political freedom motivates action and resistance, eternal freedom teaches patience and trust in God's mercy. This ambiguity places King's speech well politically. On the one hand, King's speech declares that "the day has arrived" for granting the demands of African Americans. The march to freedom and the journey from bondage provide King with a speech that calls on progressive language to energize his movement and provide it legitimacy for access to civil and political rights. On the other hand, the statement of hope that places faith in the inevitability of reward also "postpones the day," creating a matrix of patience and faith that places the movement patiently within the dominant

Judeo-Christian political system. The religious motive, therefore, becomes more powerful as a space for gradualism than as a space for dramatic social change.

The third motivational hierarchy called on for rhetorical power in the speech is the secular American political motive. The invoking of this motive is also pervasive. There are not only references to the sacred documents of American political culture, but even recitations of the hymns of secular worship—"My country 'tis of thee, sweet land of liberty, of thee I sing. Land where my fathers died, land of the Pilgrim's pride, from every mountainside, let freedom ring." The final clause becomes the chorus of King's brilliant peroration. Of course, the political hierarchy where King's fathers died was not the hierarchy of this song. As disenfranchised voters, and slaves before that, they had little access at even the lowest status of this hierarchy. The Pilgrim's pride did not extend to the African slave. In the recitations, King is, therefore, claiming an access to the hierarchy within discourse of the motive from which his people have been excluded. He makes that plea in the language of the motive to which he seeks access. A cant of the mantra to demonstrate worthiness.

But does this motive go beyond a progressive plea for access? By the early 1960s, the American political motive had split into two different languages and two different scales of social status. Franklin Roosevelt's New Deal located the highest status level of the political hierarchy in the policy bureaucracy. Power in the policy system was wielded in a heavily scientized rhetoric of policy logics that guided legislation and marshaled resources for public purpose. Arguably, by the 1960s, the unelected bureaucracy servicing administrative, legislative, and judicial officers had taken control of the discourse in government, and elected officials were lowered in the hierarchy. The bureaucrat's position in the hierarchy was justified in a fully developed language that located policy science as a branch of knowledge and established status based on the expert's claim to positivistic knowledge in specialized domains.

The language of electoral politics was a different language addressed to different audiences. The electoral structure primarily oriented the officeholder and the voter. The voter assumed a role to pick from among a small sample of candidates culled by those higher on the status hierarchy. This limited access was reinforced by financial and structural barriers to the media of communication. The language featured votes, coalitions, and political opinion. The bureaucracy was only dimly related to this hierarchy. Leaders of bureaucratic agencies were generally chosen through political processes, but from among the bureaucratic elite. In short, the American political structure insulated electoral hierarchy from bureaucratic hierarchy, requiring different languages and different strategies for access to power.

Supporting the electoral hierarchy were two important rhetorical myths. One authorized the differentiated hierarchy through the election process. This myth located the maximum power in the elected officials and imbued the elections with authority as legitimating rituals. Since the bureaucracy was seen as serving the elected officials, not as controlling them, it remained in a subordinate status. The electoral myth also expressed a kind of quality—the power of the ballot—that ironically elevated the voter to a higher status than even the elected politician. This part of the myth did function as much as it could economically—keeping salaries of elected officials low at state and local levels and creating embarrassment at the perks of status for elected officials—and had a discourse that supported it—Harry Truman left office declaring that he was being *elevated* to private citizen. Thus, a discourse existed to rationalize the status differential to give all participants a comfortable place in the hierarchy.

A second discourse provided a strong diachronic myth—the Whig history of the progress of the American nation provided the sense of the openness of the status hierarchy to advancement. American history was a story of ever more people gaining access to electoral power. The president of the United States as King spoke was John F. Kennedy, whose Irish immigrant family had been a part of this march toward inclusion. It is this second myth, much more than the first, that serves as a context for King's access to the hierarchy. King's speech is a claim that Black Americans should be the next group granted access to the political hierarchy. Indeed, the speech opens with King placing the day in that history: "I am happy to join with you today in what will go down in history as the greatest demonstration for freedom in the history of our nation." The greatest achievement of the energy released by the 1963 Washington movement was passage of the Voting Rights Act of 1965. Real progress was made based on this myth of access. King's drawing on the rhetoric of this motive succeeded in action that elevated the status of his people to voters.

King confronted the exclusion of African Americans from the political structure, but restricted the rhetoric of his journey to the electoral motive. His achievement of gaining access to the discourse and praxis of the electoral structure was substantial, but ultimately he was less successful in working past the rhetorical traps that grant access to voting discourse to block access to the upper-status levels in the American political motive. Three decades later, one African American holds a seat in the United States Senate, no African American can yet realistically aspire to the presidency. More important, African Americans in positions of power in the bureaucracy are still significant for being African Americans rather than for wielding power authorized by more than tokenism.

Obviously, Martin Luther King's "I Have a Dream" speech contains many more rhetorical resources than recited in this brief excursion into its hierarchical dimensions. But understanding the hierarchies within which the rhetoric works helps us see some of the ironies and paradoxes that provide the speech with its complexity. King's acceptance by the American power structure was difficult but successful. His cadences and images helped by demanding progressive change but affirming the motivational resources of their privilege.

In the title of this essay and of this section I used the term *investment* to characterize King's rhetoric. The complexity of the English verb *to invest* captures much of the complexity of "I Have a Dream."

> in•vest—*tr.* 1. To commit (money or capital) in order to gain a financial return: *invested their savings in stocks and bonds.* 2.a. To spend or devote for future advantage or benefit: *invested much time and energy in getting a good education.* b. To devote morally or psychologically, as to a purpose; commit: *"Men of our generation are invested in what they do, women in what we are"* (Shana Alexander). 3. To endow with authority or power. 4. To install in office with ceremony: *invest a new emperor.* 5. To endow with an enveloping or pervasive quality: *"A charm invests a face/Imperfectly beheld"* (Emily Dickinson). 6. To clothe; adorn. 7. To cover completely; envelop. 8. To surround with troops or ships; besiege. (*American Heritage Dictionary for Windows*, 3rd ed.)

There are three clusters of definition in these nine specific definitions. Definitions 1, 2a, and 2b assume an investor who acts, investing in some specific instrument with anticipation of a payoff. Definitions 3 through 5 stress a different act: the granting of authority or power to something or someone. The last three definitions move gradually toward the victim being besieged. In this movement is reflected the ironic investment of Martin Luther King. He invests in the American hierarchy, seeking advantage for his people. But in so doing, he strengthens faith in the hierarchy itself. Between the first and the final meaning of "invest" lies the irony—King acts to invest in the hierarchy that invests his people.

Treating Hierarchical Psychosis in the Twenty-first Century

If I have come at all close to reaching my objective in this essay, questions about Burke's "belief" about the "inevitability of social

hierarchy" have been so thoroughly contextualized that they have
received in favor of more critical questions about the power of discourse
engaged with social hierarchy. When discussing hierarchy in *Rhetoric of
Motives*, Burke comes as close to asserting inevitability as he ever does,
and what is inevitable is a "hierarchic psychosis":

> There is a "universal" lesson here. But it is in the fact that we
> confront a "hierarchic psychosis," prevailing in all nations, but
> particularly sinister in nations which are largely ruled by the
> "dead hand" of institutions developed from past situations and
> unsuited for the present. (281)

As the twenty-first century dawns, the sinister condition threatens the
peace and welfare of the American culture. The challenge is to respond
to the "dead hand" with creative discourse that transforms the power
relationships entailed in American social hierarchy. Read in the context
of his project, Burke seems clearly to believe more in the power of
language to do such work than in a culture doomed to an inevitable
social arrangement. But resolving that issue—committing to address the
hierarchical disease with Burke's medicine kit—only brings a critic to the
threshold of difficulty. For when the totality of Burkean concepts are
brought to bear on the problem of hierarchy, the full complexity of
language soon surfaces.

Martin Luther King's "I Have a Dream" represents one complexity:
if rhetoric works by identification, don't strong forces in support of the
hierarchy emerge fully celebrated from the performance of addressed
discourse? Indeed, so; and thus the need to mine the resources of irony
fully. How can we negotiate the ironic possibilities in such a way that we
open the possibilities of alternative social form rather than perpetuating
the oppression of the old? The foregrounding of hierarchy permits us to
turn our critical energies in that direction. I have observed that Burke's
notion of hierarchy is best considered as a contextualist notion. Contextualism turns notions that other traditions label "tools" into perspectives. The hierarchical perspective encourages the critic to consider
issues of justice in the distribution of social power and the complicity of
rhetorical forms in perpetuating or altering social power.

Burke worries in *Rhetoric of Motives* about hierarchies that are only
appropriate for outdated situations. Is there a better characterization of
the world that lies on our horizon? Having thus defined the rhetorical
situation of our age, critics can destroy the power of social ritual to
perpetuate the hierarchy by exposing the mystery that supports it. And
they can explore efforts to transform the hierarchy with an eye toward

strengthening them and bringing them to full fruition in alternative complexes of relationships that better promote justice. New pieties emerge slowly and not always as we wish, but emerge they do. Motives that perpetuate social inequality can be transformed into motives that perform social justice.

The last statement contains that combination of dream, prayer, and chart (*Philosophy*, 5–6) that we call "optimism." In fact, it may seem that we have come full circle from a rather pessimistic reading of Martin Luther King to a rather prayerful assertion of hope for the power of rhetoric. But, once again, Burke would remind us to turn our concepts back on each other. Many are the social orders that have visited horrible social oppression in the name of social justice. Seeing the common root of good and evil and the constrained power of human assertion as a risky proposition provides a construction of rhetorical discourse that merits guarded optimism. Burkean critics are always "using all that is there to use" to work their way out of inescapable complexity. The energy of Burkean criticism lies in that paradox. So the resources that Burkean criticism promises to the new century flow from the charge that closes *Rhetoric of Motives*: "let us, as students of rhetoric, scrutinize its range of entrancements, both with dismay and in delight. And finally let us observe, all about us, forever goading us, though it be in fragments, the motive that contains its ultimate identification in the thought, not of the universal holocaust, but of the universal order" (333).

Notes

1. Although I have never located a passage in which Burke makes this claim, it is a characteristic assertion by many who have worked with his method and ideas, particularly in sociology. See Duncan, 51, and Burks, 225.

2. The most explicit statement of Burke's contextualist viewpoint is in *Philosophy of Literary Form* (106), although the extended statement of *Grammar of Motives* is a better argument for his placement in this intellectual tradition. The best explanation of contextualism is in Pepper (232–79).

3. This is not to deny that there might not be places where ambiguity encourages misreading. Burke often fails to recognize that he and we live in a societal climate in which claims that do not explicitly warn otherwise are often taken as empirical claims. Nevertheless, there is no place that I can see where the empirical claim must support itself without one of the other lines of argument implied in the context of the claim.

4. Other such arguments can be developed from Burke's methodological approach to language analysis. For example, Rueckert generates a similar argument from abstraction and titling as linguistic processes (134–53).

5. It must be noted that in later years Burke recognized some of the weaknesses of this definition of man and, in fact, generally abandoned it for the more global "bodies that learn language." This abandonment further indicates his belief that hierarchy—along with other essential elements in the earlier definition—are entailed in the symbolic character of humanness.

6. The confusing use of two different definitions of "principle" should be noted in this passage. The first use of the term in the passage invokes principle as a discovered truth about human behavior, thus principle as a rule or law concerning the natural functioning of phenomena. The final, emphasized, use of the term invokes principle as a regularized and generative praxis of social behavior, thus principle as an underlying guiding structure shaping social action. The two senses are merged here in an ambiguity that is an important resource by which Burke expresses the entailment of one in the other. But seeing their variation will more clearly reveal Burke's idea about the relationship between linguistic process and social performance.

7. The naming of "inequality" as the alternative to "equality" illustrates the [linguistic] hierarchical principle at work here. The prefix indicates the imperfection and thus invokes the principle that elevates the entelechial condition of equality. Notice the reversal that results from using "authoritarian" as a synonym for "inequality" and the more neutral use of "[social] hierarchy."

8. This position is most familiar in Bitzer's formula, which maintains that language choices are a function of needs defined by social situation. But, more broadly, any rhetorical account that begins with assessment of intentional purpose lies within this framework.

9. Burke is a precursor of Foucault's move here. Burke explicitly punctuates an account of discourse as form-writ-large in *Attitudes Toward History*, where he tracks the major frameworks of motivation through three millennia.

10. In this, he differs from the project of Foss and Griffin. They actually reverse Burke's derivation of the social from the linguistic. They posit a condition of social equality and describe the rhetorical theory that would support it. The result is a formist view of rhetoric, an ethic that governs judgment of discourse, rather than the contextualist view that characterizes Burke's work. Thus, the tendency to think of "hierarchy" and "equality" as the two options for a social hierarchy. This sort of "either/or" choice characteristic of formal idealism is contrasted with a "both/and" view, which holds that the two terms express a dimension of social hierarchy upon which a range of social arrangements may be arrayed, pursued, and resisted.

11. For example, Janice Norton locates her critique of Burke in the centrality of the body in his late work and his failure to recognize the differentiation of body inherent in sexual difference.

12. Burke has posed this as the essential task of his method and the drama of human history (*Attitudes*, 27).

13. Previous studies have stressed King's success in the short-term political arena as a result of the speech and attributed this success to his identification with traditional American values. Martha Solomon [Watson]'s critique is especially

noteworthy because she conducts a metaphoric analysis of the speech. She locates a central matrix in the concept of the American covenant which the various metaphors support and from which they branch. The approach provides an alternative reading of the positive impact the speech gathers by appealing to established symbols of the American hierarchy. Watson does not explore the irony that I find in the speech's strategy. John Patton also locates the power of the speech to deliver political support in its appeal to standard American ideology, although his account of its artistic power is far wider than mere ideology.

14. J. Robert Cox notes that this seeming mixing of metaphor is resolved in its ancient origins. The terminology is drawn from the biblical book of Isaiah and probably has reference to a practice in which an entourage would precede a king, smoothing the hills and filling the ditches to ease the ride of his chariot. Thus, the up/down metaphor is converted to a journey metaphor (200). To what extent this arcane construction is known among King's religious audience is unknown, but the power of style would itself be sufficient to smooth the disruption.

15. The reference is from the peroration of Reagan's First Inaugural Address.

16. Cox focuses on time as the central theme of the speech. He argues that King sought to counter the gradualism that was growing in liberal support for the movement with a strong rationale for immediacy. Cox effectively discusses the power of the dream in American experience and King's effectiveness in invoking that power. Robert Hariman responds to Cox's position by arguing a thesis much like mine—King was not only fighting gradualism, but was fighting for leadership of the Black movement.

17. For an extended discussion of the limited assertion of economic power in the check metaphor compared to the full metaphoric complex of the economy, see Hariman (210–11).

18. King does, however, gain a pragmatic advantage from the religious motive. King elevates himself in this motive. His status as a Minister of the Gospel aids his political control over the masses spread before him. His invoking of the gospel in the language of religion that fills the speech reinforces that status. In addition, the religious motive as context positioned King's movement— the Southern Christian Leadership Conference—into power over the secular proponents of more aggressive action in the Black Power movement. And, finally, the ambiguity of King's movement as a political or a religious movement exploited the ambiguity of American civil religion to disarm the kind of political repression planned by J. Edgar Hoover and others in the political hierarchy.

References

Bitzer, Lloyd. "The Rhetorical Situation." *Philosophy and Rhetoric* 1 (1968): 1–14.

Burke, Kenneth. *Attitudes Toward History*. 3rd ed. Berkeley: University of California Press, 1984 [1937].

————. *Counter-Statement*. Berkeley: University of California Press, 1964 [1931].

————. *A Grammar of Motives*. Berkeley: University of California Press, 1969 [1946].

————. *Language as Symbolic Action: Essays on Life, Literature, and Method*. Berkeley: University of California Press, 1966.

————. *Permanence and Change: An Anatomy of Purpose*. 3rd ed. Berkeley: University of California Press, 1984 [1935].

————. *The Philosophy of Literary Form: Studies in Symbolic Action*. 3rd ed. Berkeley: University of California Press, 1973 [1941].

————. *A Rhetoric of Motives*. Berkeley: University of California Press, 1969 [1950].

————. *A Rhetoric of Religion: Studies in Logology*. Boston, Mass.: Beacon, 1961.

Burks, Don M. "Kenneth Burke: The Agro-Bohemian 'Marxoid.'" *Communication Studies* 42 (1991): 219–33.

Cox, J. Robert. "The Fulfillment of Time: King's 'I Have a Dream' Speech (August 28, 1963)." In *Texts in Context: Critical Dialogues on Significant Episodes in American Political Rhetoric*. Edited by Michael C. Leff and Fred J. Kauffeld. Davis, Calif.: Hermagoras, 1989.

Duncan, Hugh Dalziel. *Symbols in Society*. New York: Oxford University Press, 1968.

Foss, Sonja K., and Cindy L. Griffin. "A Feminist Perspective on Rhetorical Theory: Toward a Classification of Boundaries." *Western Journal of Communication* 56 (1992): 330–49.

Hariman, Robert. "Time and Reconstitution of Gradualism in King's Address: A Response to Cox." In *Texts in Context: Critical Dialogues on Significant Episodes in American Political Rhetoric*. Edited by Michael C. Leff and Fred J. Kauffeld. Davis, Calif.: Hermagoras, 1989.

Horton, Janice. "Rhetorical Criticism as Ethical Action: Cherchez la Femme." *Southern Communication Journal* 61 (1995): 29–45.

Kovel, Joel. *White Racism*. New York: Random House-Vintage, 1970.

Lakoff, George, and Mark Johnson. *Metaphors We Live By*. Chicago: University of Chicago Press, 1980.

Osborn, Michael. "Archetypal Metaphor in Rhetoric: The Light-Dark Family." *Quarterly Journal of Speech* 53 (1967): 115–27.

Patton, John. "'I Have a Dream': The Performance of Theology Fused with the Power of Oratory." In *Martin Luther King, Jr., and the Sermonic Power of Public Discourse*. Edited by Carolyn Calloway-Thomas and John Louis Lucaites. Tuscaloosa: University of Alabama Press, 1993.

Pepper, Stephen. *World Hypotheses*. Berkeley: University of California Press, 1941.

Rueckert, William H. *Kenneth Burke and the Drama of Human Relations*. 2nd ed. Berkeley: University of California Press, 1982 [1961].

Solomon, Martha. "Covenanted Rights: The Metaphoric Matrix of 'I Have a Dream.'" In *Martin Luther King, Jr., and the Sermonic Power of Public Discourse*. Edited by Carolyn Calloway-Thomas and John Louis Lucaites. Tuscaloosa: University of Alabama Press, 1993.

11

"Secular Pragmatism"

Kenneth Burke and the
[Re]socialization of Literature and Theory

Dennis J. Ciesielski

> It is not things themselves that
> disturb men, but their judgment
> about these things. (Epicitus)
> —*Tristram Shandy*, 1760

The beginning pages of Kenneth Burke's *A Rhetoric of Motives* demonstrate nicely his philosophy that "literature is equipment for living." Applying what we shall call his "secular-pragmatic" approach to "experiential" as well as literary text, Burke reveals and investigates the social textuality in our everyday lives through a sense of cultural, historical, and linguistic juxtapositions upon which all of our various discourse situations depend. It is the multiplicity of these discourse situations, in an ever-expanding social milieu, which validates Burke's investigative forays into world-text and the consequent theoretical perspectives discovered in his search, perspectives relative to the combined transactive identity of an object text, its author, and, most important, the active reader.

Stressing the social implications of art and language, Burke informs us that the key word in his *Rhetoric of Motives* is "identification" (xiii) rather than the traditional motive of persuasion. The social inquiry involved in our search for meaning (here, synonymous with Burke's "identification") implies a twofold rhetorical condition: in the act of "reading" a situation, we must identify it; in the act of identifying "other," we identify (or reidentify) self as well. And, in this process of identification, we gain new perspectives that will allow a dynamic tertiary truth that emerges ever anew with each subsequent transaction. Thus the discovery of the truths around us is also the discovery of the dynamic cultural "self" by which these truths are defined. Burke sees "identification," then, as an instrument of inquiry (*rhetorica docens*), a way to discover previously unacknowledged rhetorical motives (of both self and other) that might lead us to yet further identifications beyond the utilitarian goal of persuasion (*rhetorica utens*).

Essentially, Burke's identification is the obverse side of persuasion, its binary opposite. This binary team thus acts as a set of checks and balances in regard to the "truths" of suasive power communities, anachronistic tradition, and the established authority of a privileged hierarchal system. Hence, we might perceive the [post]modern critic's actions as an investigative and sociopolitically revealing *process* rather than the more traditional goal-oriented effort to stratify a text's meaning into a historical *product*; for, in the process of "discovering" an artist's motives or the implications of an empirical social experience (from welfare to war), the critic learns her own motives, agendas, and thus her means of interpreting the world-at-large. Hence, how one "uses" an object-text often reveals more about the user and the world from which she perceives the text than about the text itself. Rhetorical identification, then, works both ways and, in the process, it will create a dynamic truth intrinsic to both of the critical act's participants.

Burke's unique rhetorical approach to meaning and truth applies to all "texts," literary and experiential, because all movement that an ordered, socialized situation has symbolic implications which deal with our own human desire for order. In this sense, his view of symbolic action parallels Paul Ricouer's observation that the basic human ontological foundation lies in the narrative act, the (forever dynamic) sequential linearity necessary to the strategical "build-up" of truths and meaning based on previous experience and our constant need to move forward through time (56–57). Hence, our present truths are simply part of the process toward future truths in our never-ending effort to make meaning of and from the eternal dynamics of our own experience. Meaning, therefore, exists for us within its own context—it is not inextricably attached to a specific experience or signifier any more than we, ourselves, can escape our own sense of historical awareness. Burke anticipates the postmodern concept of the transcendent signifier in his observation that all action is symbolic of other action; all signs hold further implications. Hence the critic (read "experiencer") of a specific text gains a sort of transient control of text through her own unique reading, her own choice of terministic screens (*Language*, 44–45).

It is important to note, here, that Burke anticipates yet another postmodern theory in the parallel between his "terministic screen" model and Hans-Georg Gadamer's "philosophical hermeneutics." Both concepts allow for individual readings of historical texts as well the personal evaluation of contemporary experience by implying that meaning is the product of a simple *transaction* between subject and object. As Gadamer observes, understanding is not reconstruction [of a text] but a *mediation*" between the reader and the text (Linge, xvi). Because Gadamer's understanding "is bound in language" (15) (a process that necessarily implies a dialogic "other"), both sides of a transaction hold sway in the meaning-making process in their shared definition of the boundaries or terms within which this transaction must take place; both sides contribute to their respective "other's" legitimation in the world. In this sense, neither end of the subject/object dyad gains exclusive authority inasmuch as one side simply cannot exist without its "other," and, in the process, meaning occurs somewhere *between* the two extremes. Where the critic chooses to stop the plasticity of signification determines, to a large extent, her own terministic or, in Gadamer's terminology, philosophical, position. By reading as a woman, a Marxist, a secularist, or any number of identities, a reader may direct textual flow toward a specific agenda and halt the flow when enough theoretical "energy" accumulates to validate perspective. Hence, the terministic screen implies both a projection to and from a specific reality; and it is in this dynamic process that meaning emerges *between* the text and the reader rather than at one end or the other of the binary structure. By projecting our own terminology upon a preexistent object text, we reveal our own sources of identity in concert with the prompts the text brings to us. Again, we are, essentially, defined by our own means of identification. The text/situation serves as a foil for the reader's self-interpretation, which is necessary to a personal sense of legitimation in a continually changing world.

Burke sees our way of viewing an object and our way of speaking about it as a means of directing attention toward specific perspectives concerning the truth within the object-text and its relation to ideological strata specific to the reader. The way we "see" a thing is directly related to how we name it into our world. As Burke tells us, "Nomenclature necessarily directs attention into some channels rather than others" (*Language*, 45). If we view a text terministically, only pre-chosen facets of a specific gem of meaning will show in the unique light cast by each specific individual or discourse community that chooses to "identify" with it. The terministic screen, then, relates to a group's unique cultural vantage point and the terminology intrinsic to its own belief-system. The

246 Dennis J. Ciesielski

combination of these factors, rather than their direct opposition, defines base reality into truth-systems unique to each respective discourse community and implies a neo-pragmatic, social constructionist pattern for the making of meaning. Hence, we can see Burke's belief in belief as lying in the probable and the contextual. Meaning emerges from the pragmatic truths found within social concurrence, the transactive area between the choices inherent in the traditional subjective/objective model. Driving home his incipient neo-pragmatic theory, he claims that "much that we take as observations about 'reality' may be but the spinning out of possibilities implicit in our particular terms" (46). Meaning, here, is not a choice between one binary end or the other but, rather, it is the product of a conscious meeting-in-the-middle based on a reader's unique ratiocination between the either/or choices we have inherited from traditional Cartesian thought.

The quest for identification, thus, finds itself within its own activity—the symbolic action of criticism itself reveals, as well as establishes, the analyst's own needs and expectations in a world of contingencies and leaves open the door to further possibilities through future textual transactions. It is through this sense of meta-criticism that we are able to place Burke as nearly as possible in a representative school of secular theory and neo-pragmatism—secular pragmatism—which demonstrates, roughly, the idea that truth is socially (and historically) [re]constructed through a sense of communal concurrence and historical flux. This dynamic way of knowing offers us the secular equivalent of religion in maxims, myth, and tradition, as well as a quasi religious code of nonsecular piety and privilege by which specific discourse groups can define and sustain a sense of communal self that will, in turn, support a larger, more general ideological apparatus by which a culture-at-large is sustained.

Burke exercises his own critical and social identity on text in *A Rhetoric of Motives*. By applying a biohistorical approach to classical and neo-classical poets as well as their texts, he discovers a certain personal/social agenda that the ostensibly unsocial, text-centered, New Critics could not attain. Bringing in extratextual considerations, he resocializes the text in a dialogue between the author and his own socially constructed life as well as the reader and his or her own perspectives. Ideally, previously polarized historical and contemporary concerns join through a traditionally static object-text to define and redefine the human condition using the text in both its temporal perspectives: then and now. By showing how Milton (in "Samson Agonistes") may have identified with Samson's strengths, weaknesses, blindness, heroism, his socialized suicide (martyrdom), and so on (3–6), Burke gives us a positive look into the author, history, and ourselves, rather than a distanced, hermetic perusal of formal objectives designed to contain meaning within the object-text alone.

Through his secular reading, Burke discovers that the personal and political variables within Milton's perspective, in concert with the poem's scriptural and, thus, mythical origin, imply a poststructural sense of binary opposition, that is, the tension between a spiritual and a temporal authority that can be further related to the sociohistorical tension between God and king, church and state, magic and science, and the like. This theoretical (rhetorical) observation allows a historical text to speak with us on contemporary terms, thus allowing the reader to come to her own conclusions through the very oppositions Burke observes in Milton's seventeenth-century text. The text, in this sense, is "dehistoricized" and brought into the day-to-day concerns of the secular reader. Viewing binary sequencing in this way advances a positive concept of polarization and the realization that poststructuralism's deconstructive *differance* can serve to bring us together in the meaning-making process rather than keep us forever lost to meaning in light of its linguistically ever-elusive nature. Once we realize that truth lies in a dialogic transaction, that it is dynamic rather than static, we can see it as a tool to further meaning rather than as a set of authorial codes that threaten to stop Burke's "never-ending conversation" altogether. The distinction between idea and image and how this [de]combination compels us into new beliefs and parallel social action depends on the reader's own choices to remake new, socially usable images in sync with her own time and immediate cultural needs. Hence, through the manipulation of language and perspective we can redefine textual truth within the standards of our own historicity through a transactive dialogue in which we bring as much to the work as we take from it—and, in the final analysis, both the reader and the text itself become more valid in the world where this transaction takes place.

A Secular Pedagogy:
Putting Hamlet on the Map

A Burkean reading works well in the contemporary literature classroom, where many students often find canonical texts difficult and, at best, a questionable means to acquiring knowledge. By circumventing the traditional roles of teacher and text as receptacles of static meaning, we can help our students "make the text their own" by encouraging them to become, in Burke's words, "students of [a text's] strategies" (*Philosophy*, 296–97), a term that designates *how* a text means rather than *what* it means. By addressing the "hows" the readers might discover their own strategies for meaning in the contemporary world by "merging" with the text's own apparent historical, ideological outlay. In this way the text is freed from its own historicity to speak with the reader within her own experience. Hence, we discover (and confront) a basic binary team based in the terms of then/now and, in the process of relating the story's inherent human qualities that have stood the test of time (Burke refers to this as a "sociological critique"), the reader can lift the text from its hermetic setting to "apply [it] beyond literature to life in general (thus helping to take literature out of its separate bin and give it a place in a general 'sociological' picture)" (296).

By encouraging young readers to apply their own experience (now) to the text's symbolic action (then), rather than provoking a frantic search for the "right answers" to questions that might never concern them as readers and experiencers in the world, we will aid them in the setting up of a binary structure between whose points a unique reader-centered meaning can "happen" in the overlap of then/now, reader/author, experience/text, fact/abstraction. The object, here, is to move readers into a positive sense of self by allowing them to discover their own terministic screens and their own patterns of judgment based in a personal transaction with the object-text and all that it entails—to encourage them in the making of their own meaning in conjunction with the textual prompts they have just experienced. Once a student realizes a personal connection, she can enter into a dialogue with the story, and her own way of "knowing" the story, on levels pertinent to her own existence instead of simply talking about it from an impersonal academic distance.

The realization that reading and knowing are based in active trans-action rather than passive acceptance can bring a reader into his own confident sense of textual power based in Burke's theory of "consub-stantiality," the point where one gains the ability to identify both the self with other and the other with self—the joining of one's voice with an other's to become one in language by "acting together" to create a meaning intrinsic to each reader's unique textual experience (*Rhetoric of Motives*, 21). Here, the extreme ends of the binary team join in dialogue, rather than doing textual battle, to create an ultimately new reading based in active transaction. Burke realized the foundations of his consub-stantiation theory early on. In an observation of reading's transactive nature in *Counter-Statement*, published in 1931, he recognizes the reader's own power over the text: "any reader surrounds each word and each act in a work of art with a unique set of his own previous exper-iences. . . . [C]ommunication exist[s] in the 'margin of overlap' between the writer's experience and the reader's" (78). This "overlap" is the point where consubstantiation occurs, the point where the binary teams of reader/writer, experience/text meet to step beyond each other's own unique sphere into the newness of a dynamic textual meaning. When a reader (and writer) realize that meaning is a team effort, a both/and rather than an either/or proposition, the textual discussion can get under way on a positive dynamic grounding. Hence, a Burkean pedagogy begins with bringing a young reader into a strong sense of self and a deeper knowledge of how this "self" relates to textual experience. This sense of self is necessary to a successful textual dialogue—to be intimidated by a text or a contemporary situation is oppression; and the oppressed seldom control their own truth-systems.

Thus, the main hurdle in this type of pedagogy is to bring the student into a confident sense of textual power. Although we all have our own sets of terministic screens, too many students fear rejection in the classroom and must be led into areas from which they can speak with authority. A good example of this sort of textual authority occurred in a recent introductory literature class. In my attempt to bring *Hamlet* to a point of mutual interest, I questioned the importance of familial unity as a microcosm of the larger macropolitical unit (i.e., the binary structures of micro/macro family/government, father/king, good-king/bad-king, etc.) We then, as a group, discovered that Denmark's political demise might be, in many ways, tied to the demise of the family unit, a flaw represented by fratricide, an obscure king-father figure, a passive queen-mother, gender inequity in the motherless Polonius family, intrigue, insanity, and so on. In dialogue, we discovered that, on a large scale, the "general" fails because of the "particular's" disunity; the castle falls both physically and metaphorically because of foundational decay.

As students of Burke's "strategies," the students progressed into questions regarding power structures and the relationship between the "little guys" and the "big guys" and how the smaller, seemingly insignificant aspects of a whole are necessary to the whole's condition. Eventually the discussion settled into a lively debate on the condition of the contemporary American family and how this condition relates to the overall culturo-political climate in which all families must exist. Suddenly, the *Hamlet* text became a necessary point of historical reference to either prove or refute the students' own contemporary concerns based within each speaker's unique experience. At this point the once difficult, disinterested "assignment" took on a position of importance in their own making of meaning through the process of identity. Students who were once lost in the play's language and metaphor were now loudly (and correctly) quoting and citing from its previously confusing verse because of their own personal stake in its meaning. By playing the canonical text against their own life-text, they reached Burke's area of consubstantiation to discover that the text's meaning lives within their own transaction with it. By dialoguing with the text rather than holding their own monologic ground, both reader and text gained a legitimate place in the classroom and the in world outside the classroom.

One of the more interesting written responses concerning the *Hamlet* discussion came from a young inner-city African American woman who deftly paralleled the trouble in Denmark to the Rodney King riots in Los Angeles. Using her own ethnic experience in conjunction with the text, she was able to discuss the problems of inner-city relations, the dysfunctional family, and the ethically corrupt power structures that, in her estimation, both create and maintain the landscape in which this dysfunction (micro) and the riots (macro) took place. Placing Police Commissioner Gates in the role of a postmodern Claudius, Rodney King in the role of Hamlet (the marginalized stepson and true heir to the throne), and the officers involved in the beating as Rosencrantz and Guildenstern, she launched into a dissertation on the negative qualities of a political power founded on intrigue and the unstable family unit which is, itself, created by the major power's neglect of it. Yet, in her final analysis, because she had reached the point of consubstantiation through a dialogic relationship with "both sides of the story," she was forced to concede that the family (here the ethnic community) itself might have to accept part of the blame in its neglect and mistrust of the system and what it, at least superficially, hoped to achieve on the social level. Because both ends of this binary structure worked against one another, meaning was decentered, marginalized in power struggles until the inevitable firefall occurred.

The inherent political agenda here allowed my student to see a larger picture of active/passive roles in general (Gates versus King), which served to refocus her view on family matters in particular. Seeing the Gates/King dichotomy as dangerous helped her see the danger in the negative male/female, husband/wife, father/mother dichotomy. The danger she saw in these binary oppositions is that they are accepted as truth even though they reveal a lack of positive dialogue and the ability to share power-decisions in line with Burke's own concept of the poetic metaphor, where all community members are able to share in their political structures as active participants (*Permanence*, 266). This passive acceptance, she discovered, produces a hierarchy that can exist only on the basis of oppression and control, a structure that places power in an either/or situation rather than in a both/and environment where healthy dialogue will produce a positive sense of family on all levels. Her final analysis placed meaning and power in a succinct light: "Maybe if we could all just sit down and know our differences together, wouldn't be no fighting for nothing at all in the city or in the house." By allowing herself an open dialogue with the *Hamlet* text, this young writer was able to open a higher dialogue with the world and thus realize that a responsible sense of meeting in the middle is the only way to avert anarchy and total familial and political destruction—that a certain dynamic system of shared values and social "conversations" is necessary to a positive communal or political unit and that the main source of this necessary order springs from positive codes that begin in the most basic of all political units: the family.

After a short conference with the writer, I discovered that she herself was the product of a "broken home" and that *Hamlet* and the ensuing discussion of family had brought her into a sense of knowing that had eluded her during the first half of the class. Not until she was able to place her self in the picture with the "other" represented by the text was she able to gain what the text has to offer each reader—a view of self and personal values. And once self and values are brought into play the text can, as in my student's case, bring a secular knowledge that legitimates both the academic and the real world by placing them together in real experience. The textual power inherent in the realization of self, then, is necessary to the positive assimilation of binary structures that, all too often, threaten to overpower the reader and life-experience due to the academic devaluation of the subjective in favor of the historical object-text. By discussing an immediate experience through the grid of *Hamlet*'s own symbolic action, a student who was essentially lost in her search for textual (and possibly secular) meaning came to understand, not only the text, itself a necessary part of any textual discourse, but her own view of the political dimensions of community and family. By merging the objective with the subjective, rather than choosing one over the other, this young reader assimilated the text on both academic and nonacademic levels to lift *Hamlet* from simple literature into a useful commentary on the human condition. In reading *Hamlet*, she learned to read her world as well.

Metaphor: The Mechanics of Social Truth

Burke's distinction between meaning object and the symbolic action that occurs at their interface strongly informs Remy de Gourmont's fact-abstraction theory (11–16). De Gourmant's model for meaning aims to break down certain truths by exposing and analyzing a symbiotic relationship between "fact" and the "abstraction" by which these truths are ideologically validated—in Burkean terms fact and abstraction relate to object-text and a reader's perspective. De Gourmont's model, observes Burke, "nihilistically" separates fact and abstraction "to show that [fact's] factual side has no logically necessary connection with [its] abstract ideal side" (*Rhetoric of Motives*, 150–51). Thus de Gourmont drives home his point that ideas are simply "worn out images . . . which *resist* dissociation because of the part that special interests play in human thinking" (151, my emphasis). (It is in this sense that the young *Hamlet* critic observes the social acceptance of negative, yet secure, dominant/subdominant codes in the American family.) Similarly, in more [post]modern terms, our call for meaning both desires and resists change at its very source: social consensus. Our concept of truth and the power of truth are so ingrained in everyday life that we are compelled to embrace it tenaciously, on one hand, as a lifeline tethered to our own sense of cultural identity, on the other, as a reductive ballast of residual pieties holding us in a realm of positivistic stasis—and it is in this dichotomy that we find Burke's answer to the postmodern debate: held in thrall by our need for order, we must yet realize the dynamic nature of order.

De Gourmont's "decentering" of truth demonstrates the role of motive in the making of meaning; it anticipates postmodern deconstruction and informs Burke's theory of perspective by incongruity, wherein we see that all meaning is, essentially, metaphorical (*Permanence*, 89–97). Here, as in de Gourmont's polarization of fact and abstraction, Burke addresses the social dialogue necessary in the making of meaning through metaphor and its importance to communication in a dynamic, intersubjective community, an activity that our *Hamlet* critic puts to good use in her implied concept of family as political unit.

Dynamicism and intersubjectivity define truth's socially reflective nature. The objective reality around us (text) can only "mean" through its influence on us; thus, it is "fact's" influence, within specific contexts, which directs our identification of the object in accordance with our own needs. Truth is contextual. Meaning lies in the metaphors we ourselves create through what Giles Gunn sees as a deeply ingrained tendency in our speech to call things by their "'wrong' names" (80). A key word here is "things," the objective facts toward which our perspective is necessarily directed. George Lakoff and Mark Johnson distinguish between de Gourmont's fact-abstraction and Burke's object-perspective in terms of existence and meaning—how an object "means" lies on a higher plane than mere existence. Pure objectivism can only establish the true or false of an empirical situation (201); but, by fitting language and perspective to an object, we essentially define the truth of that object on affective terms. Thus, the truth-value of the *Hamlet* text for a young inner-city African American woman emerges in metaphors of family and culturo-political agendas—concerns that reach deeply into her own history. And, in the final analysis, we must see the object-text as a metaphor for the contemporary ideals that are the reader's own driving force. *Hamlet* the play (object) takes a secondary role to the "play" that it inspires in the reader (perspective).

Burke's pragmatic tendencies work in concert with secular criticism. Legitimate truths are those that allow an object to work for us. In this sense, the truth really can set us free—however, this freedom must be reinvested in the maintenance of a dynamic truth-system rather than the institutionalization of static authorial codes. Thus, an object gains meaning through the conditions of probability by which it becomes true or false for us; or, in the Jamesian sense, the basis of our usable truths lies in how reality influences us both culturally and personally. Objectivity is necessary to intersubjectivity. In this sense, truth is found in the melding of binary oppositions into a higher sense of social knowledge. As William James avers, "Pragmatism is uncomfortable away from facts" (38); pragmatic reality could not exist without the backdrop of empirical reality any more than could the metaphors through which we gain our necessary sense of identity.

We can find a literary illustration of James' "fact" and Burke's secular interpretation of the objective in Robert Frost's "Mending Wall." Frost's poem sets up a binary structure for pragmatic meaning that works around the premise "good fences make good neighbors." Formally, this phrase can, itself, be seen as a sort of textual fence or divider when we consider its placement in the near center of the poem (l. 27), when the maxim comes to light, and then again at the end (l. 45), when it is repeated with a sense of finality after the speaker's questioning of the necessity of boundaries and the validity of the neighbor's traditional stance that walls are, indeed, necessary to a positive social situation.

From the pragmatic stance, the reader must deal with two compelling "realities," the text itself and the wall which is the problematic object within the text, and is forced into a usable conclusion concerning the social validity of both. From Burke's secular (or, in his own terms, "sociological") stance, we can see the text as a "proverb writ large" (*Philosophy*, 296) and, indeed, poem's reigning message does take on the sound of a proverb or maxim based in enthymematic principles, that is, previous consensus is the basis for further consensus—truth is based in what we already "know" to be true. The idea of the enthymeme is important to the poem's meaning here, for if proverbs are, as Burke claims, strategies for dealing with situations (293–94), we readers must identify both the strategy and the situation inherent in each textual [re]presentation. By acting on the poem's enigmatic theme, "good fences make good neighbors," we can divide the proverb into its two working parts: "good fences" becomes the strategy; "good neighbors" becomes the situation. To paraphrase, a positive means of demarcation and identity allows for a positive social condition. Here we can see how *differance* can bring us into a dynamic sense of shared meaning in the maintenance of the distinction (rather than its deconstruction) between the "I" and "Thou" of traditional Cartesian thought—each neighbor's identity is both reinforced and influenced by the "other" on which this identity must necessarily be projected. Thus, when seen from a postmodern perspective, Frost's wall becomes the "slash" between two binarily opposed yet inseparable positions (+/-) whose only point of reference is their own oppositional interface, which they must create and maintain together in order to survive: "I let my neighbor know beyond the hill/ And on a day we meet to walk the line/And set the wall between us once again/We keep the wall between us as we go" (ll. 12–15).

The separatory wall-slash becomes the main factor in each side's own sense of identity and legitimation. Although natural forces tend to erode our "walls" ("Something there is that doesn't love a wall") we, as order-seeking humans, cannot exist without them; because we must live within the larger, inassimilable sphere of Nature we must find a usable sense of order within it through the creation of smaller assimilable spheres of our own by placing a contextual meaning on the base realities Nature supplies. Referential boundaries are necessary to human identity inasmuch as they imply a sense of control through Burke's "fiction of ownership" (*Rhetoric of Motives*, 33), a process by which we merely allow an other to *own* his identity through material and ideational means so that we ourselves might have a way to gauge our own sense of control in the world we must necessarily share. Without this sense of owning there can be no parametrical marking-off of the sociocultural walls by which we are defined. As Burke observes, "The cult of property comes to reflect public norms, norms identified with social classes which are differentiated by property" (130). What we "own" privately, from land to ideas, represents where and how we exist publicly. Hence, Frost's wall allows for both a private and a public identity in its position as the interface of binary terms; and the transactional nature of this interface creates the dialogic energy by which human order is created and maintained.

However, if a reader is not able to accept the irony of the fence metaphor, that what has traditionally been seen as an oppressive barrier can become a positive point of social interface, she will be forced into a reductive either/or model for meaning, a condition echoed by Frost's speaker when he wonders what his wall will be "walling in or walling out" (l. 33). This either/or position, the inability to see, as it were, both sides of the fence, brings dialogue and thus dynamic human order to a grinding halt. The dualistic reader must find her meaning either through a pantheistic hermeneutic where Nature (chaos) holds forth and the fence becomes not only a negative divider, but a scar on Nature's purity or through a static human-order model where all tradition becomes unerring law. However, in either case, the fence will come apart. On the one hand, if the neighbors remain totally separate, out of dialogue, they cannot come together to maintain what Nature "doesn't love," that is, their own sense of order. Hence total separation of identities will bring nothing but a pervading chaos which is, for all purposes, the binary opposite of identity. On the other hand, a total sense of monologic order on either side of the fence will block out the dynamic communication necessary to the fence's maintenace; for, in the process of erosion, some of the wall's "boulders" have fallen to one neighbor's side while others have fallen to the wall's other side. Hence each neighbor has a responsibility to replace what has fallen from his side of the social boundary—it takes two to maintain a positive sense of identity in the larger sphere of the natural world. If the neighbors neglect dialogue, truth can never be shared and will, thus, become the basis for a negative power struggle between those who would know the truth—in this sense the term *wall* takes on its oppressive connotations as a barrier rather than a forum.

Although a dualistic reading of Frost's poem pivots on the desire for a positive social situation, the reader must divest self of the idea that a positive social situation rests in codes of power and control. If not, the fence (strategy) will work negatively to keep people separated, away from the "other," while the fence's removal will keep people scattered with no sense of public space or shared forum from which a sense of human identity will emerge through the dialogue they invite. Hence, even from the enthymematic consensus that good neighbors are desirable and that boundaries promote good social relations, we must investigate the strategy (fences) and how it works in concert with the situation. We must look to the divider rather than the divided.

The poem and the wall share the same theoretical space—they are lines of demarcation, points of interface, which serve to bring together, rather than separate, the two sides produced through their very existence (i.e., reader/text, neighbor/neighbor). The poem addresses the importance of humanity's self-set parameters of identity in a naturally chaotic world, while the poem's speakers question the necessity of material boundaries in a natural environment that does not need them—"Something there is that doesn't love a wall/That wants it down." (ll. 35–36). Moving through the text, we discover a series of unreconcilable dichotomies (or differ-

ences) that bring us to the realization that there really are no easy
answers here; what exists for the speakers is simply an ongoing dialogue,
and it is this dialogue that maintains the wall as much as it is the wall
that keeps the dialogue alive. This symbiotic energy illustrates Burke's
dialectic action of merger and division, the give-and-take action of
dialogue that allows the constant building and rebuilding of consensus
(the wall) at each stage of interface which, in Frost's poem, is set in the
spring, a symbol of cyclic rebirth. In this sense there is no real monologic
answer here because there is no real sense of a monologic individual
distinct from the rest of humanity—self is always defined through a
strong sense of "other"; we are known through our differences; we meet
in the between created at the interface of unique identities. Because we
know self through other, we must necessarily recognize the boundaries
we, together, create and realize Burke's observation that "the so-called 'I'
is merely a unique combination of 'corporate we's'" (*Attitudes*, 264)
produced in dialogue. Meeting at and maintaining the wall intrinsic to
both sides allows these "we's" to occur; and with each new meeting new
"corporations" obtain.

In the "Mending Wall," the speaker's neighbor will not move from
tradition while the speaker, even though it is he who calls the neighbor to
the task of repair, cannot truly accept tradition; yet they discourse on the
nature of the parameters they both honor; and through this discourse,
each neighbor creates an identity for self as well as for his partner-in-
dialogue. The speaker sees his ultratraditional neighbor as an unenlight-
ened yet well-meaning fellow who "moves in darkness" (l. 41) "like an
old stone-age savage" (l. 40) bent on a primitive sense of territorial
demarcation. In painting this somewhat negative picture of "other" he
identifies himself in the light of his own self-implied wisdom. Here, the
speaker can be seen as symbolic of unbridled philosophy, base
intellectuality that has lost touch with empirical experience; while the
traditionalist neighbor, in his taciturn repetition of one simple thought,
might symbolize the utilitarian value of static order and tradition
["behind his father's saying" (l. 43)] over philosophical contemplation.

Although the poem's symbolic action serves to create a series of
complex multi-oppositional teams, the major binary team on which all
others rest is time/being in its relation to Nature and humanity. The
speaker, who questions tradition and static order, leans toward the
Nature category while the traditional, order-prone neighbor relates to
the more human side of the model. To further this distinction, we might
see the philosophical speaker identified with time (in this sense, I refer to
time as Heidegger's "large-time"—the undivided, nonsegmented space
within which our own sense of time exists) and the traditional neighbor

identified with being (the human ability to find a place in the world by setting up parameters of meaning in both abstract and material models). For the sake of illustration, we could take this strategy yet further by relating the poem's implied extremes as: speaker = chaos and neighbor = order. In this light we are able to see the absurdity of choosing one side over the other: either total no-meaning or abject order. And, in the process of this realization, we must see the necessity of a dialogue between the two, a dynamic transaction where one side keeps the other in check. The speaker legitimates the wall through his questioning of it, while the neighbor legitimates the wall through a passive acceptance of traditional values.

This transaction happens at Frost's wall, the point of interface between the two extremes. That the two neighbors meet each spring to repair the "gaps" in their own tenuous order brought about by Nature during the cold, symbolically dead winter months when little dialogue takes place, shows the value each of them places on the situation and the cyclic rebirth of the point where they meet each spring. How they see the strategy is, as Burke, James, and Gadamer might claim, historically inconsequential. The fence works for each side on different levels of knowing; and this is the bottom line—whereas the speaker is suspect of too much order, the neighbor fears impending anarchy, a binary opposition that brings to light the tenuous balance between liberal and conservative views. Each neighbor's terministic screen is focused on the situation of "good neighbors" and social harmony, and the wall is the means to this end because it allows each side to maintain the identity necessary to the neighbor concept. Without fences, lines of demarcation, the slash (/) between binary teams, the term *neighbor* would not hold meaning; dialogue could not exist. Meaning can have no meaning in a world without interface, and all interface is founded on rhetorical identity.

The implication that silence breeches the wall of positive interface and dialogue reinforces Burke's constant call for participation, conversation, and the symbolic action of language through the dialectic merger and division of ideas in a world that needs walls and texts which serve as self-created public space where ideas meet to create and maintain our own sense of legitimation. On the secular level the proverb, "Good fences make good neighbors," allows for a more in-depth view of the necessity of ownership, both abstract and material, as a means for identity within the larger, un-ownable, natural world we, as seekers of order, have wrapped in language so that we might know it. If the world is a place from which our meaning emerges and in which it must work for us, textual experience is the wall at which we must meet to maintain and [re]align our position in the world. As critic Lois Tyson observes, "a literary text . . . is a site for cultural production in which multiple unstable meanings vie for dominance" (230). It is in this friendly competition for meaning, this give-and-take volley of necessarily un-ownable truths across the wall and back again, that Burke would have us see in the reading of Frost's poem. The poem's usability here lies in the reader's realization that dialogue is both the builder and maintainer of an ownable public space within the non-ownable space of the natural world which presents to us the base realities we, as humans, are compelled to interpret contextually, that meaning lies in the dynamic interface between question and answer, subject and object. The secular-pragmatic approach to text insists that we remain "in the between" if we are to move beyond the static truths of foundationalist thought. By seeing the "sociological" impact of a text, rather than its purely academic value, we can lift it "beyond literature into life in general" (*Philosophy*, 296), where it truly can become equipment for living. In maintaining Frost's metaphorical wall, the positive space between all of us, we maintain each other's sense of identity in a never-ending search based in Burke's rhetoric of identification wherein we become participants in meaning— where we act rather than allow ourselves to be acted upon.

The "secular-pragmatic" investigation of fact/text is not aimed at what the text speaks to us or what we speak to it but rather how we *transact* with it on a practical social plane. If metaphor informs meaning, the critic, by discovering and "decentering" privileged objectives within metaphor and text, will create a tertiary textual meaning through the manipulation of previous orientations and readerly perspectives. By juxtaposing dissimilar orientations (such as the liberal and conservative views of Frost's rural neighbors) we can gain a new perspective on an object-text and use this perspective in a subjective value judgment to [re]socialize previously static interpretations. Hence, perspective not only creates the metaphors by which we believe; it also serves as a tool by which we might rhetorically manipulate objectivist "reality" to create a tailored truth designed to augment or maintain certain ideological standards necessary to the cultural task at hand; and these standards reveal themselves, as Burke tells us, in a culture's specific views of art and literature.

The Postmodern Conversation

Burke's sense of "secular pragmatism" emerges in his view of art and literary text: true art, rather than addressing a preplanned cultural agenda ought to reoffer a culture's sense of self back into its own ongoing dialogue. In this sense the artistic/textual "message" is found not in the artist's reification of a cultural standard, but in the culture's own acceptance of the work as a candidate for art in conjunction with the artist, the reader, and various shared historical, cultural, and communal perspectives. This pragmatic validation of art within the community, the transactive process necessary to the shared definition between art and its purveyor, illustrates the necessity of a reader's own textual power in the interpretive act. Here we see Burke's theory of interpretation in parallel with John Dewey's concept of active experience, which necessarily joins the "reader's" own terministic evaluation with the art-object in order to attain an aesthetic truth-value that will raise both the reader and the object to new levels of meaning; and it is in this new meaning that we discover (or create) aesthetic experience. Hence, it is the reader's own creative action that discovers the object's aesthetic qualities within the context of each viewing. Dewey recognizes the necessity of active interpretation as a sort of reconstruction of the object: "Without an act of re-creation, the object is not perceived as a work of art" (54). This "re-creation" of the object into the viewer's perception of art applies to the written text as well. Louise Rosenblatt, a contemporary of both Burke and Dewey, relates Dewey's active experience to textual experience, observing that a work cannot become a poem until the reader places a sense of self-interpretation upon the "un-activated" text (12–13, 16–17) Only when this active transaction between reader and text occurs can the text become for the reader what Dewey's sense of art is for the active viewer. In each sense the object, on all levels, becomes an invitation to interpretation rather than a static source of authorial meaning—art/text does not tell us what to know; rather, it invites us to know on our own terms, to create our own sense of what art is for us. Pragmatically speaking, the "experiencer" holds an interpretive responsibility to the same extent as the artist does. Thus, the art of text and the text of art must join with the reader's life to create a meaning unique to the ratio of two specific parts which, when joined, create a much larger, socially productive whole. This secular demystification of text brings art into a dynamic world where it can join Burke's ongoing conversation rather than remaining on static display, mired in its own historical "truth."

Secular pragmatism's message is clear. Meaning is not found in the static, foundationalist attitude of pure objectivity, but in the dialogue of binary forces that contribute to each other a sort of miasmic, yet definitive energy that changes with each reader and with each reader's successive readings as well. Because cultural experience is not static, neither can truth be static. Thus, theoretical investigation into social and cultural concerns within literature as well as empirical experience becomes essential. From religious ritual to scientific development, a culture operates on the energy of its storytellers. John Schilb's recent observation that "Literature emerges as a culturally produced category for texts, [and thus provokes] questions of history, philosophy, politics" (60), echoes Edward Said's secular intentions when Said asks a text how it "works for the reader." Said claims that the socializing tendencies of specific texts can demonstrate how cultures are "ennobled and validated" (2) by the [new] texts which they generate through the personal and group grids of unique, creative individuals—both authors and readers.

The multiplicity of questions generated by the secular pragmatists implies a move toward postmodern dialogue through interdisciplinary tactics and a multitheoretical approach to answer for the social as well as the literary validity of an object-text. But the bifurcation of text here implies an extended set of binary sequences created and maintained within the very social structure that seeks to dismantle them. In his anticipation of both the social-constructionist call for the breakdown of foundationalist patterns of meaning and poststructuralist deconstructive patterns, Burke is able to maintain a sense of nervous equilibrium between the images and ideas, the facts and abstractions, within the shared text of community and culture.

Unlike the poststructuralists, Burke values human meaning and sees its necessity for our cultural existence. His social (pragmatic) side compels him to see textual ambiguity in the nature of a never-ending dialogue between experiencer and experience. Meaning occurs as a sort of "moveable feast," the product of all the dynamic integers that will arise through all of the various textual transactions that might take place in the interpretive experience. In this sense all [post]modern critics are, as William Covino observes, rhetoricians:

> I have tried to portray an emergent, interdisciplinary critical theory, fundamentally a theory of discourse that devalues certainty and closure while it celebrates that generative power of imagination. Kenneth Burke reminds us that [postmodernists] with their acute sense of relativism and ambiguity of every statement are our rhetoricians. . . . Burke recognizes that rhetoric partakes from and contributes to the many voices of social inquiry and equates rhetoric with "identification," social cohesion that results when a multiplicity of views interact. (28)

Thus, Burke's secular pragmatic view of Milton's "Samson Agonistes," in *A Rhetoric of Motives*, finds meaning within de Gourmont's fact/abstraction juxtaposition as well as the then/now breakdown of historicism.

Instead of cleaving one part of the binary "team" from its under-privileged "other," he finds a probable truth in the interactive gray area between magic and spell, religion and prayer, the political act and the social act.

In light of the probable nature of social truths Burke marks the distinction between idealism and pragmatism. Idealism's optimistic "bureaucratization of the imaginative" tends to see a pure sense of good in the reification of an abstract ideal; whereas pragmatism (in the Jamesian sense) notes the necessary presence of the ideal product's binary opposite or, as Burke refers to it, an "unwanted by-product" (*Permanence*, 282). Thus, on our quest for meaning and identification, we create a series of dyadic truths existing as both privileged and nonprivileged concepts that, over time, gain a sense of piety and "correctness"; and through this sense of right thinking, they maintain themselves through the systems of their own creation. Often, an unwanted by-product will gain certain advantages over its privileged side. (Although this action would seem evolutionary on the term's part, in fact, the term remains static while our own dynamic perception of it evolves). But the privileged base resists change in the name of tradition and piety, allowing power exchanges to take place only in the areas of privileged access defined by those who attain power through them. The modern court system is a good example of this process. Law, originally a concept designed to protect people, has evolved into a means of social control in order to protect those who hold the reins of social and economic power—the truth-value of law, then, is how we now perceive the concept in opposition to the motive involved in its original "creation."

Since Burke sees truth and meaning as the product of perspective, his way to a healthy social dynamic is through the redirection of perspective. As we have seen, a good way to promote this process lies in setting the groundwork of secular reorientation in the literature classroom. It is here that the vicarious social experience within literary texts and the potential for rearranging the sociocultural hierarchies they represent will demonstrate the probable nature of truth and the reader's own power to choose and create a meaning unique to her own experience through responsible social and textual analysis.

Secular Pragmatism and the Postmodern: A Lesson Plan for the Future

Pragmatism and poststructuralism hold the concept of binary opposition in common; both base their operations on a two-sided truth. But there is a major distinction between the two theories: on one hand,

262   Dennis J. Ciesielski

poststructuralists (in the narrow sense) claim that we have no choice but to escape pluralistic, predetermined meaning. To destroy the over-privileged perspective we must destroy the whole truth-system and defray meaning to the point of no meaning. Pragmatists, on the other hand, hold that truth is a series of contextual "trade-offs." Meaning lies in a carefully weighed social concurrence. Pragmatic truth is dynamic, dialogic. The pragmatic "reader" sees the same binary oppositions that the post-structuralist sees, but the pragmatist sees them in the knowledge that a certain order is necessary to the human condition. Thus, she will make choices based in the transaction between self and both sides of the binary team and stop the process when a pleasurable sense of Burke's identification obtains. Rather than a rule-laden critical model, Giles Gunn sees pragmatic interpretation as a hermeneutic theory whose central issue is "neither what texts say about us nor what we say about them, but what we can learn from the forms of otherness they mediate to us" (68).

Burke's incipient deconstructive tactics combined with his pragmatic tendencies place him in a position to apply a poststructuralist grid in a pragmatic approach to text; in other words, by employing deconstructive strategies, the critic can expose the binary oppositions in a text in order to pragmatically dismantle and reassemble them according to his own immediate needs—deconstruction, on Burkean terms, becomes a sort of reconstruction, and truth/meaning is altered rather than defrayed. Thus, a text's cultural/textual building blocks are tumbled and restacked in a reassessment of text, author, reader, and the world in which they presently operate.

Anticipating the postmodern concern with the ambiguities in language and text, Burke discusses, in his "Definition of Man," the role of antithesis in what he calls "polar terms," and comes to the conclusion that the negative side of the binary sequence is "principle" because, "1: Yes and no imply one another; 2: In their role as opposites they limit each other" (*Language*, 11–12). The idea here is one of linguistic checks and balances; by replacing "yes and no" with good and evil, true and false or, in the social sense, I and thou, we can better see how one side literally creates and supports the other. And because of this symbiotic relationship, it is entirely impossible to recognize only one side of a particular situation or experience. Hence, it is the critic's goal to investigate the dynamic relationship between the two binary extremes and how they work together to compel us into a sense of our own meaning.

The secular value in a pragmatically controlled deconstruction of hierarchy lies not so much in the presentation of a finished analysis (product) as it does in the pedagogy behind it (process). Once a student learns to reassess perspective on and through a text, she becomes her own critic of the pan-text, the world in which we must all exist. Approaching a text as an interdisciplinary construct necessarily brings with it Burke's concept of binary checks and balances that must be either accepted or altered. Reading through a secular lens, the student soon realizes that she cannot turn her back to culturicity; we all see the world through unique terministic screens; we all take sides. And, it is this taking of sides itself that must be investigated through the vicarious action of the text in conjunction with the reader's transactive experience with this action.

By discussing the concept of ideological priorities, class codes, and so on, the literature "guide" can validate the abstract through the lens of an approachable, referential text. For instance, the juxtaposition of magic, religion, and science symbolized by the frozen turkey hearts and their failure to produce the desired effect as a love potion in Louise Erdrich's novel *Love Medicine* (see the appendix) represents a young Native American man's cultural confusion against the backdrop of his strong regard for family unity—which, in itself, is the foundation for cultural and political unity. The cultural, economic, and religious juxtaposition of Eurocentric ideals as opposed to Native American culture and history, if accepted from the privileged position of the "dominant paradigm," will maintain the perspective that compels one to see Erdrich's young "hero," Lipsha Morrissey, as a "dumb Indian" who can't keep his life together even in a welfare state—I've had students read the text in this way. But we can "decenter" this type of interpretation if we can lead the students who subscribe to dominant utilitarian models to participate in the text from the dramatistic position inherent in Burke's rhetoric of identification. If one can relate the polarized causal objects, the elusive, magical wild geese whose lifetime mating habits are symbolic of the marital devotion Lipsha desires for his troubled grandparents and the dead, frozen turkeys he substitutes for these unachievable talismans, to the sense of love, family, and warmth, the symbolically unattainable geese are supposed to bring, the elusive geese, and their inherent ritualistic magic, win out as the desired objects. And, much to the students' surprise, they are forced to either redirect their perspective from White to un-White, from the power of money to the nobility of stoic poverty, from science to magic and ritual, or to abandon their own deeper preferences for family, warmth, and nurture. The Native American belief-system inherent in the symbolic geese represents the unprivileged position of the ethnic underdog while simultaneously symbolizing the universally privileged ideals of home, hearth, and familial love.

Suddenly, the young critics see that the dominant authorities of church, state, and general good-ole-boy consensus hold privilege prisoner in a world of language and ideological power; political and economic "piety" subverts the more natural implications of virtue, family, and Burke's "poetic metaphor." And through the juxtaposition of polar terms, perspective by incongruity, the secularization of piety, bureaucratization of the imaginative, and any number of what Gunn calls Burke's "menagerie of critical terms" (80), the student discovers that she can reconstruct, rather than simply accept or destroy, the pieties that define our sociocultural being. She learns that she can redirect perspective to redefine the previously unbreachable objective "realities" around us and redistribute priorities to re-create a "user-friendly" social environment that might accept and abet the Lipshas of our world.

By upending hierarchal systems and codes we can place new value on previously devalued concepts; and, in this freedom, our literary experiences will transfer to the "real world." If life imitates art, the secular pragmatist's effect is obvious: in socializing the text, we reassess and resocialize our world and the strategies by which we know it; we maintain dynamic textual transaction and thus continue the conversation of socially constructed meaning in a poetic dialogue between art and experience.

This is the bottom line of secular pragmatism: it brings meaning to the point of public access; it releases the reader into her own meaning rather than holding meaning within the text itself or "behind the lines" of academic foundationalism. By seeing a culture between the pages and the means by which that culture can be experienced, dismantled, "corrected," an "experiencer" can gain the means to reconstruct (or repair) a flawed community or a confused personal existence. The pragmatic evaluation of text informs the relation between reality and truth and the perspectives that define truth. The secularization of text and theory, and its inherent "taking it to the streets" action, brings a dynamic, consensual truth to the people, where meaning truly does become the product of a rhetoric of identification.

Burke's visionary approach to art, literature, and sociopolitical experience relates to a transactive, social experience with text. Obsessed with humanness, he necessarily leans toward the social, the intersubjective, the transactional. And it is this interest in humanness that lifts him out of mere criticism into a theory based in the reader and the reader's world in conjunction with the vicarious world of art. Hence, our terministic screen, secular pragmatism, raises no ground rules, no positivistic constraints in an increasingly postmodern environment. The interdisciplinary attitude inherent in critical theory sits well with Burke, who is pragmatic but not a pragmatist, secular, but not wholly a secular critic, postmodernistic, but not a totally a postmodernist. Wonderfully lost in language, he invites us into our own meaning, to the edge of the abyss where the word of God becomes the God of word and the modern critic maintains the title of rhetorician.

References

Burke, Kenneth. *Attitudes Toward History*. 3rd ed. Berkeley: University of California Press, 1984.

———. *Counter-Statement*. Berkeley: University of California Press, 1968.

———. *Language as Symbolic Action: Essays on Life, Literature, and Method*. Berkeley: University of California Press, 1966.

———. *Permanence and Change: An Anatomy of Purpose*. 3rd ed. Berkeley: University of California Press, 1965.

———. *The Philosophy of Literary Form: Studies in Symbolic Action*. 3rd ed. Berkeley: University of California Press, 1973.

———. *A Rhetoric of Motives*. Berkeley: U of Calif. P, 1969.

Cahalan, James M., and David B. Downing, eds. *Practicing Theory in Introductory College Literature Courses*. Urbana: NCTE, 1991.

Covino, William. *The Art of Wondering: A Revisionist Return to the History of Rhetoric*. Portsmouth, N.H.: Heinmann, 1988.

De Gourmont, Remy. "The Dissociation of Ideas." In *Remy de Gourmont: Selected Writings*. Edited and translated by Glenn S. Burne. Ann Arbor: Unversity of Michigan Press, 1966.

Dewey, John. *Art as Experience*. New York: Minton, Balch, 1954.

Erdrich, Louise. *Love Medicine*. New York: Bantam, 1984.

Gadamer, Hans-Georg. *Philosophical Hermeneutics* Edited by David E. Linge. Berkeley: Unversity of California Press, 1976.

Gunn, Giles. *The Culture of Criticism and the Criticism of Culture*. New York: Oxford Unversity Press, 1987.

James, William. *Pragmatism*. Cambridge, Mass.: Harvard Unversity Press, 1975.

Lakoff, George, and Mark Johnson. *Metaphors We Live By*. Chicago: Unversity of Chicago Press, 1980.

Linge, David E. Introduction. In *Philosophical Hermeneutics*. By Hans-Georg Gadamer. Berkeley: University of California Press, 1976.

Ricoeur, Paul. *Time and Narrative*. Chicago: Unversity of Chicago Press, 1968.

Rosenblatt, Louise. *The Reader the Text the Poem: The Transactional Theory of the Literary Work*. Carbondale: Southern Illinois Unversity Press, 1978.

Said, Edward. *The World and the Critic*. Cambridge, Mass.: Harvard Unversity Press, 1983.

Schilb, John. "Text, Reader, Author, and History in Introductory Literature Courses." In *Practicing Theory in Introductory College Literature Courses*. Edited by James M. Cahalan and David B. Downing. Urbana: NCTE, 1991.

Tyson, Lois. "Teaching Deconstruction: Theory and Practice in the Under-graduate Literature Classroom." In *Practicing Theory in Introductory College Literature Courses*. Edited by James M. Cahalan and David B. Downing. Urbana: NCTE, 1991.

Appendix

Recognizing Binary Opposition: How to Challenge the System

Hierarchies are socially (and in some instances scientifically) construed categories of order based in sequential thought. They always begin with the smallest, weakest, and most insignificant, and gradually work their way to the "top." All hierarchies recognize a weak and strong, an unfavored and a favored, a bad and a good; and all hierarchies attempt to order the gray area in between two extremes.

The idea of socially constructed hierarchies prompts questions of POWER: Who originates them? Who perpetuates them? Who profits from them?

One type of extreme hierarchy is called *binary opposition* (binary referring to a two-part system) in which one concept is favored over its counter-part. In most instances this value-system is based in social concerns—value is a group concurrence; and if value = truth, we can see how truth and knowledge might well be the product of a people's own desires to attain them at a certain cost to an "other." Some examples of "accepted" binary oppositions are:

Man/Woman	Up/Down
White/Black	At Rest/Moving
Good/Evil	Light/Darkness
Consumer/Producer	Rich/Poor
Young/Old	Process/Product

These time-honored privileged/nonprivileged sets have become so ingrained in our perceptual habits that they often go unnoticed and unchallenged.

By finding sets of binary opposites in literary works, we can weigh and measure the validity of our social (ideological) truths by taking them apart ("deconstructing"), analyzing, and [re]evaluating the values that established the initial premise against our own personal or group ideals, and, in the process, lend a larger share of power to the "subdominant" side of our model.

Another use of the +/- model lies in its ability to open up a new dialogue with the text (and the author) by finding the "hidden" messages and references "between the lines"—for example, the goose/turkey opposition in *Love Medicine*. By analyzing and redefining each side of the extreme, we can follow the author's ideas about the nobility and spirituality of nature, loyalty, and the idea of movement (process) of the living geese over the dead, cold, static commercial (product) nature of the turkeys. The geese are Native American symbols; the turkeys are White Man symbols. Here we see how Erdrich has upended the hierarchy to place a new value on previously devalued concepts—the heart of the White Man symbol kills (chokes) the patriarch of Lipsha'a tribe, just as European occupation destroyed (choked) the Native American culture.

Social patterns, then, establish truth for those who need it. It is interesting to note that Erdrich, a Native American, uses symbol and metaphor to show her points, while the European culture uses language and words to tell or order the underprivileged into submission.

Contributors

DAVID BLAKESLEY is Associate Professor of English and Director of Writing Studies at Southern Illinois University, Carbondale, where he teaches and writes about Burke, rhetorical theory, and film. His edited collection, *The Terministic Screen: Rhetorical Perspectives on Film and Film Theory*, is due out in late 1998. At present, he is writing a book-length treatment of Burke's rhetorical theory and its historical, cultural, literary, political, and philosophical contexts in the early to mid-twentieth century.

BERNARD L. BROCK is an Emeritus Professor of Communication and Director of the Center for Art and Public Policy at Wayne State University. He received his Ph.D. from Northwestern and taught at University of Minnesota, Minneapolis. He is interested in contemporary rhetorical theory and criticism with application to political campaigns and social movement and specializes in Burke's "dramatism." He is co-author of *Methods of Rhetorical Criticism: A Twentieth Century Perspective* and *Kenneth Burke and Contemporary European Thought: A Rhetoric in Transition*. His articles have appeared in speech communications journals such as the *Quarterly Journal of Speech*, *Communication Quarterly*, *Communication Education*, *Communication Studies*, and *Argumentation and Advocacy*.

GEORGE CHENEY is an Professor of Communication Studies at the University of Montana-Missoula. He received his Ph.D. from Purdue University in 1985 and taught at the Universities of Illinois and Colorado before moving to Montana in 1995. He specializes in the area of organizational communication, and his teaching and research draw on both humanistic and social-scientific traditions. His specific research interests include issues of identity and power in organizations, employee participation and workplace democracy, the analysis of corporate public discourse, and business ethics. He received the National Communication Association's Golden Anniversary Monograph Award in 1996, and is currently chair of NCA's Organizational Communication Division.

JAMES W. CHESEBRO is Professor of Communication at Indiana State University. He was President of the National Communication Association in 1996 and President of the Eastern Communication Association in 1983. He is the author of *Computer-Mediate Communication*, *Public Policy Decision-Making*, and *Orientations to Public Communication*, and co-edited the third edition of *Methods of Rhetorical Criticism*. He has also published articles in national communication journals such as *Quarterly Journal of Speech*, *Critical Studies in Mass Communication*, *Communication Monographs*, *Communication Education*, *Text and Performance Quarterly*, and *Journal of Applied Communication Research*. He has received outstanding research and service awards from the National Communication Association and Eastern Communication Association.

DENNIS J. CIESIELSKI is an Assistant Professor of English and Rhetoric at the University of Wisconsin*-Platteville. He is the author of *Between Philosophy and Rhetoric: Aesthetics and Meaning in the Postmodern Classroom*, forthcoming from Peter Lang Publishing. His recently published "[Re]presenting Writing across the Curriculum: A Case for Faculty Development and Dialogue," appeared in *Connecting with Your Creative Self* (Nebraska Teaching Improvement Council, 1996).

KAREN A. FOSS is Chair and Professor of Communication and Journalism at the University of New Mexico, where she also served as Director of Women Studies. She earned her Ph.D. from the University of Iowa in 1976 and taught at Humboldt State University in Arcata, California, before moving to New Mexico in 1993. Her research and teaching interests include rhetorical theory and criticism, gender and communication, social movements, and feminist perspectives on communication. She is particularly interested in discourse at the margins and its possibilities for transforming communication theories. She is the co-author of *Contemporary Perspectives on Rhetoric*, *Women Speak*, *Inviting Transformation*, and *Feminist Rhetorical Theories*.

KATHY GARVIN-DOXAS is a Doctoral Candidate at the University of Colorado–Boulder. She recently completed a two-year fellowship with the National Institute of Standards and Technology, where she assisted with the design and implementation of workplace participation programs. She is currently working on her dissertation, which examines the management and negotiation of the meaning of participation, team, and teamwork for members of a government organization, and she is working with the Solar System Collaboratory project at the University of Colorado to develop an introductory astronomy course centered around collaborative learning and web-based technologies.

GREIG HENDERSON is Associate Professor of English at the University of Toronto. He is the author of *Kenneth Burke: Literature and Language as Symbolic Action* and is currently co-editing *Poetics, Dramatistically Considered* along with a volume of essays commemorating Burke's centenary.

PHYLLIS M. JAPP is an Associate Professor of Communication Studies at the University of Nebraska*-Lincoln. She is interested in contemporary rhetorical theory and criticism and frequently writes on feminist issues. She has been active in the Kenneth Burke Society.

JAMES F. KLUMPP is Associate Professor of Speech Communication at the University of Maryland. He is a rhetorical critic, pursuing the relationship between discourse and social practices. He is a founding member of the Kenneth Burke Society and author of numerous essays developing the work of Kenneth Burke and applying it to contemporary discourse. Recent work has appeared in the *Quarterly Journal of Speech*, *Argumentation and Advocacy*, *Argumentation*, and *Southern Communication Journal*, and in *Making and Unmaking the Prospect of Rhetoric*. He was editor of the recent special issue of the *Southern Communication Journal* paying tribute to the ouvre of Kenneth Burke.

STAR A. MUIR is an Associate Professor of Communication at George Mason University and received his Ph.D. in Rhetoric and Communication from the University of Pittsburgh. His research focuses on environmental communication, and he has published in ETC.: *A Review of General Semantics*, *Philosophy and Rhetoric*, and *Speech Communication Teacher*. He is co-editor of the recently published *Earthtalk: Communication Empowerment for Environmental Action*. He is the Publication Director for the NCA Environmental Communication Commission, and is now editing the newsletter *Ecologue*. He was the Conference Planner for the 1996 Triennial Conference of the Kenneth Burke Society.

DINA STEVENSON's desire to explore and map the common ground between contemporary rhetorical and literary critical theories has led her through the study and teaching of rhetoric to her current pursuit of a Ph.D. in Literature and Criticism at Indiana University of Pennsylvania. Her research applies semiotic, Burkean, and Lacanian theories to the interpretation of contemporary American literary texts.

RICHARD H. THAMES, an Associate Professor of Rhetoric in the Affiliated Departments of Communication and English at Duquesne University, considers himself fortunate to have studied with Kenneth Burke during Burke's visiting professorship at the University of Pittsburgh. An organizer of the original 1984 Burke conference in Philadelphia and the 1996 conference in Pittsburgh, he serves as Editor of the *Kenneth Burke Society Newsletter* and the forthcoming *KB: A Journal of the Kenneth Burke Society*. His publications include "The Writings of Kenneth Burke, 1968–1986" and "A Selected Bibliography of Critical Responses to Kenneth Burke, 1968–1986" in *The Legacy of Kenneth Burke*. His interest in Burke encompasses his interests in the rhetoric of science and the rhetoric of religion. He is a founder of the Kenneth Burke Society.

KATHLEEN TORRENS is Assistant Professor of Communication Studies at Kent State University's Stark Campus. She earned a Ph.D. in Speech Communication in 1997 from the University of Minnesota and has taught at the University of St. Thomas and University of Colorado. In addition to the work of Kenneth Burke, her research interests include the critique of popular culture and rhetoric, the rhetoric of social movements, the rhetoric of visual forms, and women's history.

CINDY L. WHITE is Associate Professor of Communication and Co-coordinator of Women's Studies at Central Connecticut State University. Her primary research interest is the rhetorical negotiation of identity. She is currently working on a project that examines the rhetoric of nineteenth-century African American women activist/intellectuals.

Index

Familial, 263; destruction, 251;
  hierarchy, 201; unity, 249
Fascism, 164; fascism-democracy, 81
Femininity, 108; feminism, 11, 12, 13;
  feminist, 100, 102, 109, 116, 118,
  123, 125, 127, 219; critical
  strategies, 121; critics, 116, 123,
  126, 129; perspective, 12, 100,
  109, 116; reclamation, 114, 116,
  117, 118, 123; revision, 122;
  rhetoric, 114, 167; scholars, 103,
  108, 114, 123, 125, 128;
  scholarship, 100, 113, 114;
  theologians, 114; theories, 102;
  theorists, 108; feminists, 105,
  108, 122, 127, 209
Ferri, Joseph Michael, 171, 173, 174,
  178, 184 (n.3), 185 (n. 6), (n. 7)
Figural, 162; meaning, 153; motives,
  161; reading, 154; figurality, 152;
  figure, 152, 153, 154, 163, 164,
  231
Fiorenza, Elizabeth Schlussler, 114,
  118, 119, 120, 121, 123, 124,
  129 (n. 1); critical system, 118;
  critical feminist approach, 118
Flaubert, Gustave, 2, 93
Form, 44, 49, 152, 163, 167, 170,
  173, 175, 176, 177, 183, 196,
  227; alternative social, 236;
  apostrophe, 171; bathos, 171;
  chiasmas, 171; concept of, 170;
  contradiction, 171; conventional,
  163, 171, 175, 176, 177; of
  definition, 160; developmental,
  228; disclosure, 171; discussion
  of, 182; expansion, 171; of the
  journey, 227; linear, 176, 177;
  major, 170, 171, 175, 177; minor
  or incidental, 163, 170, 171;
  nature of, 181; paradox, 237;
  paradoxes, 235; paradoxical
  power, 232; parallelism, 228;
  pattern, 177; perspective of, 182;
  progression, 163, 171, 174;
  qualitative, 182, 183; quality,

229, 234; reasoning, 177;
  repetitive, 163, 182, 183; 171,
  175, 177; rhetoric of, 163;
  reversal, 171; scheme of, 170;
  spiral, 176, 177, 178, 179, 180;
  syllogism, 177; syllogistic, 82,
  174, 183; syllogistic progression,
  171, 181, 182; symbolic, 122
Formal idealism, 219; motives, 163;
  formalism, 163; formalist, 152;
  critics, 152; formalist-aesthetic,
  82; formalist/Marxist, 82
Formless, 196; formlessness, 193, 195
Foss, Karen, 122, 124
Foss, Sonja, 114, 122, 124, 125, 127,
  138, 139, 218
Foucault, Michel, 133, 134, 139, 238
  (n. 9)
Foundationalism, 264;
  foundationalist, 258, 260, 261;
  epistemology, 161
Frame, 64; frames, 226, 230; of
  "acceptance," 36, 51, 59, 89, 175,
  222; interpretive, 71; for language,
  10; of orientation, 79, 80; frames,
  tragic, 10; framing/roles, 11
Freedom, 53, 54, 226, 228, 229, 231,
  232, 253, 264
Freud, Sigmund, 4, 29 (n. 2), 30 (n.
  10), 93; Freudian; insights, 144;
  displacement, 152
Frost, Robert, 253, 254, 255, 257, 258

Gadamer, Hans-Georg, 245, 257
Gearhart, Sally Miller, 102, 103, 105,
  106, 107, 108, 109
Gender, 11, 216; dominance, 138;
  inequaity, 249; gendered, 213
Generalization, 210, 211
Giddens, Anthony, 133; theory of
  structuration, 143
God, 8, 20, 21, 22, 25, 136, 216, 225,
  231, 232, 247, 265; godhead,
  202; god-terms, 24, 25, 136;
  divine Logos, 82; faith, 232; final
  word, 49